Nicholas Farley

Handbook of
Garden Machinery and
Equipment

Drawings by Valerie Stiles

J M Dent & Sons Ltd London Melbourne Toronto

Printed in Great Britain by
Billing & Sons Ltd, London, Oxford, Guildford & Worcester
Bound by Western Book Co, Maesteg, for
J M Dent & Sons Ltd, 33 Welbeck Street, London

This book is set in 11/13pt VIP Plantin by
D P Media Ltd, Hitchin, Hertfordshire

British Library Cataloguing in Publication Data
Farley, Nicholas
Handbook of garden machinery and equipment
1 Gardening – Great Britain – Equipment and
supplies
I Title
635′.028   SB454.8

ISBN 0 460 043811

1

Contents

Acknowledgements Writing a book such as this needs the co-operation of many people to make it possible and I am very grateful for the help and support which I have received from so many people. Particularly I would like to thank those companies and their representatives who have supplied me with technical information and advice as well as the machinery to test and evaluate. In some cases not only was I allowed to test machinery but also to see round the factories and to judge for myself the quality or otherwise of the workmanship which goes into producing some of our equipment. To all the people in the trade who made these things happen I owe a great debt.

Advice and information from consumers were equally important and I thank all the gardeners whom I visited and the many more who wrote to me while this book was being researched, especially Mr Monteath who endured my two prolonged visits to his large mechanized garden in Surrey.

Throughout the preparation of this book two people have been particularly helpful and to Kay Nichols of J. M. Dent & Sons who has guided, advised, controlled and encouraged me and to Valerie Stiles, who turned my odd descriptions and diagrams into splendid drawings, go my thanks.

Finally, the biggest thank you goes to my wife who has typed, re-typed and typed again the notes, drafts, final drafts and absolutely final drafts of this book and who has also endured the swearing and tantrums which invariably accompany any work which I do. Without her help there would have been no book. (Which you may judge to have been the better outcome when you have read it.)

Most of the fifty-seven photographs in the book were taken by my wife or by me and nearly all were taken in our garden. However, the seven listed below are reproduced with the permission of the companies mentioned and we thank them for giving their consent to the use of these photographs.

Plate 10 reproduced by permission of Wolf Tools Ltd
Plate 20 reproduced by permission of Wolf Tools Ltd
Plate 21 reproduced by permission of Nupla Products Ltd
Plate 26 reproduced by permission of Allen Power Equipment Ltd
Plate 35 reproduced by permission of Wolf Tools Ltd
Plate 50 reproduced by permission of Honda (UK) Ltd
Plate 51 reproduced by permission of Link Hampson Ltd

All but two of the drawings in these pages were done specially for the book by Valerie Stiles but we thank Honda (UK) Ltd and Ledger Selby and Co. Ltd for allowing us to reproduce Figures 28 and 90 respectively.

List of Plates

Introduction

There are probably more books written on every facet of gardening than on any other subject, and it is difficult to name a plant which has not had at least half a library devoted to its likes, dislikes, diseases, habit, colour, taste and so on. Despite the feverish activity of gardening writers, however, I could find no up-to-date book devoted to the likes and dislikes of garden equipment. Yet there are available today more machines, tools, gadgets, gimmicks and gizmos for use in the garden than at any time in history and they are all as much a part of gardening as the ground and plants which they are designed to look after. Having many times needed the help of a book on the subject before buying some piece of garden equipment, and having many times failed to satisfy that need, I know how frustrating it can be. This book will, I hope, help those in a similar position.

Before getting stuck into any book, however, it is considered necessary to wade through that part known as the 'Introduction'. It is a part which I am often tempted to avoid, reasoning that nothing of importance will be contained therein and reasoning further that by reading it I am keeping myself from the pith of the real chapters. My status as one of the great non-readers of 'Introductions' has over the years cost me dear; rather than saving time I have wasted it because, although it is true that I can be immersed in the real matter of a book while other more cautious types are still digesting the introduction, it is also true that by skipping the introduction I get to the real matter without understanding how exactly to receive it or use it. This problem would be overcome if instead of heading the opening blurb 'Introduction' it was entitled 'Instructions'; I always read instructions before using anything and, after all, instructions for use is really what an 'Introduction' to a book is.

In order that you may understand this book, therefore, it is necessary that I outline here its purpose and aims, and also gives some background to the subject and to the research that was done before the writing.

The purpose of the book may be stated thus: to persuade gardeners to use more garden equipment and machinery and to help them choose the right equipment from the colossal range on the market. Simple enough it would seem, but there is actually much more to it than that. It is easy, you see, to give advice and guidance but nothing is more quickly guaranteed to get the elbow than unsolicited advice distributed willy nilly to all points of the compass.

Since you are reading the book it is reasonable for me to assume that you feel yourself to be in need of some advice on matters related to garden machinery and equipment; but through which section of that vast subject you require the guiding hand I do not know, and therein lies the problem. If you are in need of the hot word on tree sprayers you will, I hope, absorb that part of the following which is relevant to your problem and go on your way rejoicing but, books costing what they do these days, I think it likely, if only to avoid waste, that you will read some other sections – perhaps on hedge trimmers or maybe cloches – and while reading these extra sections you will unknowingly put yourself into a different reader category. In other words, there are times when I shall be giving advice that you want to read and at other times I shall be unwittingly committing the cardinal sin of flinging all sorts of unwanted stuff at you on subjects which you believe you are fully informed about anyway. At this end of the operation I shall not know which part is which, although it may be possible to make one broad assumption and this I do: I am assuming that most people will want most advice about the more complex mechanical gardening equipment and only a cursory paragraph or two on such fundamentals as rakes, forks and other common hand tools.

Having made that assumption do not for one minute suppose that I intend to write only a cursory paragraph or two about the fundamental hand tools. Far from it. I raise the matter only because I want to persuade you now not to ignore the sections on those tools which you believe to be too simple to warrant discussion. If, as I suggested earlier, the stop press on tree sprayers is your prime requirement then everything in the chapter on sprayers will be as grist to your mill; but your singleminded pursuit of sprayer knowledge will not, I hope, blind you to the counsel offered in the section on the more mundane tools.

While stating the purpose and intent of the book it is just as important to state quite clearly what it is not intended to be: it is not intended to be the horticultural equivalent of *Jane's Fighting Ships* because it does not list every piece of equipment made and it does not pretend to. In each appendix there will be a list of manufacturers, but it is quite likely that you own or know of worthy machines which are not included and there are good reasons for this which will be explained later.

The book is also not intended to be a 'best buy' report of the type *Which?* magazine attempts to publish. It is true that on some occasions I shall state quite clearly that I believe a particular model to be a good buy, possibly even the best buy, in its field. But the background to such judgments needs to be borne in mind by the reader, who must necessarily use his own experience to qualify any remarks made here. There is at least one good reason why it is not possible to write a best buy guide, which is that the number of products in the field is so big that it is just not feasible to try every make and model of every implement available. This point may be illustrated by the fact that there are over 200 lawn mowers available in this country which would take the most ardent tester the best part of a decade to test adequately – by which time, if you waited, your grass would be as long and tangled as his would be short and moss infested. What is intended, however, is that this book should equip you to make the choice of the right tools for your particular need and, obvious though it may seem, it is worth saying that everyone's needs and requirements will be different and what is right for one person will be wrong for another. In some sections the lists of manufacturers will be a helpful guide to what and who is in the market but, as I have said, these lists are not exhaustive.

You may reasonably be wondering what criteria were used to assess whether or not a manufacturer should be included. The answers to that throw some light on a peculiar industry. Obviously the first requirement was that I should know of the existence of the company and thus most of the familiar household names are here somewhere. Many obscure ones have been located by diligent tracking and others, I am afraid, will have escaped notice altogether. Two directories which purport to help those seeking company names and addresses were used – *Where to Buy Agricultural and Horticultural Equipment* and *Farm and Garden Equipment Guide* – but both are incomplete and out of date and as a critique of directories one cannot say more, or perhaps I mean less.

Some companies have been left out for the very good reason that although I may know of their existence they have gone to great lengths to ignore mine, by which I mean that they have ignored repeated letters asking for information on their products. I am forced to conclude that they do not want me, or indeed readers of this book, prying into the secrets of their products. They may rest assured we shall pry no further; and lest you think that in a fit of pique at receiving no reply to my first overtures I abandoned further attempts to wring information from such churlish companies, let me assure you that nothing is further from the truth; to be left out of this book a company must have ignored at least three letters and possibly a phone call or two as well. In short only those who tried hard to be left out were left out.

You may well be thinking that a company receiving an enquiry from someone intent on writing about its products in a book would be at the least moderately interested in seeing that the someone in question was fully equipped with the specification of the company's every last nut and bolt. But, as I said, this is a peculiar industry and some companies obviously do not choose their products to be highlighted here, leaving us inevitably to conclude that their products are not good enough. We shall not miss them.

Yet other companies have grudgingly supplied information but have clearly taken the view that they are too big to be concerned about what goes on between these covers. I ask myself, and indeed you too, what the response of these companies would be to a request for a small spare part from some poor unfortunate user several years hence when he represents no positive commercial value to them. Shortish shrift is what he'd get I fancy. In some cases, where the product made by these companies is not special, I have not included them in the appendices but in one case, where the product offered is, in my view, of some particular interest, I have included the company but an asterisk beside the company name in the address guide will indicate that I have had great difficulty in obtaining any information about them. Do not imagine, however, that companies which are not asterisked are therefore automatically going to fall over themselves to help you. They might, but many will not. I have found two reasons for makers or distributors not being helpful: the first is that they do not care and the second is that the company is small and everyone (which might mean both of them) is so busy making their particular gadget that they never seem to have time to answer letters or the telephone.

It is probably the recommendations on which model, make or type of equipment to buy which will prove of most interest and value and it is therefore important that you understand the basis on which they are made. You may assume that all recommendations are based on my own experience of the equipment in question or occasionally the authenticated experience of others. The limitations of this approach are obvious not the least being that I cannot possibly have tried everything for the reasons stated earlier. Therefore if I say that X is very good it means exactly that and no more. It does not mean, unless specifically stated, that machine Y is not as good; it means only that I have no personal experience of machine Y.

The matter of my impartiality in making any recommendation also needs to be qualified by saying that I cannot possibly be impartial; I can only set down my subjective opinions, much as a theatre or film critic does, and in many cases you will modify those opinions in the light of your own experience. There are some machines which I find particularly nice to use, not because of any demonstrable working superiority which they might have, but because they have an indefinable character or quality which appeals to me. The Hayter Ambassador mower is one such machine. Such appeal is of course subjective and biased, but the facts on the machine's performance and quality will be objectively assessed and recorded too, thus enabling you to decide whether or not such a machine is a likely candidate for your fleet.

You may wonder how I came to test the products mentioned in these pages and what the test or trials comprised. Such knowledge will naturally be vital to you in forming your opinion of my opinions and subsequently in making decisions on what is worth buying and what is not. The machinery and equipment tested fell into three categories. First there was the equipment which I own and use constantly in the maintenance of my garden. Second there was the equipment which was loaned to me by manufacturers specifically to help with the research for this book. Third there was the equipment which I bought or hired in order to test. It is clear, therefore, that the tests were necessarily of varying length and value; my own machinery constantly used over several years has been thoroughly tried and my opinion of that equipment is a mixture of admiration, affection and even awe. Implements loaned by manufacturers spent varying periods in my hands ranging from days to months and even, in the case of some of the less expensive bits and pieces, for ever.

Let us first consider the equipment which has been loaned; the manufacturers have volunteered to let me use machinery and form my own opinion of it, and that opinion can be good or bad. If the manufacturer knows he makes a dodgy product, and many do, it is very unlikely that he would have allowed me or anyone else the opportunity of finding out about it. On the other hand a good product can only benefit from being objectively tested and where my opinion of some implement has been unfavourable I have gone to some lengths to check with other users and with dealers and repairers to see if their opinion coincides with mine. The longer the test period allowed the more thoroughly I came to know the equipment and this will be reflected in my comments. In a few cases the test may have been restricted to using the machine in question at a trial ground for an afternoon on a visit to the factory. At such trials, of course, no more than an impression of the machinery can be gained, but a useful impression nonetheless.

In other cases I have relied on the comments and experience of the gardeners who have written to me and whom I have visited. Very often during such visits I have been able to try their machinery and this has helped broaden the scope of the book. But remember that this book is not trying to find the 'best buy'. It is, above all, trying to tell you what to look for when buying equipment, what to expect from various types of garden machinery and equipment and what equipment is available for you to choose from. At the end of most chapters there is a list of *Buying Points* which I think will help to collect the thoughts of the chapter together and are the points which should be considered before you decide whether or not you need a particular item; if you decide you do they are the points to consider when deciding which model.

Seeing, testing, proving and recommending is, I realize, only part of the story; the one crucial factor beside which all others become insignificant is cost, and it is the one constantly changing feature of this market, just as of any other market. Some of the machinery available to you has not shown any fundamental change in twenty years or more, except in price, and inflation has made the price change significantly every year. The problem of putting prices in a book such as this is that they will be out of date before the ink is dry and laughably out of date in six months. Therefore I have given an indication of prices in the appendices. The description *high*, *medium* or *low* will usually appear under the list of a manufacturer's products. This means that, for the category of goods listed, his products are high, medium or low compared with others in that market. This is further qualified in the appendix.

Before allowing you to stagger, instruction weary, into Chapter 1, a word about the appendices is called for. It is there that the lists of manufacturers and models will appear, with some specifications where applicable. Other manufacturers' information, including addresses, will be given in an address list after the appendices. By applying the principles outlined in the text to the information in the appendix you should be able to shortlist the manufacturers making equipment suitable for your garden.

Finally a word about the measurements which are used throughout this book. Although we are being at once Americanized in language and Europeanized size-wise I am sticking to feet, inches, yards and pounds for three reasons. The first is that I do not understand the metric measurements and have no feel for them, second I believe that you will be more at home with feet and inches than with cms, mms and ms and thirdly I am a chauvinist and rather enjoy the confusion which twelve inches to the foot, and three feet to the yard induces in the European bosom. However, the best 'yardstick' I have heard came from a gentleman at the Howard Rotavator Company who said, 'If you plant your rows two-and-a-half wellies apart you can just get the Howard 350 between them' (the rows that is not the wellies). Now two-and-a-half wellies is something we can all understand, a truly international standard – although certain of our common market cousins may not care for a standard based on a Wellington.

1 The Reasons for Buying Garden Equipment

Buying garden machinery is one of those things in life which, it seems to me, we often do for the wrong reasons and with insufficient thought or care. Yet when selecting a restaurant for the birthday dinner, for example, no stone is left unturned in the quest for an illusory culinary perfection. Mr Ronay's guide will be pored over and, no doubt, Monsieur Michelin's too, while supporting testimony will certainly be sought from friends who may have been to the restaurant in question, or who will at least know someone who has. If, after due deliberation and discussion, the evidence is favourable a reservation will be made.

Now if we will gladly undertake all that work to minimize the chances of the teeth coming into contact with soggy chips or crestfallen soufflés, why will we not do the same product research when we are about to spend money in other fields? Since the admirable Ronay does not operate in non-foody fields other sources of information have to be found if we are to avoid the horticultural equivalent of a soggy chip introducing itself into our gardens. You might consult *Which?* magazine, as it has built up something of a reputation for dishing out advice on what to buy, but if you are like me, you will find *Which?* is a mirage or illusion. I believe I can see help on the horizon – in the very next paragraph will be revealed the name of the best machine to buy and my problem will be solved – but somehow I never seem to reach that paragraph and before I know it the report is finished leaving me still uncertain and muddled. I want *Which?* to tell me unequivocally to buy something because it is best, but it never does and I always feel somehow short-changed after reading its reports. But when *Which?* does name a best buy I nearly always disagree so it cannot win whatever it does.

You could, if you feel the urge to buy new garden equipment, just biff off to your nearest dealer and hope that some divine hand will guide you mystically to the right machine or gadget; or you could simply rely on your dealer for help. When consulting dealers you will, if you are fortunate, get some good advice. But remember the dealer has commercial interests and even if he were equipped to give impartial advice there would be little point in his recommending that you buy a 'Such and Such' mower, it being the best for your purpose, if he is not a 'Such and Such' stockist. It is also unlikely that any dealer will sell you a £150 item if he believes that you have a £300 wallet, although the £150 model might possibly be better suited to your needs. Despite my cynicism you may have a dealer in whom you feel able to place your trust (they do exist), but that will still be of little help when buying garden equipment by post, and today a great deal of garden equipment is only available by post. Thus, at last, I come to my point; since you are going to get no worthwhile help from anybody else you had better help yourself and the first thing you must have clear in your mind before attempting to buy any new equipment is *your reason for wanting it*. It is probably fair to assume that you have a lawn mower of some description but if asked why you bought that particular mower I wonder what your answer would be. Apart from knowing that you wanted to cut grass did you consider *how* you wanted to cut the grass? Mowers are offered today which enable you to cut your grass quickly, effortlessly, energetically, cheaply, badly, electrically, manually and noisily. Which of these qualities were you looking for? There are mowers on the market which have at least one of those qualities and possibly some which have the whole lot, if we are to believe the advertisements. (Believing advertisements, by the way, is an unsatisfactory pastime and generally leads to disappointment. I don't recommend it.) In other words knowing exactly what you want of a machine before you start is of the utmost importance.

You may think it unnecessary for me to go over the often quoted reasons for buying garden equipment but they are not quite so straightforward as they seem, as I have found to my cost; while it is easy to say that garden equipment will save time, effort and even money, this is only true if certain conditions are satisfied. It is also true that a piece of equipment is not bought for one reason alone. Usually it is a combination of factors which persuades someone that they need a new piece of garden equipment. However, it is easier to consider the reasons separately here and to allow the reader to blend them according to taste and need. (This tediously practical approach to the problem may bore those of a more romantic and adventurous disposition but, as I aim to please all, I urge those of you in these categories to wait for livelier things later on.)

In virtually every part of the garden equipment market there is an embarrassment of riches; the choice of products is usually large, which makes selecting the right model very difficult. Remember, too, that not only does one have to choose between brands of machine but also between types because there is very often more than one way of tackling the same job and machines working on different principles will be available ostensibly for similar work. An example is the spade.

It has been one of the tenets of the British way of life that spades could, by and large, be considered to be spades. (The spade being singled out for duty in this old saying by virtue of its simple, unchanging, no-nonsense qualities. You can easily see why a front-loading washing-machine, for example, would not do half so well in such a proverb.) But remember this is the twentieth century and I regret to have to tell you that spades can no longer be relied upon to be spades. A spade can, on the one hand, be a sort of cross between a large draw hoe and a pick axe and, on the other hand, a complicated sprung device which owes much to the engineering of medieval siege catapults, with all shades of spadely opinion being represented in between.

Now if the twentieth century can throw up the sort of chap who can tamper with the simplicity of the spade (and also ruin one of life's rules at the same time) just think what the same fellow could do with the already complex lawn mower. He has indeed wrought havoc. Thus we have rotary mowers, cylinder mowers, electric mowers, petrol mowers, push mowers, pull mowers, metal mowers, plastic mowers, diesel mowers, noisy mowers, mowers you sit on, mowers you don't, mowers which hover, sickle mowers, flail mowers, green mowers, red mowers, mowers which start, and mowers which won't. All of which means that before you set foot outside the front door to buy garden equipment you need to have your reasons for doing so pretty clearly ordered, ready for presenting to the dealer. It will not be enough to point at the pretty blue mower in the corner saying that you want that one because it looks nice and you think it will *save* you time lawn mowing.

The magic word save; we British are people who since birth have it instilled in us that saving is a good thing. It does not really matter what we save or how much we save or indeed whether our saving is worthwhile, it matters only that we should at all times be saving something, somewhere, somehow. It is only natural, then, that the deeply rooted desire to save should intrude itself into our gardening and it would seem that the best way of selling anything to we gardeners is to tell us that it saves something, be it time, or work, or money, or even all three.

Saving time

You may now be asking yourselves how on earth this fellow is going to fill the next few pages on saving time; after all a machine either does the job quicker than it can be done by hand or it does not. It is precisely *because* so many people believe the subject to be simple that it is worth taking some time to point out that it is not. Before acquiring a new piece of garden gadgetry designed to save you time, consider carefully why you want to save time, how much time you will save and, having saved it, what you will do with it.

Why do you want to save time? The answer to this question will differ from job to job. You may wish to save time hedge cutting because you find it such a ghastly job that even a minuscule time saving will be welcome, whereas you may want to save time lawn mowing because you are too busy to allow the two hours every Saturday which it takes. If we stay with grass cutting for the moment, as it is a job which practically everyone has to do, we can see that there are a number of ways in which time can be saved and they don't all involve investing in new machinery.

The first thing to consider is cutting the grass less frequently; cutting the lawns fortnightly instead of weekly halves mowing time at no cost and it just might be the answer to your particular needs. It is true that this is not likely to be satisfactory for the very formal garden but it may do very well in some gardens or areas of garden. In my own case I used to cut the grass under the fruit trees every week.

As demands on my time grew I decided on fortnightly cuts and have recently stretched this to a three-weekly cut.

Cutting less frequently is not, however, likely to be a satisfactory solution to most people and therefore other means of time saving can be sought. Another method which costs nothing is to stop collecting the grass thus saving (the magic word) the nuisance of emptying the grass box and the trudging to and fro which this can involve. A useful saving can be made on a big lawn but on a small lawn this may only save a few minutes, which is of no great matter to anyone.

Your most likely course of action is to buy a bigger mower and, if the rule which states that a good big'un will beat a good littl'un has any substance, you will save time. The question is not whether you will save time but how much and at what cost. To illustrate this point let us examine the time taken to mow a lawn using mowers of different blade width. Using 14 in., 18 in. and 21 in. mowers to cut the same lawn should result in time savings of 23·5 per cent and 35 per cent respectively calculated purely on a mathematical basis. But factors such as turning at the end of each strip and making an allowance for mowing round irregular shapes as well as island flower beds will, in practice, affect these times. However, it is reasonable to assume that moving from a 14 in. to an 18 in. mower will give you a time saving of about a quarter, moving from 14 in. to 21 in. will save about a third, while moving from an 18 in. to 21 in. will result in a 15 per cent time saving.

It would therefore seem that the answer to such problems is to buy the biggest mower available, but this is patently false for other factors need to be considered too. The point which I am labouring so intensively to make is this: that bigger mowers will save time but the savings may not be great unless you are dealing with big lawns. Remember also that bigger mowers do bring problems of manoeuvrability which must be taken into account, particularly if your lawn is broken by flower beds, shrubs, trees or other obstacles to the mower's smooth passage.

The type of mower you choose can also be an important factor affecting the time you will save and it is worth deliberating at some length before deciding this point. The traditional cylinder or reel type mower unquestionably gives the grass a better finish and in most circumstances I have found it to be as quick at cutting any given lawn as a rotary of the same size. However, the cylinder mower does have limitations which affect its use; it cannot, for instance, cut such long grass as a rotary nor can it cut wet grass so well as a rotary.

No one in their right mind, of course, cuts grass when it's wet. But I do, not only when it's wet but in pouring rain too, if needs be. If you are managing a garden at the weekend and there are household jobs, gardening jobs and family duties not to mention sleeping and eating intervals all competing fiercely for your time you will not be wanting delays in one part of the programme caused by a mower which is not capable of cutting wet grass; keeping to schedule demands that wet grass be cut come hell or, as it were, high water. Thus you will see that the correct choice of mower can prevent time being wasted and in this sense can save time.

There is another very important point to be considered before we move from time saving and that is that work takes as long as you have got: if you have one hour per week to weed the vegetable garden or trim the lawn edges then one hour is what you will take regardless of equipment. While I do not hold this to be universally true it is undoubtedly true of many people and situations, and you would do well to ask yourself whether or not it applies to you, before, rather than after, taking delivery of your latest time-saving machine. There is no point in doing a job more quickly than you need to, especially if the extra speed has cost money.

A section on time saving is inevitably a statement of the obvious. Precisely because it is so obvious, it is not often thought about and so I have tried to show that there are many reasons for wanting to save time. It is something which requires thought on your part, otherwise you will not make the right decisions when it comes to buying. Furthermore, it is essential that the thinking should have been done before you get to the dealer, not when you arrive. Whatever the result of your thinking it is unquestionably true that equipping yourself with the right mechanical aids will save you time and enable you to do other things and to maintain a much larger garden than would otherwise be the case.

Saving work/effort

Earlier I said that it is unlikely that any one reason will be offered for buying or using garden equipment. Rather it is likely to be a combination of reasons and this becomes obvious when you buy a time-saving machine, *not* **because** *of the time saving* but because time saved has the incidental benefit of *saving work*. If by using a wider mower you cut the lawn more quickly it follows that you will walk less far and thus use less energy and this may be a much more significant saving than the time saving. It will be particularly important if you are not in good health or in any way disabled.

If because of age, ill health or disability it is necessary for you to save work you will naturally be keen to find equipment which will help you. But, unfortunately, it is not easily found, for while there are plenty of labour-saving devices on the market many of them first require quite large inputs of elbow grease before they show any savings of that same commodity. Powered cultivators are perhaps a good example of this because, although a cultivator will save enormous amounts of work, it also, paradoxically, requires quite a lot of effort from its master while it is in use. A powered cultivator is, you see, a singleminded sort of beast and left to itself tends to want to go forever in a straight line. This is desirable in one sense, provided that we are able, periodically, to redirect its efforts by turning it through 180° at the end of each row of work and it is this task of redirection which can sometimes be akin to going fifteen rounds with a goodish wrestler. But if intense activity for one hour will actually save me several more hours' work I am definitely your man, and it is for this reason that I am sold on using a cultivator for digging; it can be extremely hard work using a powered cultivator but it is hard work for, perhaps, an hour whereas digging the same plot with a spade could be hard work for many, many hours.

If, on the other hand, you are unlike me and a glutton for hard work but because of age or illness you cannot do all that you want, you will find, as I have said, that many labour-saving machines require, like the power cultivator, a good deal of energy and strength to operate and unfortunately you may not be able to use them. It seems quite unfair that the fit and idle should be able to use labour-saving machines whereas those people that could benefit most from such equipment will, in many cases, not be capable of using them, but that is the unfortunate truth. In the chapters on particular equipment you will see models to suit most people's needs, however matching needs to pocket may be a different matter.

It is worth mentioning *en passant* the head-on clash of two of the fundamentals of British life; one is the save creed discussed earlier and the second is the 'hard work never did anyone any harm' which goes with 'if a job is worth doing it is worth doing well' (where 'well' usually means that the doer should slip discs, blister hands, suffer extreme fatigue and be generally discomforted in the doing of a job). If there be such virtue in hard work it is difficult to see how there can be virtue in doing less hard work or saving work and yet saving is a good thing too. I cannot resolve this problem but thought it an interesting philosophical point worth mentioning.

The old school will have it that doing things the old way is invariably best and, as the old way was usually the hard way, it is they who are most frequently heard to chunter on about hard work being good for a chap. This does mean that very often you will see old hands advising against much new machinery because it does not do as good a job as the old (and remember if a job is worth doing etc.). This is quite simply not true. I am all for doing a job well but, by and large, I am against slipping discs to achieve that end and it is not necessary to do so.

It cannot have escaped your notice that the farmers of this extremely efficient agricultural island do not go out with a spade and double dig a fifteen acre field and yet they grow remarkably good crops. So if you are worried because a cultivator cannot double dig forget it because you do not need to dig two spits deep. There are those gardeners who derive some physical and mental therapy from churning around in the sub-soil and I would not wish to stop them but there really is no need to join them. Apart from any other consideration the soil two spits down in my garden is a particularly glutinous yellow clay, the less of which I see the better.

Some of the labour-saving equipment, it must be admitted, will not do such a good job as the more labour-intensive methods of old, and attention will be drawn to these in the appropriate sections. Very often a compromise between quality and quantity is necessary if we are to cope with the work of the garden and if that is the case you may have to accept doing a job not quite as well if it means doing it quickly. Most labour-saving equipment will, however, work as well as many of the more laborious hand tools which it replaces and indeed often very much better.

The combination of saving time and work is probably the reason why most of us buy garden equipment and if you consider very carefully what you require of the machinery you will make the right choice and will find life a lot easier as a result. The confirmation for this is in a letter which I received from a seventy-year-old gardener who, with his wife, but with no other human help, manages a magnificent three acre garden.

Saving money

When trying to convince the bank manager that it is a good idea for him to advance you two or three thousand pounds to buy a sophisticated garden tractor it is useful to be able to say in support of this outrageous request that it will save money. Bank managers can, I am told, be impressed by such arguments and if this is true the following may be used to embellish your story.

For some years it was relatively easy to find somebody, often of uncertain vintage and not always in possession of the standard four limbs, who would for a few shillings do work of doubtful value in the garden. Hedges might be cut and lawns mown while occasionally even vegetable gardens would be dug and certainly vast quantities of tea would be drunk by such characters. But not any more. It is now almost impossible to find such help or at least to find reliable help at an economic (for you) rate. Many people who managed their gardens for years quite adequately with a 'little' help find themselves hopelessly bogged down when the 'little' help is no longer available. If you have to call in the real professional jobbing gardener you will need, as you may already have discovered, a pretty healthy bank balance, for labour costs are extremely high.

There was an occasion some years ago when it was necessary for me to pay someone to cut my lawns. The man who did the work made a reasonable job of it and relieved me of six quid for his efforts. Considering the time, petrol – not only for his mower but also for his delivery truck – and wear and tear on the machinery I do not suppose he made much profit on the deal. On the other hand six quid to have my grass shortened seemed rather steep. Assuming that the grass is cut about thirty times each year and each cut costs £6, the total for the year is £180. Not a king's ransom but well on the way to a decent lawn mower, and if by buying a decent lawn mower you can cut your own grass you will, over two or three years, be financially in clover, if you understand my meaning. This is the sort of saving which is particularly applicable to people who believe they are not able, for some health reason, to cut their own grass: buy a ride-on lawn mower and you will very soon recover its costs.

There is another area where, in theory, money can be saved and that is the growing your own fruit and vegetable game. But I believe it to be a myth. We grow a good deal of our own soft fruit, top fruit and vegetables and although I have never kept an accurate check, I believe it costs us a small fortune to do so. It is perhaps odd to be writing how not to save money in a section entitled 'Saving Money' but it is important to highlight such areas because I do not want you to invest in a barn full of powered equipment and attachments in the belief that you will automatically save money. You might, if you are careful, but it is by no means certain. I would still encourage you to buy a cultivator but for other reasons altogether.

The cost, for example, of cosseting our apple trees into productive growth is a bit like developing an arborial Concorde. It seems that if you turn your back on an apple or apple blossom for so much as one second it is being attacked by everything short of Israeli jets. This means spraying, netting, bird scaring and eventually, I think, night nursing. The cost of sprays being what it is I would think that in an average year each maggot-ridden apple costs about £1.50; and while it is true that we managed to harvest about £22 worth of raspberries this year the cost of the fruit cage which protected them from the birds was £80 and we therefore need another four years before we are into the black.

Many will argue that home produce is cheap and does represent a saving but if you calculate the cost of seed, pesticides, fungicides, stakes, netting, wire, tools and machinery not to mention petrol for the machines I cannot believe that it pays. Of course there are many other reasons for growing your own fruit and vegetables which make it an extremely worthwhile occupation but I doubt that saving money is one of them. I am sure that many people who have diligently recorded their expenditure and crop weight over several years will prove me wrong and naturally I would like to be proved wrong on this point, but try as I might I cannot convince myself that the large quantities of fruit and vegetables I grow actually save me money.

You can make out a very credible, indeed plausible, case for buying, say, a cultivator, or greenhouse or fruit cage because it will save money in the long run and you may win spousely approval for the scheme; you may also succeed in convincing yourself for a short while, but deep down you must know that although money might be saved in the long run, it is one hell of a long, long run. The real money savings which garden equipment can bring are made by being able to do jobs which you would normally pay a gardener to do.

So far the reasons for buying and using garden equipment have been tediously practical and it is a fact of life that we British do seem to need such reasons to justify our actions. But if you can bring yourself to be irrational, extravagant and adventurous there are, in my view, much better reasons for doing something or wanting something.

Pleasure

Most gardening writers, be they writers of books or magazines, seem to assume the satisfaction and pleasure of gardening is in the end product – in the good onion crop, the continuously colourful herbaceous border, the prize winning rose or the symmetrically striped lawn. Yet we can take as much pleasure in the work necessary to achieve these results as in the results themselves. I actually enjoy cutting the grass with my lawn tractor. It is not a chore to be dreaded nor is it a means to an end, it is an enjoyable pastime in its own right. This is not true of every job in the garden but it is true of many.

The point is that if using a particular tool or machine is enjoyable that is a good reason for buying and using said tool or machine. Gardening is something which, I imagine, most of us do because we enjoy it and if you can increase this level of enjoyment by your choice of garden equipment the more 'sensible' reasons such as saving work, time and money become irrelevant, or at least less relevant. Very often quite horrible jobs can be made tolerable, even pleasant, by using the right tool for the job and I am certain that among your existing armoury of garden weapons you have one or two favourites which are, for some inexplicable reason, nicer to use than their mates. The hoe is an example of the sort of tool which you need to develop an affinity for: hoeing with a strange or new hoe can be a chore whereas hoeing with your own hoe can be a pleasure.

This same principle, although more noticeable with hand tools, applies equally well to the larger mechanized tools and this can be a source of trouble. It is obvious that if there is a lack of empathy between you and your garden shears you can hand the aforementioned shears their cards and look around for suitable replacements without too much trouble or financial strain. But if you find yourself metaphorically bickering and arguing with a £250 lawn mower it is not so easy to make a change without suffering a marked biff in the balance of payments. The first law of buying garden equipment, therefore, states that the time given to considering, trying and testing prospective purchases is directly proportional to the cost of prospective purchase. It follows naturally from this that if you are not allowed to try a machine adequately before buying, then don't buy. It is also the reason why so many people buy the same machine as their neighbour; because they have been able to try the machine at some length and know whether or not they can use it and enjoy it. The importance of trying a piece of equipment in your own garden before finally deciding to buy is very important and is a point which is re-emphasized many times in later chapters.

Manufacturers too frequently ignore the concept of enjoyment when designing and marketing their wares. They believe that as long as they demonstrate that their goods satisfy one of the 'save' rules it will sell. I would suggest that no matter how efficient a tool is, no matter how much money, time or effort it saves, it will not be worth buying unless it is a pleasure to use.

This matter of enjoyment or pleasure is, of course, subjective, and those qualities which may make a machine attractive to one user carry no weight with another. In my own case I find the noise which most garden machines make is almost intolerable and the noisier they are the less I like using them. Some degree of noise is, I suppose, inevitable although I am not convinced that it needs to be very much, but the rudimentary 'silencers' which are fitted to most garden engines are next to useless. There are doubtless those among the gardening fraternity to whom this matter of noise is of no consequence at all and these bods will be able to use the petrol engined chainsaws of this world without a care. Among chainsaw manufacturers it would seem that vibration, or rather efforts to eliminate vibration, are considered important, which leads me to suppose that the average chainsaw user is deaf, but sensitive to vibration. In my case I find using a chainsaw such a debilitating experience, and the noise makes such an assault on my ears that my sensitivity to vibration or, indeed, anything short of a nuclear explosion, is somewhat dulled. As I said, it is subjective.

The single furrow plough which attaches to my Honda tiller is an example of a tool which is a pleasure to use. Incredibly efficient, it satisfies all sorts of sensible reasons for use but I would use it even if it took twice as long, was twice the effort and cost twice as much as digging by an alternative method. I like using it; I even invent excuses for ploughing if no genuine excuse exists. Pleasure may also be derived from things which are not used in the sense that tools are used, such as cloches; for some quite irrational, inexplicable, nonsensical reason I like to see a row of glass cloches and I am sure that this fact rather than any practical reason explains why I generally use glass rather than plastic cloches.

Some tools and machines will give pleasure because of their construction and workmanship as well as for their efficiency and practical value. If such tools were to be judged only on their usefulness and cost efficiency they would never find a home with the private gardener who could not sensibly justify spending about £500 for one product when a similar but cruder model would serve him just as well at £250. But if you are the sort of bod who does appreciate good engineering and you can afford to indulge yourself I urge you to do just that when buying garden equipment: there is something very satisfying about seeing and using good tools which cannot be measured in pounds and pence (which explains why I am looking for a second hand 'J.P. Super' mower to add to my own fleet. This mower, which sadly is no longer made, is a delight to the eye and although I have never used such a machine I would still like to own one for the satisfaction ownership would bring.)

It is, I believe, as important that one's garden tools should give pleasure as that they should be ruthlessly efficient, particularly in this country where ruthless efficiency has never been a quality we much admire on its own. It is very necessary that you should look after your tools and this is much more likely if you are able to work up some affection for them, daft as that may seem. This is not to say that I am suggesting efficiency is something to be ignored; far from it. What I am saying is that given the choice between two roughly similar products do not automatically choose the cheaper one if you feel the other one will be, for the want of a more accurate adjective, nicer – and of course you can afford it.

At all times remember that for whatever practical reason you are buying garden equipment, be it to save time, work or money, try to garnish the practical with a liberal sprinkling of pleasure. It will make the subsequent use of the equipment much more worthwhile.

I want

In the last section I linked pleasure to the practical reasons for buying and using garden equipment; but it can also stand alone as a reason for buying. You may have no need, no real use, for a particular machine but you want it nonetheless. I have made a couple of significant buys on this basis and not regretted them for a minute. Such purchases are, of course, pure luxuries and should be recognized as such. But why not have luxuries in the garden shed as well as in the drawing room? If you admit they are luxuries it saves the tedious business of having to justify them either to yourself or anybody else. After all, you do not try to justify the purchase of another new putter because it is considered, rightly, as a luxury which is fun to have. If gardening is a hobby the same rules apply.

Which brings us to the question of what is a luxury and what is not. The answer is that there is no clear cut rule, but the following may help you decide, if decide you must. It seems to me that almost no garden equipment can be said to be on the one hand a pure luxury nor yet on the other hand a basic necessity. You could ignore your garden and let it become completely wild in which case any tending of the garden becomes unnecessary which makes any garden tool a luxury. (The occasional suburban wilderness indicates that there are those who incline to this view.) However, most people would regard keeping their garden neat and tidy as part of their responsibility to others in the community and therefore the tools necessary to maintain this basic state of neatness and tidiness are necessities. But where does one draw the line? When does one begin to exceed this basic standard of tidiness? It is vital to know because any tool used for gardening the extra bit above the basic state must be considered a luxury. All of which is patently silly and I hope indicates that it is not really possible to say whether this or that implement is a luxury or not; and does it matter anyway?

In my own garden I have a number of expensive mechanical aids which might be classified as luxuries by some – but I do not think they are, as I shall explain. You see in my garden the single most important factor affecting its maintenance is time; there is quite simply not enough time. The garden, which is about two acres in size, has to be maintained at the weekends so I use all the mechanized help I can lay my hands on. Most of the grass is cut with a lawn tractor because it is the only practical way of covering the area in the time available for mowing. However, if I had five days a week to look after the garden I could consider using a less expensive piece of equipment to cut the grass. This would take longer, but since I would have longer that would not matter much. But if I had five days each week to tend the garden and still used the lawn tractor I think I would have to classify it as a luxury (I would still use it because it's great fun churning round the garden on such a machine – but that is another story).

In other words the judgment as to whether or not some of our garden equipment is a luxury is a subjective one which depends entirely on the circumstances of each individual gardener. The value in discussing it here is because I have so often seen people using inadequate machinery for their particular needs because they feel that the bigger or more expensive items are luxuries and there is something faintly 'not nice' about luxuries. Whereas if you are able to convince yourself that the item is a necessity you can buy and use the thing with a clear conscience. One gentleman whose garden I visited while researching this book has his own cement mixer, which he regards as an essential garden tool. When you learn that his garden is fourteen acres in area and is maintained almost singlehanded you will not be surprised to learn that he can justify a cement mixer as an essential item. It is used for cementing in fence posts, repairing paths, laying foundations for outbuildings and greenhouses and for the construction of garden features; and when it is not mixing cement it is mixing compost in bulk. Makes you wonder how any of us has managed without a cement mixer all these years.

You see it does not matter whether you need garden equipment to save time, work or money; whether it's to give you pleasure or to relieve drudgery; whether it's a luxury or a necessity. There is garden equipment to satisfy every conceivable need and choosing it, buying it and using it are all, in my view, great fun and almost as interesting as the earthy side of gardening, perhaps sometimes, dare I say it, more interesting.

2 Cloches

The original cloches were made of glass and were bell shaped which is how they got their name, *cloche* being the French word for bell. Glass is, of course, still used but in recent years many of the plastics which have been developed have proved themselves suitable for making cloches and it is now probably true that the majority of cloches sold to gardeners are made of some kind of plastic.

Plastic, being tough, light and difficult to break, is a good material for manufacturers to use and also for shopkeepers to stock and handle. Glass, on the other hand, is not. The result is that in most garden shops it is easy to see examples of plastic cloches and almost impossible to find glass cloches which in turn means that most people buy plastic cloches because that is all that most people ever see. Furthermore, if you are one of those people who buys gardening sundries by post you too will find your choice limited to plastic cloches of one kind or another for the very good reason that light, strong plastic cloches stand a good chance of surviving the rigours of a long journey by courtesy of the GPO and arriving on your doorstep intact. However, it is a good idea if we remind ourselves that cloches are bought for the benefit of plants and, therefore, indirectly for our own benefit: our requirements and the requirements of our plants are more important factors to be weighed when buying cloches than the expedient requirements of the garden trade and the GPO.

So what exactly do we and our plants require of a cloche? Most people have a vague idea that cloches keep plants warm with the result that the plants, overcome with gratitude for this attention, grow quicker, bigger and better. While I would not deny that this is very often the case, there is, as always, a bit more to it than that: it is true that the function of the cloche is to protect plants, not only against cold and frost but also against the effects of fierce sun or birds or wind or rabbits or next door's cat or too much rain or too little rain or anything else nasty which the world decides to throw at them. The requirements differ from plant to plant, and from month to month, so that a cloche may be keeping the wind off in January and keeping the sun off in July, or holding moisture in for some plants and keeping moisture out for others – and if there exists a cloche which gives optimum performance under all these conditions I have not yet heard of it.

The convenience to the gardener must also be taken into account and I find that the single most important feature to me is ease of handling: in other words I like to be able to pick up a cloche easily by a handle and move it from place to place as required. Ease of lifting is particularly important in an opaque plastic cloche because the condition and health of the plants in the cloche can only be judged by looking underneath and thus one frequently needs to lift the cloche. With glass or clear plastic one can see the plants through the cloche and it is therefore less often necessary to lift it.

It is also important to me that cloches should be stable and able to withstand very strong winds without blowing away. Some of the lighter plastic cloches are not very good in this respect and require a means of pegging or weighting them down to make them practical. Such arrangements are irritating if the cloche needs to be lifted often but are no great trouble if the cloches can remain in place for long periods.

In my opinion no one type of cloche is so good that it makes itself the obvious choice for most gardeners – although there are a couple which come close – and so we are in a position, which will become familiar as you read this book, of having to weigh carefully our particular requirements and our money before making the inevitable compromise between what we should like, what we can afford and what is obtainable.

Glass cloches

My favourite is the Chase High Barn glass cloche which seems to come nearest to satisfying my own requirements. The Chase Barn is an all glass cloche comprising four sheets of glass held together by an arrangement of wire which looks complicated but, against all common sense, works extremely well. The advantage of this cloche for my purpose is that it is very easy to move about the garden because each cloche has a carrying handle; it is possible to adjust the roof glass to provide ventilation; it is all glass which means that it is inherently heavy and stable and does not require pegging or weighting to resist wind; it is a big cloche, being 24 in. long, 23 in. wide and 19 in. high at the centre; it is easy to see how well or otherwise crops are doing without lifting the cloche and by the easy removal of one of the roof panels it is possible to tend the plants or to harvest melons, for example, without lifting. This last point becomes particularly important when you are growing marrows, melons and other such

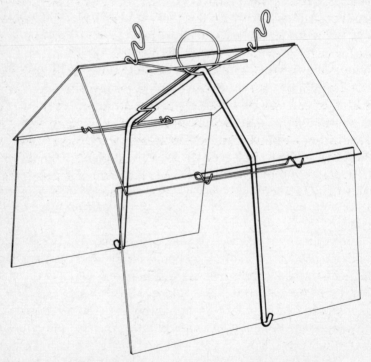

Figure 1 The big Chase High Barn cloche showing the complex wire framework which holds the four sheets of glass together. The Low Barn is similar except the side panels are smaller. These cloches are usually made of glass but can also be made of Correx or with Correx sides and glass roof. One of the roof panels can be slid into the notches on the roof wire to provide ventilation

unruly plants under cloches because it is never easy to replace a cloche over a good marrow or melon plant. The plants flop and straggle about all over the place when the restricting cloche is lifted so that it does not seem possible that all the greenery can be crammed back under cover again – and indeed very often it cannot. Cloches doing work of this kind are best left in place until the job is done and the ease with which a roof panel can be removed from a Chase Barn cloche makes it ideal for this. There is also a Low Barn version of the Chase cloche which is much favoured for smaller plants and which is slightly cheaper as it uses less glass. The most important factor, however, is that the plants seem to like growing under Chase cloches.

The simpler Chase Tent cloche is very good for covering small plants and seedlings and is of course much cheaper than either of the Barn types as it uses only two sheets of glass and a much simpler wire frame. I find my Tent cloches are invaluable and when not in use they have the virtue of being very easily dismantled and stored.

The problem with Chase cloches is that they are not easy to find in shops and it is almost certain that your nearest garden dealer will not stock them and will probably not even have heard of them. Some dealers will tell you that they are no longer made, which is their way of saying they do not know about something and cannot be bothered to find out, or that they want to sell you another, quite different, article. Rest assured that Chase cloches are still made and if you are unable to locate them in shops contact the manufacturer, Expandite,

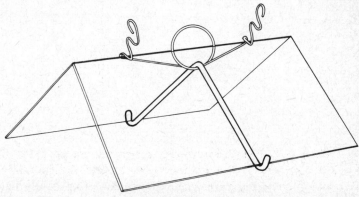

Figure 2 The simple Chase Tent cloche can be made from glass or Correx and also has the ventilation facility of the bigger Chase cloches. Note that it is impossible for the glass to fall out of the hooked feet of the frame

whose address is in the appendix. It is usual to buy only the wire frames for these cloches and to obtain the necessary glass separately from a local glass supplier. I should warn you, too, that assembling a Chase Barn cloche is a job which needs to be approached in the right mood otherwise things can get out of hand: it is the sort of task which I imagine an average saint might accomplish on a good day without swearing. But if you are, as I assume, only mortal make sure that your more sensitive and genteel brethren are out of earshot when you attempt to assemble your first Chase Barn cloche – or when you assemble your 101st come to that. I would only add that the effort is worth it.

A much more recent recruit to the cloche ranks is the Westray, which you will probably see much advertised in the gardening periodicals. This is an excellent product which has a number of novel features that make it particularly useful. Like the Chase, the Westray cloche comes in High Barn, Low Barn and Tent forms. The Westray also has that vital part, a carrying handle, but its particularly interesting feature is that it incorporates a fine mesh netting as well as the conventional glass or plastic covering. Thus in the summer months the normal roof may be taken off the cloche while the netting remains to give the plants continued protection against the birds, which are such a pest in some gardens.

The sides of the Westray cloche are made of a double skinned polypropylene called Correx, of which more later; suffice to say that having plastic sides to a cloche is very sensible because it does mean

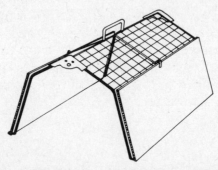

Figure 3 The Westray High Barn cloche showing the bird-proof netting incorporated in the roof. When the roof glass is removed the netting remains. The sides are Correx. This cloche has more features than any of the other makes. The Low Barn version is similar

that when hoeing near cloches or when walking down the rows the chances of the spouse's clumsy feet damaging the cloches are greatly reduced. As one who does occasionally accidentally kick in the sides of glass cloches I find the plastic sides of the Westray a very good idea. When delivered to you these cloches come with a thin polythene sheet for the roof panels but it is suggested in the instructions that this be replaced by glass at the earliest opportunity. I have done this with mine and the extra weight keeps the things grounded in strong winds and also makes the cloches more efficient and permanent.

All good things require a bit of effort on our part and, like the Chase, the Westray cloche is a bit awkward to assemble; indeed the instruction sheet does say '. . . the first one will test your patience a bit but the rest will be easy', and I think that is about right. The present models have been made simpler, I believe, but in any case the effort is again worthwhile. I have been much impressed by the Westray cloches which I have been using and if I were to restock with cloches now I would find it extremely difficult to choose between the Chase and the Westray; perhaps I would have some of each.

The Westray is very versatile for, in addition to its built-in bird netting, it also has provision to be staked upright to act as a wind shield for tender plants and shrubs. The Chase and indeed other cloches may be similarly used but the extra stability achieved by staking the Westray does make a difference.

Both of the cloches discussed are principally intended to be glass cloches and I realize that glass, desirable though it is in many ways, is not the answer in a garden where there are boisterous children or animals on the loose, nor indeed on allotments where there is a risk of damage from passing yobboes. Plastic cloches are the answer in such circumstances because although they do not relish being caramboled by footballs, cricket balls, housebricks or other missiles deliberately or accidentally launched, they will probably survive such attacks whereas glass cloches will not.

Plastic cloches

As I said most cloches offered today are plastic and all sorts of plastic have been used from thin polythene sheet to quite rigid clear pvc and all of them offer protection to your plants with varying degrees of success at widely different cost.

Perhaps the cheapest cloche is the continuous polythene tunnel type which is widely used by commercial strawberry growers. It must be said that this form of cloche does allow a lot of ground to be covered for a small initial outlay and that fact alone will be sufficient recommendation for some uses. However, there are a number of drawbacks which do not bother the commercial grower unduly but could concern the private gardener. First, the polythene sheet deteriorates in sunlight and there is nothing which you can do to prevent this. The sheet may last two seasons but no more and then it will have to be replaced. (Of course the more rigid plastics also deteriorate in the light but not so quickly as the thin gauge polythene sheet which becomes brittle and useless relatively quickly.) Second, it is quite difficult to tend crops under tunnels as there is no really satisfactory method of lifting them. Although it is true that the sides may be pulled up for ventilation and access to the crops this is usually when damage to the polythene starts. Last, polythene gives less protection against frost than the other, more robust cloches. In short unless cost is an overwhelmingly important factor in your choice I would leave tunnel cloches to the commercial men whose priorities are very often quite different from ours – a factor which will re-emerge several times during this book.

One of the widely used plastics is Correx, already mentioned as forming the side panels on the Westray cloche. The 'Supacloche' made by Pilc Productions Ltd is made entirely of Correx with a very simple wire frame. I have been testing these cloches for the past year and am very impressed by them. Although they are very light the wire frame, which also serves as the handle, digs several inches into the ground and the cloches are thus able to resist fairly high winds. It

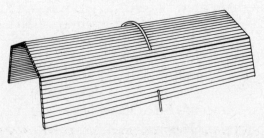

Figure 4 The effective and relatively inexpensive Pilc Supacloche, made entirely from Correx. Note the very simple wire frame

is, however, necessary to weight them in gales. The Supacloche is at once simple, cheap, effective and fairly durable – what more could one ask of a cloche? The real drawback is that Correx is opaque and therefore the Supacloche has always to be lifted to examine the progress of the crops underneath. Perhaps this compromise is worth it in view of the relatively low cost. Other manufacturers also use Correx for their cloches and I think you may be sure that such cloches work well, but as there are a number of similar products I recommend that you compare prices before buying as this would seem to be the main area of difference.

Another of the plastics commonly used is the clear pvc 'Novolux' corrugated type which I have not used but which I understand is very good. Certainly this type seems to fulfil many of the requirements of a cloche being quite large, transparent, and having carrying handles as well as long anchors to hold it to the ground. ICI offer this cloche in 3 ft and 6 ft lengths and without question the 6 ft length is the better value as the cost index in the appendix will show. Unlike Correx, ICI Novolux is transparent and allows good light levels to be maintained but it is an expensive cloche. (The cost per square foot of ground covered is more than the Chase High Barn glass cloche which is bigger and has several other advantages.) Novolux is guaranteed for five years against discolouration or deterioration and ICI will replace it free within this period should it be necessary. The Novolux cloches are expensive by any measurement but they are one of the better cloches available and do have the advantage of great strength and resistance to accidental or deliberate damage. If you need the qualities of a transparent, relatively long lasting, rigid cloche which must also be virtually unbreakable the Novolux cloche is for you.

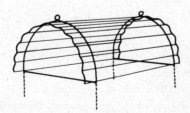

Figure 5 The ICI Novolux cloche comprises a sheet of clear corrugated pvc which is sprung into two wire frames. The frames dig into the ground to give a measure of stability. Two hands are needed to lift this cloche

Marmax Plastics Ltd offer the 'Marmax Self-Watering' cloche which is made of a double skin of clear cellulose film reinforced by wire which enables the cloche to hold its shape without any additional framework. Naturally it needs pegs, which are supplied, to hold it to the ground. Its self-watering properties are of doubtful benefit in my view as the sideways movement of water allows adequate irrigation under most cloches and where this is not the case I suggest using seep hose (see Chapter 3 on watering equipment).

There are countless others, all of which are variations on the themes outlined above. The important thing to remember about all plastic cloches of whatever type is that they deteriorate in sunlight and there is nothing which you can do to prevent this from happening. You must be prepared to replace the plastic as it becomes old. The thin polythene types may be useless after one season, although if you are careful they will last for two, and while the other plastics may last for several years before requiring replacement they too will eventually need it. It is not possible to say how long such deterioration will take, nor is it possible to calculate the cost of replacement in several years when inflation is likely to have made nonsense of all price estimates.

Home-made cloches

Cloches, being by and large simple things, are quite easily made at home by the reasonably competent do-it-yourself man and this is particularly true of the plastic cloches. What is really required to make a satisfactory cloche is a means of joining two pieces of glass or plastic together to form a simple tent shape and there are several such devices on the market. A much advertised one, which also has the doubtful accolade of being selected by the Design Centre in London is the Rumsey Clip. This metal clip is claimed to be able to hold glass sheets of up to 18 in. × 12 in. to form a tent cloche but in my experience it does not do this satisfactorily. All the time the cloche is resting on the ground there is no problem but when the time comes to move it the trouble begins: the clips are not rigid enough to hold the glass apart and the weight of the glass is sufficient to bend the clip and make it unusable. In some cases the glass will fall out of the clip. On the face of it the Rumsey Clip, you might think, is one of those things that looks like a good idea but actually fails to live up to its early promise. But no: it actually *is* a good idea and if it makes a less than satisfactory glass cloche no matter, it has other tasks to perform which it does very well. One of these tasks is to build those special structures for the protection of large individual plants or small shrubs which are getting established, and which are too big for conventional cloches – tomato plants or tender herbaceous plants in exposed positions, for example. The Rumsey Clip enables you to surround such plants with a 'keep' made of glass or rigid plastic and to tailor the structure to suit each particular plant. I have used the clips as illustrated to hold together glass sheets 24 in. × 18 in. with no bother because such structures do not need to be moved like an ordinary cloche. Moreover it makes the task of offering protection to tender plants relatively easy and one is therefore more inclined to do it rather than neglect the job and hope the weather stays good.

Having said that the Rumsey Clip makes an unsatisfactory *glass* cloche does not mean that it cannot be used for tent cloches at all. On the contrary, it is a very good way of holding two sheets of Correx together to form a really good, low cost tent cloche and, in my view, this would be a much better alternative to the polythene tunnel cloche and would not cost much more.

Whatever cloches you use I suggest that a few Rumsey Clips and odd bits of glass and Correx make a worthwhile addition to any

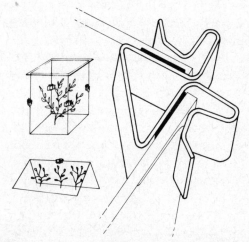

Figure 6 The Rumsey Clip is very useful for forming large glass box constructions, for protecting big plants or for forming simple tent cloches of Correx or other rigid plastics. (I think it unsuitable for glass tent cloches)

garden to cover those extraordinary jobs which always seem to crop up.

Another device which is designed to form a tent cloche from two sheets of glass or plastic is the Calvert Cloche Maker and this does not work satisfactorily with glass either. It does, however, work well with light plastic such as the ubiquitous Correx and has the advantage over the Rumsey Clip of having a good carrying handle, although it is less versatile in other ways. Nonetheless it offers the means to make a decent tent cloche from plastic at very low cost. Naturally such cloches are very light and need to be pegged or weighted to prevent their being blown away.

Yet another device for forming tent cloches is a grooved plastic strip into which glass is slid and held. Two of these things are needed for each cloche and having used them I can find nothing to recommend them at all.

Although the Rumsey and Calvert clips are cheap and easy to use there are always those bods who will want to make everything themselves and that being so I can do no more than suggest that you buy some of the already much mentioned Correx from Pilc Productions Ltd, who will send not only Correx but instructions on how to make cloches, compost bins, seed trays and a host of other things as well. Correx has made life much easier for the do-it-yourself cloche maker but of course you can also buy clear plastic rigid sheets and the corrugated pvc like Novolux and then adapt it to use with your own wire hoop supports.

Correx has received a lot of attention in this chapter and a word about what it is and what it does is perhaps necessary. It is an opaque

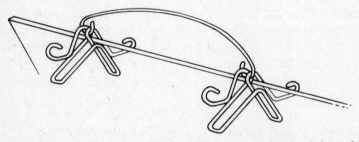

Figure 7 The Calvert Cloche Maker which, for clarity's sake, is here shown with only one sheet of plastic being held. This clip has the advantage of a good handle

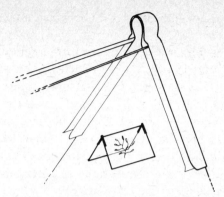

Figure 8 The grooved plastic cloche clips. These are not at all satisfactory

polypropylene sheet which, as Figure 9 shows, has a double skin with a number of ridges running between the skins and it is from the ridges and the double skin that it gets its useful properties. Because of the ridged construction the sheet is rigid and strong although it does have the ability to flex and thus absorb shocks such as bricks, boots and so on. Its rigidity, however, means that only the simplest wire hoop is necessary to make a passable cloche from a sheet of Correx and because it is thin plastic it is very easily cut with a knife, making it an easy material with which to work.

The double skin gives it very good insulation properties and this is what makes it particularly suited to cloches where heat conservation is often all important. It is usually held that glass cloches conserve heat better than plastic ones but I have found the reverse to be true when using Correx. Over a period of three weeks in September I conducted a test to discover whether or not glass was better than plastic at retaining heat. Two Chase High Barn cloches were used for this test, one made entirely of glass and the other entirely of Correx. The cloches were placed side by side on bare soil in a completely open position and the maximum and minimum temperatures under each cloche were recorded every twenty-four hours. The results were interesting:

(a) The Correx cloche always recorded a higher minimum temperature than the glass cloche.
(b) The glass cloche always recorded a higher maximum temperature than the Correx cloche.

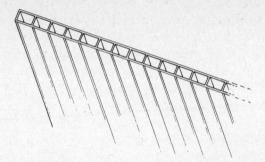

Figure 9 An end view of a sheet of Correx showing in detail the double skin and ribbed construction

(c) On days of prolonged sunshine both cloches achieved similarly high temperatures with the Correx perhaps 2°F lower than the glass.

(d) On days when there was only a short period of sunshine the temperature difference was greater, with the glass cloche achieving a temperature as much as 10°F higher than the Correx.

The temperatures for some sample days are recorded below to illustrate the difference (all temperatures in Fahrenheit).

	Glass		Correx	
	High	Low	High	Low
Day 1	93°	60°	86°	61°
Day 2	103	45	98	47
Day 3	100	48	89	50
Day 4	93	50	88	52
Day 5	96	55	94	57

These sample days in the table are not consecutive but picked at random from the three weeks of the test. The two thermometers used were alternated from cloche to cloche to eliminate any bias which a faulty thermometer might have introduced into the results. Of course I do not pretend that a simple test such as this has the scientific pedigree which a laboratory controlled experiment has. Nonetheless I think it safe to draw the inevitable conclusion that Correx is a better conserver of heat than glass and if heat conservation is your first requirement of a cloche Correx would seem to be the stuff for the job.

Moreover, it subjects the plants in its care to less violent temperature fluctuations than glass does and this will be an important factor for some plants. Correx is, then, a very good material for home-made cloches but if you prefer glass roof cloches and still wish to benefit from the Correx heat conserving properties you can cut panels of Correx to fit over the glass and, in the late afternoon or early evening, fix the Correx to the glass with spring type clothes pegs.

Finally, before leaving home-made cloches, it is interesting to consider that after many years the cloche wheel has turned full circle because we can once again have bell-shaped cloches and at no cost. The many plastic containers in 1 gallon and 2 gallon sizes now used for such things as vinegar or liquid fertilizer make excellent cloches for single plants if you cut the bottom out and, moreover, the neck will unscrew to provide ventilation. These cloches are the nearest things to the originals which we can have and they are very useful, albeit rather unsightly.

Which cloche?

The question now to be asked is which cloches should you buy? Should it be the posh Westray High Barn, or the very cheap ICI polythene tunnel, or perhaps you should cobble your own together from coat hanger wire and scrap glass. The answer is probably that you will need different cloches for different jobs and as I do not know what plants you grow nor where you grow them nor yet the state of the exchequer I cannot possibly say what is right for you. What I can offer is a list of arguments and points for you to consider before you make your choice or choices.

Unlike the *Which?* report on cloches published in February 1978 I do not think it very sensible to consider the cost of cloches being set off against the savings in buying plants or vegetables. It is such a very difficult thing to measure and if this was the reason for our gardening I doubt that many of us would bother. However, if such a consideration is to carry any weight it must mean buying the more expensive glass cloches which will last for ever and will, therefore, easily pay for themselves. Again, unlike *Which?*, I do not consider it worthwhile for the gardener to go for the cheapest cloche, the polythene tunnel, unless, as I have said, he has a very large area to cover and cost becomes the only important factor.

The apparently expensive cloches such as the Westray High Barn and the Chase High Barn cost the most but give the most. They are both very durable, both have the facility to ventilate, while both are big enough to allow even large plants to reach full maturity under the cloche because at about 20 in. high they are bigger than anything else available. With their near vertical sides they offer a large amount of usable space, they are stable in high winds and yet very easily moved when necessary. The Westray also has the unique feature of being able to continue work as a bird defence even when its glass roof is removed. The factor which makes them appear disproportionately expensive is their height: they offer a very large volume of protected space and it is possible to grow three rows of large plants under one row of these big cloches. If such cloches appeal to you but seem expensive then I suggest using the Chase fittings with Correx or other rigid plastic instead of glass and this will make them about 20 per cent cheaper.

Large luxury cloches are all very well where they are needed but if you only want to give early protection to emerging seedlings the simpler and much cheaper tent cloches are probably the things to consider. The cheapest way of having tent cloches is by using Rumsey Clips to join two sheets of Correx, although if funds allow the more rigid and more easily moved Chase tent cloches are a better investment. Whether you use glass or Correx in them will depend on such factors as whether or not you want to be able to see your crops without lifting the cloche.

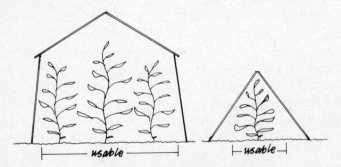

Figure 10 This diagram indicates the usable space difference between the barn type cloche and the tent. The barn uses twice the glass but gives three times as much usable ground growing area and about five times the protected volume or cubic capacity

One of the more expensive cloches is the corrugated pvc type such as the ICI Novolux; the cost per square foot index in the appendix shows this type to be about the same as the Chase and Westray High Barns but without having any of their other advantages. However, these pvc cloches do have one big advantage over most other types and that is their toughness. Therefore if your prime requirement of a cloche is its ability to resist children, dogs, vandals and everything this side of nuclear attack you will have to stump up the necessary cash with a grin and bear it.

The appendix at the back of this book lists some cloches with their sizes and other features as well as some cost indices. I have calculated the cost of a 30 ft row of cloches for the total cost index and calculated the cost per sq. ft of ground covered in a 30 ft row for the other index.

Using the appendix in conjunction with the list of points for consideration below should enable you to select the cloches which are most suited to your needs and pocket.

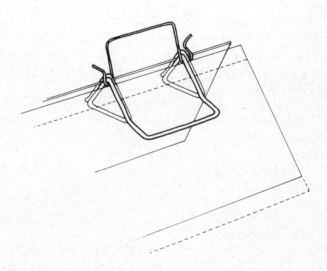

Figure 11 Chase cloche clip: the most expensive of the clip variety but probably the best. It will support quite large panes of glass, e.g. 24 in. × 18 in. Lifting the side handle and sliding the glass down to the dotted line gives ventilation. The cheapest way of having a reliable glass tent cloche

Cloches: buying points

1 Height: do you wish to grow large plants to maturity under the cloche?

2 Width: usable width is much greater with barn cloches and others with near vertical sides. Tent cloches give least usable width.

3 Length: not usually a consideration for individual cloches.

4 Weight/stability: glass cloches resist the highest wind. Weights and pegs on plastic cloches are a nuisance.

5 Carrying handle: much more important than it seems.

6 Ventilation: the ability to allow top ventilation is very important for some plants and at certain times of the year.

7 Access: the facility to allow access to crops for attention and harvesting without removing the cloche.

8 Transparent: saves lifting cloches to judge condition of crops. Also necessary when plants require high light levels in winter.

9 Heat retention: glass better than most plastics but Correx better than glass. Polythene tunnels relatively poor.

10 Cost: polythene tunnels are unquestionably the cheapest but Rumsey Clips and Correx offer a good cheap alternative.

11 Strength: rigid pvc such as ICI Novolux are probably better than anything at resisting attack.

12 Stacking: ease of stacking can be important. It is not easy to find a home for a large number of temporarily out of use cloches.

13 Durability: the *only* permanent cloches are all-glass types.

14 Special use: home-made or glass/plastic and Rumsey Clips.

15 Aesthetic appeal: some cloches, particularly the opaque plastic type, are rather unsightly whereas a row of glass cloches can look rather pleasing.

3 Watering and Irrigation Equipment

A gardening friend of mine says that there is nothing he enjoys more than standing outside on a balmy summer evening idly squirting the hose over his fortunate beans while he sucks on a therapeutic cigarette and contemplates the pleasures of the simple life. Each to his own I suppose. For me watering is one of the gardening jobs which I do not much like and nothing puts me into a worse mood than having to fiddle about with taps, hoses, ill-fitting hose joints and watering attachments. I have long promised myself an elaborate fully automated system but the cost would be roughly equivalent to the national debt and I therefore doubt whether it is a promise which I shall be able to keep. In between this automated, watery Shangri-la and the simple watering can there exists a vast range of watering gadgetry demanding our attention, and some of the bits and pieces are very good.

Watering cans

Starting with the least complicated watering system we should first consider the watering can. An ancient vessel which has, like so much in the garden world, lately caught the eye of the plastics industry with the result that watering cans are now available in all sorts of brilliant colours which I find quite ghastly. However, no one can deny that plastic watering cans are a useful addition to the garden: they are light, cheap and will stand ill treatment without becoming damaged. Despite these excellent qualities they have not displaced the traditional galvanized cans and the best of these, the Haws cans, are still made. The Haws watering can has long been a favourite of

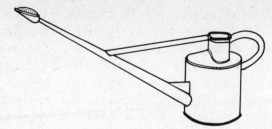

Figure 12 The traditional Haws watering can available in galvanized steel or japanned steel. Note the narrow neck, very long spout and fine rose

gardeners and its very fine brass rose is still so much better than any plastic equivalent. The Haws cans with their narrow necks and long spouts are particularly useful where reach is important, such as when watering in frames or the greenhouse. The galvanized finish makes the cans unsuitable for mixing the copper based sprays and the alternative japanned finish cans are needed for this. However elaborate your watering arrangements are you will need at least one watering can and the Haws metal cans are undoubtedly the most satisfying to use; if you are the sort of person who derives satisfaction from watering cans, that is.

Hoses

Whether or not you need any or all of the watering equipment described below will depend on many things not the least being the unbelievably high price of most of it. The most basic piece of the watering armoury is the hose without which most of the other gadgets are useless. There are varying qualities of hose and big differences in price but, contrary to current opinion, even the cheapest hose is quite good provided it is treated well. Most hoses are of ½ in. bore and most fittings are for ½ in. hose but some companies offer bigger bore hoses and fittings to match. Under certain conditions you will need bigger hoses as will be shown later. Apart from a choice of size you also have a choice of quality and the most expensive hoses will be the braided type shown in Figure 13. This type combines flexibility with great strength and durability; indeed, so durable is this hose that one company, Polygard, guarantees its braided hose for ten years. This braided hose will cost nearly three times as much as the cheapest hose but for some applications it will be essential. If, for example, you incorporate 'water stops' in your system you will certainly need the strength of braided hose. (Several companies offer water stops and their purpose is explained fully later.) In my garden the water pressure is low and I do not use top quality hose because I do not need it: ordinary medium quality stuff has been more than adequate for my purpose and good thick walled ribbed hose will, I suggest, be adequate for most work.

If you need to pipe water over a long distance and if you have good water pressure you will need to consider something more adventurous than ½ in. hose: you will need perhaps ¾ in. hose or bigger. Such hoses are not likely to be found neatly wrapped in your local garden shop and you will need to contact one of the companies supplying watering equipment to the commercial grower. These firms will have hoses of between ½ in. and 1½ in. bore. Tricoflex, sold in this country by Valentine Plastics, is an example of this commercial quality hose.

The reasons for needing bigger hose than the standard ½ in. are complex and are influenced by flow rate, pressure, friction, turbulence and probably the phase of the moon as well but one thing is

Figure 13 This cut-away diagram shows the structure of braided hose. The inner pipe is surrounded by a fabric mesh which is in turn protected by an outer plastic tube. Such hose will last longer and withstand rougher treatment than a simple single wall hose

certain: you will not automatically improve things by buying bigger bore hose. Only if your present ½ in. hose is in any way constricting the water flow will you see any improvement by using bigger hose (more boring hose?). The friction caused by the water passing through the hose will slow the rate at which the water moves. Therefore in the best hoses the insides are very smooth to reduce this friction to a minimum. Even so, the drop in pressure between the tap and the hose outlet can be significant for various reasons, as the following example shows: if a sprinkler requires, say, 40 lb/sq. in. pressure to drive it satisfactorily and it is delivering about 12 gallons per minute at the end of 200 ft of 1 in. hose it will be necessary to have about 52 lb/sq. in. pressure at the tap. The pressure loss between the tap end of the hose and the sprinkler end will therefore be about 12 lb/sq. in., which is almost 25 per cent. Other things, such as the number of bends in the hose, also affect the friction caused and turbulence of the water, both of which further slow the rate of flow and affect the performance of the sprinklers at the end of the hose. Such effects will be slight in short lengths of pipe but over big distances the effects of friction and turbulence can be marked. This can be reduced by having a big bore hose. However, if your tap is delivering water at a feeble rate small hose may cope with it well enough and there will be no need to invest in anything else.

A rough way of indicating whether or not your hose affects the water flow is to fill a bucket at the tap and note the time taken to do this. Then attach your hose to the tap and fill the bucket from the other end of the hose. This will take a little longer. If it takes a lot longer it is an indication that the hose is unduly restricting the flow and you could probably benefit from bigger hose. If the difference is slight do not bother to change. In my garden the difference in time at the end of 100 ft of ½ in. hose was almost negligible and when 100 ft of ¾ in. hose was used the time recorded was identical or as near identical as the crude timing allowed. But in other tests elsewhere in the country bigger differences were noted: in one case there was a 40 per cent difference between filling at the tap and at the hose end. In short, get the right hose for your work because all else depends on it.

Having got yourself rigged out with hose the next problem is to decide what device or devices you should be stuffing in the business end of it. The solution to that problem can only be found by careful consideration of what you want to do with all the water, which was once at point A and which is now a hose length away at point B.

Sprinklers

The easiest watering job to tackle is watering a large lawn because virtually any of the gadgets on offer will do the job reasonably well. Some will, however, be better than others. The traditional sprinkler throws water out in a circle either by means of a spinning arm or, more simply, by a fixed 'squirter' which is only slightly more sophisticated than holding your thumb over the hose end. Whichever of these things you choose do check that the water distribution is fairly even by placing a few jam jars in the fall-out area; they should all fill at about the same rate. If they do not it means that the sprinkler is not much good. The trouble with these and any other circular pattern sprinklers is that in order to water a lawn completely one cannot avoid also watering the surrounding flower beds. This may be at once unnecessary and undesirable.

The oscillating sprinklers overcome this problem by watering in a rectangular pattern which, in theory, can be closely controlled. In theory yes, but in practice no. Oscillating sprinklers have an awful habit of getting stuck in one position and instead of watering a large lawn they flood one end and leave the rest dry. They work not at all in my present garden because there is insufficient water pressure and although some are supposed to work on low pressure I can assure you they do not. If you are going to have an oscillating sprinkler it is worth buying the best to avoid any disappointments. A further problem with the cheaper types is the frequency with which they contrive to get blocked jets. This causes irregularity in the spray pattern and is difficult to cure because the jets are not easy to clear satisfactorily. Two good designs which I have not tried but which look worthy of investigation are made by Melnor and Wolf. The Melnor Time-A-Matic – awful name – is able to deliver a set number of gallons and then automatically turn itself off. This could be very useful. The Wolf Swingfan does not have this facility but it is the only sprinkler that I know of which can deliver either the normal heavy water droplets or a fine mist spray. It is, moreover, easy to clean the jets on this model and it will supposedly work on low water pressure; but of that last claim I am sceptical until I see it proved.

Both of these models have brass nozzles inserted in the spray bar for accurate spraying. Do not bother with any cheaper models that do not have these brass nozzles or jets.

A cheap alternative to the oscillating sprinklers, if you want to water various rectangular patterns, are the fixed pattern sprinklers also offered by Melnor and Wolf. Figure 14 shows how these simple devices work. A variety of spray patterns is available.

Another way of controlling the spray pattern is to use one of the adjustable pulse sprinklers which have long been used by the professional groundsman. I like these sprinklers because of their range of adjustment and for their trouble-free behaviour. It is true that the water pattern can only be controlled to the extent of various segments of a circle but this is often good enough. In Figure 15 it can be seen how the semi-circle pattern is used for watering a lawn but not the adjacent flower bed. The other good thing about these sprinklers is that they operate reasonably well on low pressure and when operating on good water pressure they will give huge coverage of large droplets or a lesser coverage of fine drops. There is no more satisfying

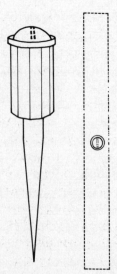

Figure 14 This is a Melnor pattern sprinkler. The spike digs into the ground and the water is forced through the holes in the dome-shaped top. The dotted outline on the right shows the watering pattern; there are a variety of patterns available

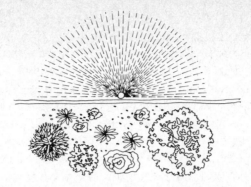

Figure 15 This plan of a pulse sprinkler set to water a semi-circular pattern shows how a lawn may be watered while the flower border remains dry

sight or sound on a hot day than a pulse sprinkler working flat out, whooshing its pulses of water across the lawn. These sprinklers have been late coming to the ordinary gardener but now they are with us I feel sure they will replace some of the traditional rotating sprinklers.

Having pinched the pulse sprinklers from the professionals it is worth looking at the rest of their kit to see if other things are of value to us. H. Pattisson, T. Parker and particularly Cameron Irrigation are the companies supplying the professional and their catalogues are well worth looking through if you are seeking more sophisticated equipment than that usually obtainable from garden shops. The Cameron catalogue is devoted to irrigation in one form or another and the range of sprinklers, hoses and couplings should be sufficient to satisfy the most demanding gardener. These catalogues are also valuable because, unlike most ordinary garden brochures, they give the operating pressures necessary for satisfactory working of each gadget and in some cases the delivery rate per hour and area covered at a variety of different pressure settings. This is the stuff for the perfectionist. The travelling sprinklers listed in these catalogues would be a great help in the garden but Melnor also make several versions for garden use. These machines automatically move round the garden, on a course decided by you, and switch themselves off when their job is done. They are driven by water pressure and actually move back along their supply hose, winding it up as they go.

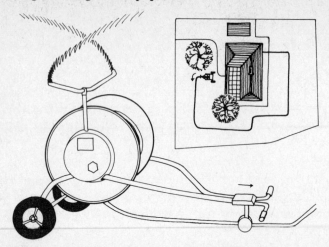

Figure 16 One of the mobile sprinklers made by Melnor. This machine moves back over its hose in the direction of the arrow and it reels the hose in as it goes. The plan shows how the hose is laid out in the track you wish the sprinkler to follow. It cuts off automatically when it reaches the end of the hose

Imagine that. The advantages are obvious. Such things have been used by groundsmen for a long time so they do work, but how well they will cope with uneven or sloping ground in the garden I do not know. If you think one of these chaps is for you insist on a demonstration in your garden before committing yourself. They are expensive, so be certain that both your terrain and water pressure suit the machine and vice versa.

One of the simplest of all the watering gadgets is a hose which has been punctured at various points and which therefore sends out a series of fine jets of water in a rectangular pattern. You might think that this sort of thing could be made at home by pricking holes in a length of hose, but it is not quite as easy as that. You see, round section hose is not suitable as it is likely to roll on the lawn and there would be no way of keeping the outlets in their correct position. What is required is special flat bottomed hose, or three small bore hoses joined together as illustrated in Figure 17. This type is sold by Valentine Plastics and there is also an aluminium version of this idea available from Barrie Grist. These punctured hose type sprinklers are very effective lawn sprinklers and have the advantage of spraying

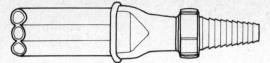

Figure 17 Sprinkler hose showing the attachment for the supply hose and cross-section through the three small bore hoses which comprise the sprinkler section. Perforations in these three hoses allow water to spray out as shown in Plate 4

a rectangular pattern, although some makes give uneven water distribution. This needs to be checked. This type also works well on low water pressure and I find them to be simple and trouble free. Do not roll them up, however, because once they acquire a coil or kink they become quite useless until the sun softens them sufficiently to allow them to lie flat again.

Nice though all these things appear they are really only suited to lawn watering because, with one or two exceptions, all the sprinklers deliver fairly large water droplets which are too big and heavy for the satisfactory watering of some vegetables, flowers, seedlings and seed beds. Plants are so easily damaged by heavy overhead watering while small seedlings can be flattened completely and exposed ground can become panned and unworkable. This being so, alternative watering methods are needed and this is where mist watering units are useful. Two which I find simple and effective are the Torspray and the Agriframes spray.

Mist watering units

My favourite watering gadget of all is the Torspray which is a mist watering unit mounted on aluminium tube with a spike for holding it in the ground. This simple, cheap and well-made tool gives a very, very fine and intense mist over a small area. The mist is so light that no damage is done to the plants or the ground but care is needed to prevent over watering. The Torspray needs very frequent moving. There are other mist devices which are made of plastic and which are not as good as the Torspray. Of course the watering pattern is circular but I am prepared to put up with this for the fine spray. The Agriframes sprayer has a similar effect but can be controlled to deliver either a circular spray pattern or one narrow segment of a

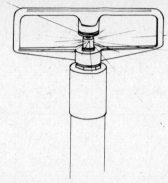

Figure 18 The head of the Torspray fine mist watering unit. This head stands on a 3 ft length of aluminium pipe. The very fine mist is ideal for gentle watering but remember that it delivers large quantities of water over a small area and needs moving frequently

circle. Its spray is not so fine as the Torspray but I find it a simple and useful watering tool. The trouble is that the very fine and gentle mist which is so kind to the plants is also easily blown about by the wind and this can make accurate watering a problem.

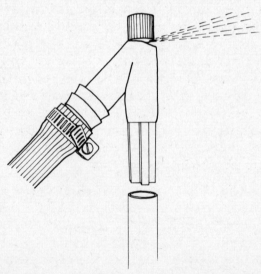

Figure 19 The Agriframes mist watering device. The knurled brass put on the top is screwed into the plastic body of the unit and water is forced from one side in a fairly fine mist. By using an alternative body full circle watering is achieved. The plastic top of the unit plugs into a steel tube for support

Seep-hose

No matter how fine the spray which the sprinkler delivers there are plenty of occasions when overhead watering of any kind is inadvisable because of the risk of scorching the plant leaves, or for a variety of other reasons. This is where the seep-hose enters stage left.

The seep-hose, which is made by Access Irrigation Ltd, is very good and it can be used at any time of the day regardless of wind or sun. The principle is simple: water is allowed to ooze or seep very slowly from the stitched edge of the hose and as the hose is lying right beside the plants the water soaks away into the ground just where the roots are. There is no danger of soil panning or of plant damage. It is also worth noting that this method of watering is not nearly as wasteful as the sprinkler methods. This type of watering is done at very low pressure and even the pathetic pressure in my garden is too much and the tap has to be turned down. This is, of course, no problem because one of the joys of the seep-hose is that it does its work slowly over a long period and does not therefore require the constant attention of its master. Another advantage of the seep-hose is the ease with which the ground under cloches can be watered. Before placing cloches over a row of plants first lay a length of seep-hose down and all you need to do when watering is required is plug in the ordinary hose to the seep-hose and the job is done. Indeed I find the best way to use seep-hose is to leave it permanently in position beside vegetable rows and to plug the main hose in as required. To make this easier I throw away the useless hose connectors which Access supply and with a Jubilee clip I fix a 3 in. length of ½ in. hose to the seep-hose. To this short piece of hose I attach a hose joint ready for plugging into the main hose end. Which raises the question of which hose joints to use.

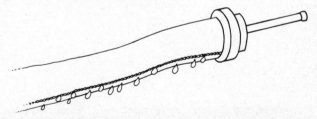

Figure 20 A section of seep-hose by Access Irrigation. Water seeps slowly from the stitched seam of this hose. Excellent in the vegetable garden. The poor hose fittings shown here are best changed, as described in the text

Hose attachments

There are several brands of hose attachments on the market, most of them in plastics of different quality, and they all do a reasonable job in the garden. For something better you will need, once again, to go to the companies who supply the professionals. The single most important piece of equipment in the system is the already mentioned 'water stop': not all companies include such a thing in their range and that limits their use as far as I am concerned. Among those that do are Voss, Al-Ko, Wolf, Poly-Gard and Gardena. The water stop is a magical device which stops the flow of water the moment you disconnect the sprinkler from the hose end. This saves a lot of trouble. Normally you lay out your hose, attach the sprinkler or whatever gizmo takes your fancy, run back to the tap and turn on. Some time later the whole outfit needs moving or changing to another sprinkler unit so you trot to the tap and turn it off, then walk to the other end of the hose, disconnect device A and connect device B, then walk slowly back to the tap to turn on and finally crawl back to whatever job you were doing before all this started – only to repeat the process several times throughout the afternoon. The alternative is to try and effect the change without shutting off the water which means you get very wet and, in my case, very bad tempered too. With a water stop that is all in the past because the instant you disconnect device A the water stops and the instant you connect device B, lo and behold, water flows again. No trips to the tap and no soaked shirt.

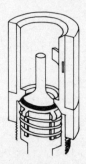

Figure 21 Cross-section through a Voss water stop. When the next hose length or hose attachment is pushed into this the peg is depressed against the spring and the valve is opened. When the attachment is removed the spring forces the valve back on to its seat and the water flow is stopped

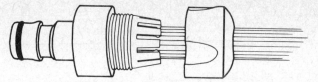

Figure 22 This is a typical claw type hose fitting made entirely of plastic. The large nut on the right is screwed on to thread on the left and this forces the claws to bite into the hose, thus gripping it very tightly

Once you incorporate these water stops into your system the weaknesses in it will be shown up because when the water is stopped the hose is full of water *under pressure* and any weakness in the hose fittings, the hose itself or the tap fittings will become apparent. Therefore you need good hose, probably braided hose if your pressure is high, good hose fittings of the claw type illustrated, and good tap fittings. Indeed without good tap fittings the water stop will not work. The only thing that will happen is that the hose will blow off the tap and if that tap is in the kitchen trouble may be only a wife-stride away. The only satisfactory way to use a hose is to have an outside tap with a screw nozzle so that the hose adaptor may be screwed to the tap and will thereby be able to withstand any pressure. Which of the brands of hose fittings you use is probably not too important; some are made of better quality plastic than others and this is important because the joints must be screwed up very tight and poor quality fittings break when treated thus. I have been using the Voss fittings for about a year and find them very good.

One important thing to remember when using a water stop system: always release the pressure in the hose before rolling it up. A hose full of water under pressure which is subsequently heated by the sun can expand from ½ in. bore thick-walled hose to 1 in. bore thin-walled hose. I speak from experience.

Usually I do not roll the hose up but leave it straggling untidily across the lawn; I find hose reels a bit of a nuisance. If you want a hose reel at least buy one with wheels or have one attached to the wall – in either case you should have the water delivery type – but I am willing to bet that you will not use either after a time, especially if your hose is 200 ft long. Hose reels are, on the face of it, a good idea but they do not solve the problem of what to do with a hose, they merely make a tidy coil of what is otherwise an untidy tangle. A hose of any

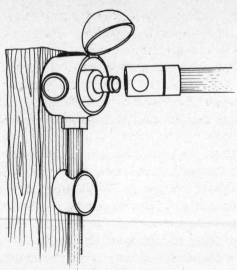

Figure 23 A Voss water point mounted on a wooden post. With the covering cap lifted the hose can be plugged into the point and water flows immediately. There is no need for a tap. When the hose is disconnected the flow is immediately shut off by the valve in the water point

reasonable length which is used frequently is, frankly, an annoying thing to be constantly reeling in and winding out and the better method is to leave it out but *hidden*. This means laying a proper watering system in your garden using the various plastic hose fittings available from Voss and other companies.

The hose is laid around the garden and sunk a few inches underground; it does not need to be very deep. At strategic points a water plug is put in the system so that you have a water circuit with plugs at various points like the electricity circuit in the house. All that is then required is a short length of hose to be plugged into whichever is the most convenient point for each watering job. By doing this water is taken to every part of the garden without any visible hose and without the need to be reeling and unreeling miles of the wretched thing all weekend. Each flower bed, the vegetable garden, the greenhouse and the garage can all have their own water point conveniently placed. The only thing to remember is that the system cannot be plumbed permanently to the water main. It must be connected to a tap at some point and in the winter it must be drained to prevent damage to the hose fittings. This is achieved on level ground by pumping water from the system using a small hand pump which Voss supply or, if the layout is on a slope, a drain outlet at the lowest point will allow gravity to clear the system.

If the idea of a hidden system appeals to you and you want to go the whole hog you can have a very elaborate arrangement with a control panel which looks as if it would fly the Atlantic if it were fitted with wings. The thing bristles with twenty-four-hour clocks, fourteen-day clocks, remote control solenoids and a host of other goodies which will cause an army of sprinklers automatically to pop out of hidden holes in the garden, and water their appointed areas before disappearing whence they came. This automated aqua show is the 'Rain Bird' system from California (where else?) and it is available from The Plastic Tube and Conduit Co. Ltd, in the UK.

In contrast to this I should point out that if, despite all that the plastics and the electronics industries are doing for you, you still prefer the simple traditional brass hose fittings and nozzles these can still be obtained from Parker, from Pattisson and from Cameron Irrigation. Furthermore you can make your own metal sprinkler from brass or copper if you are able to do a little soldering.

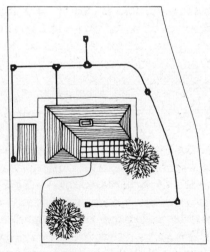

Figure 24 A plan view of an underground water system using ordinary braided garden hose and plastic fittings such as those made by Voss. At various points water plugs are installed which enable a short length of hose to be used to water places convenient to each plug. Sprinklers may be plugged directly to water points in some cases

It is unlikely that either of the extremes, the 'Rain Bird' or the home-made system, will find their way into many gardens. The ordinary plastic systems, on the other hand, are within the reach of most people and the versatility of the products allied to the ease with which they can be handled means that watering should be a pleasurable gardening activity and not the battle with leaks and poor fittings which it so often is. Moreover, as it is such a vital part of gardening, perhaps we should make a greater effort to find the right equipment for the various watering jobs in every garden. Certainly if you look hard enough the right equipment does exist and even if that equipment is a well you could contact Al-Ko because they offer to search for water, sink a well and supply all the bits and pieces necessary to make your own water supply. Well well.

Watering and irrigation equipment: buying points

1 Hose quality: braided hose best and strongest for water stop system and high pressure.

2 Hose bore: good water flow, high pressure and long hose length could mean bigger bore than standard ½ in.

3 Lawn watering: any sprinkler will do. Check for even distribution of spray patterns.

4 Plant watering: mist watering and seep-hose.

5 Cloche watering: seep-hose.

6 Hose fittings: look for rigid plastic fittings of the claw type. Water stop essential. Brass is available for those who prefer it.

7 Oscillating sprinklers: only buy the best. Look for brass nozzles.

8 Hose reels: wheels necessary or wall type. Must be a through hose type connected to water supply.

9 Automatic watering: moving sprinkler type. Fully automatic remote control system.

10 Special equipment: specialist suppliers, Cameron, Parker, and Pattisson.

11 Water pressure: ensure that your pressure is sufficient to drive the gadgets you choose.

1 To show that garden tractors are not toys this Wheel Horse is fifteen years old and is still going strong in a large garden near Haslemere

2/3 The contrast between the very fine mist of the Torspray and the larger droplets of the Melnor pulse spray are clearly seen in these two photographs. The pulses of water can be seen as whiter parts in the spray from the Melnor. Both sprinklers are excellent for their varied uses

4 This end view of a pierced-hose type sprinkler shows the three-pronged spray shape and also that the droplet size is smaller than that of the pulse sprinkler but much coarser than the Torspray mist

5 Another mist sprinkler, the Agriframes, here used to water a part-circle pattern. This is a useful device for watering borders

6/7 Two extremes of grass cutting. At the top my own John Deere tractor cutting through very long grass and weeds and below the unusual triple reel Nickerson Turfmaster. The John Deere also cuts our lawns and other short grass but the Turfmaster, as its name implies, is for lawns only. Notice how the cutting cylinders remain level despite the camber of the ground and the leaning of the tractor

8 This photograph of a Hayter Harrier shows what a rotary lawn mower will do if necessary. Although designed for lawn cutting this mower will cut quite long rough grass when this is occasionally required. Cylinder mowers are not as versatile as this

9 If cutting long rough grass is a regular task you need a mower such as the Hayterette which is designed for the job – and it does it very well, even under the extreme conditions shown in the photograph. This was taken as I prepared some rough ground for a new vegetable plot

10 Grass collection with some rotary mowers is not as efficient as it should be. This photograph of a Wolf Rotondor grass box shows what can be achieved

11 This puzzling photograph shows the attachment on the end of the rotary blade of a Snapper mower which creates the lift or suck that makes these mowers such efficient grass and leaf collectors

12/13 The underside of the mowing deck of a Hayter Osprey showing a different type of rotary cutter from the usual propeller blade type. This type is common on cutters used for rough work because the little knives attached to the large central disc can swing back if they strike some hard object hidden in the long grass. This minimizes damage to the knives and the engine of the machine

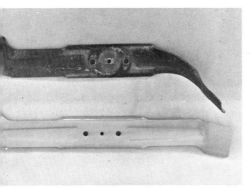

14 What can happen to the conventional rotary blade when it meets something hard in its path. The bottom blade shows the true shape

15 These two blades show the difference between a worn blade, top, and the replacement blade, bottom. You should not allow blades to wear to the extent shown here because as they become worn and thin they can break and fly off causing damage to mower, plants, windows and, not least, people

16 The completely enclosed blades and relatively low profile of the Flymo mowers make them particularly suitable for cutting under shrubs and similar inaccessible places. Such work is much more difficult with orthodox mowers

17 The Andrews Spin Trim which is a very good battery-driven lawn edger

18/19 These before and after pictures show how well the Spin Trim cuts the grass edges. (The wavy appearance of the edge is due to my earlier inaccurate work with the half-moon edging spade and is not the fault of the Spin Trim)

4 Grass Cutting Machinery

Quite how we are going to get through this chapter I do not know but perhaps if we take a good run at it our momentum will carry us through. The problem is, you see, that there are more than 270 different mowers presently available in this country all competing for your valued custom and all hoping to be given a fair chance in that competition. The figure of 270 includes the small ride-on mowers, but does not include the lawn and garden tractors (which are dealt with separately, in Chapter 15), nor does it include small gang mowers and similar devices. Now when you take yourself off to the nearest mower dealer and announce cheerily that you intend to do him the honour of buying a mower, you can see how you might be making a mistake. Do not imagine that I am suggesting that you bore yourself to death by carefully scrutinizing and testing 270 or so mowers first. I am not. What I am suggesting is that if the right one is to be plucked from such a collection then it will be a good idea to do a little homework first otherwise somebody will sell you the wrong thing. It happens all the time.

There are so many ways in which it is sensibly possible to divide this chapter but the most basic is probably by grass type, namely lawns and other grass. By *other grass* I mean anything which is not kept as a short smart lawn.

Rotary or cylinder mowers?

Nearly everybody has some grass which they think of as lawn so we shall consider first the machines which are available to cut lawn. They fall into two groups, the rotary mower and the cylinder, or reel, mower. The last named is the traditional mower which has spiral blades revolving horizontally and cutting against a fixed bottom blade. The rotary mowers are a much more recent machine and, as the name implies, they work by having a rotating blade, like a propeller, which in theory cuts the grass as it moves over it. In practice it is an action which beats the grass into submission. Between the supporters of the rotary and the reel mower there is a constant war with neither side prepared to hear a good word said for the other. I do not propose to be drawn into such an argument which is as futile and dangerous as discussing religion or politics, but I can point out the arguments for and against each as I see them.

The cylinder mower does have a better cutting action made possible by one blade, the revolving one, bearing on another, the fixed one. The result is a slicing action similar to that of a pair of scissors or shears and the grass, which is trapped between the two blades, is cut neatly and cleanly. The rotary's spinning blade in theory also cuts cleanly: the sharp blade edge moving at phenomenal speed comes into contact with a stem of grass and slices it straight through. If a steel blade came into contact with your neck at 200 mph it would go straight through but the question is, would it go through cleanly? Herein lies the substance of one of the arguments between the two sides. The rotary blade, moving as it does at speed and with some weight, is bound to remove the top of anything it comes into contact with. Because that object is not held still during this brutal act, however, the decapitation is likely to be ragged rather than clean even if the blade is extremely sharp which it mostly is not. The cylinder mower, on the other hand, slices grass with a clean neat cut all the time. So who, you may wonder, cares whether the cut is clean or ragged? Apparently a lot of people do. Grass which is cut cleanly heals quickly, recovers and grows away lush and green. Raggedly cut grass, however, does not heal quickly and is therefore, it is said, more susceptible to disease. Moreover the tops of the ragged grass tend to go brown and spoil the appearance of the lawn. All of which is good stuff in an ideal world but there are other factors for we gardeners to consider in the real world in which we struggle.

The first practical point is that a cylinder mower, depending as it does on the precision action of its blades, will only cut well when its blades are maintained in very good condition. This is something very, very few gardeners ever bother about and, worse yet, some cheap cylinder mowers will not cut properly anyway because the quality of their materials does not allow them so to do. Whereas a rotary, depending as it does on brute force and ignorance, will knock the top off grass whether the blade is sharp, blunt, bent, rusty or made of plastic, which is one reason why such mowers have found favour in recent years.

The next practical point concerns rain and the considerable quantities of the stuff which we get in this country. Wet grass should not be cut and if you have a reel mower, especially a roller driven one, you will find it almost impossible to cut wet grass. Yet to the weekend gardener such a limitation is hopeless. He has to cut his grass at the weekend because that is the only chance he gets and if during that time the grass is wet, well too bad, it has to be cut anyway. A rotary will cut wet grass quite satisfactorily. Whether this does the grass any harm or any good or neither is a moot point but in any case that will not always be the most important consideration.

The third practical point, and a telling one it is, concerns the versatility of the rotary mower. If you not only have lawn to cut but also some *other grass*, you will either need two types of mower or alternatively one mower which can cope with both conditions. The rotary will cope with both, the reel mower will not. It is that simple – well almost: there are some rough country cylinder mowers which we shall come to.

By now your first choice should be plain: if you have a very good lawn which you treat in a manner befitting a very good lawn and if you are prepared to maintain a mower in very good condition and if you buy a mower of reasonable quality and if you do not need a dual purpose machine, then buy a cylinder mower because nothing else will satisfy you. But if you have to compromise any of the qualifications above then join the rest of we grassy heretics and buy a rotary mower.

Cylinder mowers

If you opt for the cylinder mower you are confronted as ever with the means of powering such a machine. Do you have petrol power, electrical power or human power? If you can possibly afford it I would have a motor mower and not a push mower. If you want a push mower they are still available from Qualcast, Webb, Husqvarna and

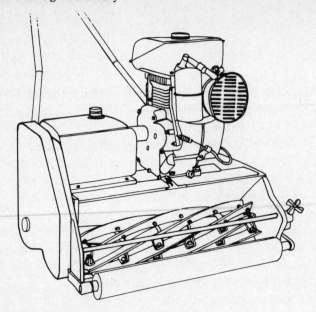

Figure 25 The Lloyd Palladin cylinder mower

Ginge, with the last two having the grass collection box behind the mower instead of in front which is more conventional. Having a rear mounted grass box has a number of advantages not least of which is the ability to drive the cutting blades of the mower close to obstructions. But these rear mounted boxes do not collect well and one must remember that such machines are side wheel types not rear roller types and they do not, therefore, give the striped finish of which most people are so fond.

When testing a hand push machine remember that the ease or difficulty with which it can be pushed is affected by how well the blades are adjusted: if the revolving blades bind too tightly on the fixed bottom blade the thing will be very difficult to push. This may seem painfully obvious but is easily overlooked. Only compare one machine with another when you are certain that both are in perfect adjustment (for which assurance you will have to rely on your dealer who will, I hope, know enough to be able to give you such assurance honestly). It is also a fact of life that the mower which will give you the best lawn finish in this category, the Webb Witch, is also the mower which will take most pushing. This is because it has an 8 bladed cutting reel, instead of the 5 or 6 of the others, and gives 60 cuts per yard rather than the 30 or 40 cuts of the others. There is more friction and therefore more resistance to be overcome by the pusher.

Correct blade adjustment is, of course, crucial to all reel mowers but it is particularly important on hand mowers because of the strain it imposes on the pusher, namely you. On power mowers no strain will be transmitted to you by poorly adjusted blades but the motor could be overloaded and, particularly in the case of electric motors, much damage could be done.

Not all power mowers are self-propelled. Some use their engines only to power the blades and still rely on you to push them along; this is all right for very light mowers but I think the whole point of having power is to save pushing. I would always choose a mower which is self-propelled, and this is particularly true if you are cutting grass on anything other than dead level ground. Whether the mower is electrically powered or petrol powered will depend on the area to be cut. If you have to take the mower far away from the house it must be petrol. If you do not, then mains electric is at once a quieter and simpler means of power. Battery power is making a revival and it is a good idea, but the price of the batteries makes such machines expensive and you must make certain they are capable of cutting all your grass on a full charge. If you choose a mains electric model make sure it is double insulated and *not earthed*.

Other things to look for in a cylinder machine include the quality of the blade reel and bottom knife, the method of height adjustment, the grass box material, engine size, gearing and weight.

The blade reel should be robust and properly welded – some are very poor in this respect – or better still riveted. The bed knife should be extremely rigid and strong. If not it will flex while mowing, making it impossible for the mower to achieve a good cut. The curved blades should be touching the bottom knife at *at least* two points all the time. The bottom blade adjustment should be simple, strong and accurate, which means that a central adjuster is probably not good enough.

Height adjustment, too, is difficult on some machines. Look for simple but strong height adjusters. If they are wing nuts, ensure that you can move them easily by hand; some require a spanner which rather defeats their purpose I always think. The grass box these days *must* be of some lightweight fibreglass or plastic: there is no excuse for having heavy rust-prone steel ones any longer.

Engine size, or rather engine power, is much more important than you might imagine. The power of the electric motors is measured in watts and if they are of the brush type such machines will develop their maximum torque and power at maximum rpm. This speed must be compatible with a sensible walking pace for the operator. If the machine has an induction electric motor, which is very unlikely, it will work well and powerfully almost regardless of the rpm, so you will easily adjust it to a comfortable walking pace. A petrol engine must provide sufficient power to turn the blades in the worst conditions likely to be encountered and propel the machine at the same time but with the proviso that it does these things at a comfortable walking speed. If the gearing of the machine is such that for the engine to drive the blades in difficult going without stalling requires it to rev very fast and consequently make you run behind it, then the gearing is all to pot and the machine probably needs a bigger engine. Also know that mowing on a slight incline can have a much greater effect on mowers which are underpowered than you or the salesman might at first think. If you already have such a mower you can have an engine conversion carried out which could change the whole thing and save you from buying a new mower.

When considering the weight of the machine it is a relative matter because most mowers are heavy; it is just that some are heavier than others. You are the one who has to heave it in and out of the shed so remember this, because during such operations the engine will be of no help whatsoever. One way of saving weight is to have a small mower. Do not therefore choose the biggest and widest there is unless you are really able to benefit from its greater mowing capacity because all you might get from it may be extra weight to manhandle in the garage.

Finally when contemplating and comparing various cylinder mowers think about the number of cuts per yard which the machine will give you. This is an important point and not all manufacturers seem to be keen to divulge such information although I cannot think why they should not. There is no hard and fast rule about how many cuts per yard there should be and it will depend on the work you do with your mower; but there are some broad rules.

For the very best of fine lawns, the sort rarely seen, a machine giving about 100 cuts per yard will give a very good finish. Some machines go to 150 or so but this is for cutting the nap off a snooker table and really has no part in the garden. However if you have a lawn of snooker table fineness and you want to shave it daily then by all means buy such a tool. At the other end of the scale the big side wheel cylinder mowers, which are used for cutting long rough grass, give about 30 to 40 cuts per yard. The number of cuts per yard is governed by two things, the number of blades on the reel and the number of times the reel spins round for every yard the machine moves forward. So by having lots of blades going slowly or by having a few blades going fast you can achieve the same number of cuts per yard. With either method there are secondary problems not the least of which is rapid bearing wear with the few blades going fast method; but it is the many blades going relatively slowly which is more likely to cause you trouble. Such machines will have ten blades on the reel, will not cut damp grass and will have great difficulty in cutting anything but the shortest grass. They do literally shave the top of the grass and so if you use one of these your lawn will need to be cut on alternate days when it is growing well, perhaps even daily. They also have difficulty in clearing grass quickly enough from the cutters because of the relatively slow reel speed. Probably for goodish garden lawns a mower giving about 65 to 80 cuts per yard will give a fine enough finish, compatible with the mower being able to cope with at least a week's growth of grass and possibly damp grass too. Cutting rates of 50 per yard or lower will leave the ribbing effect on lawns which looks so bad. Only buy a mower with a high cutting rate if you are certain you and your lawn can cope with it.

Fine lawns are not the only grass areas areas cut by cylinder mowers. Indeed, some people still demand that very rough areas be cut by cylinder mowers because they believe they do a better job and so there are big robust cylinder mowers for heavy work such as road verges and similar places. These machines are usually side wheel types or special adaptations of pedestrian tractor units. All of the machines in this category are primarily designed for the professional groundsman, greenkeepers and local authorities but if you are sold on the cylinder mower you could well use them in the rougher parts of your garden. They will cut grass up to 7 or 8 in. long but they are expensive. Lloyds and Ransomes are two companies making mowers in this special category.

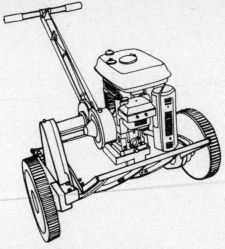

Figure 26 An example of a very large cylinder mower for rough grass. This is the Lloyd Pennsylvania side wheel mower

Among the more usual garden machines are the names which have been part of gardening, it seems, since Eden was a horticultural show place. Companies like Atco, Qualcast and Webb are still producing a good range of cylinder mowers for the garden (Qualcast and Atco, along with Suffolk, come under the corporate umbrella of Birmid. However they have maintained their separate characters and identities). It is the 12 in. Suffolk Super Colt which is probably the most common petrol engined lawn mower of all time – and with good reason. This small machine gives the advantage of power blades and power propulsion at a very low cost. It may not be the most sophisticated mower available but it is simple, durable and very good value for money. My own totally neglected and criminally abused Colt has been working well for ten years now and, although it is ill treated and often required to do work for which it was not intended, it has been no trouble. If you want a cylinder machine cheaper than this you will have to buy a small electric one and none of these will give the service of a Colt. They are altogether lighter, less robust and not nearly as powerful. They work fairly well but are for quite small areas only. The fact that they are popular is indicated by the fact that Qualcast have sold 1¾ million of their Concorde in the few years that it has been made.

The fact that Atco and Suffolk are from the same stable will be obvious when you compare the Suffolks with the bottom of the Atco range. They are basically the same machines. However, the Atco range is much wider and extends into the area of the professional user and it is at this end of the range that you will find the bigger cylinder mowers, some of which are able to pull a small roller seat which enables you to sit down for your mowing.

Among the cylinder mowers the Hayter Ambassador is one which I found particularly pleasant to use. The fact that it is very quiet and smooth contributes to this pleasant feeling but it is also one of those machines which, for no obvious reason, is just a nice machine. I tested this mower on a wide variety of grass in my garden throughout last summer and although it took longer to cut the grass with this than with my lawn tractor I nonetheless found myself using it because it was such an enjoyable machine to handle. By and large cylinder mowers are pleasanter machines to use than rotaries, and this could be another factor in making you decide whether a cylinder mower will suit you.

If you want a small cylinder model of the very first quality you could contact Lloyds of Letchworth who might, for considerable sums of money, sell you one of their beautiful Palladin mowers. These machines I have not used but I have seen them being painstakingly made and that was impressive enough. If you can afford such a machine you will also have to be prepared to wait for it because, as with all good things, demand far exceeds supply.

For really big lawns, particularly those with few mowing obstacles such as beds, trees or shrubs, the big cylinder mowers normally used by groundsmen are the perfect machines. In this category Ransomes, Atco and Hayter are the companies offering suitable models, although the Nickerson Turfmaster machines, which are dealt with in Chapter 15 on tractors, are also ideal for this work. Despite being of fearsome size, some of these big cylinder mowers are quite simple to operate provided the controls are good. You should not be deterred by their bulk; if you have the work for such equipment it would be folly to attempt to do it with anything less. My fairly brief trial of the Hayter Condor in this class showed me that it is no more difficult to control than a mower half its size and, incidentally, it too is a pleasant machine to use.

If your need is for a big cylinder mower it is worth considering a second hand machine which has served its time with a professional

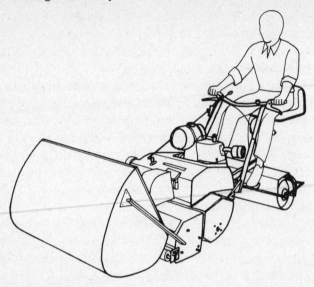

Figure 27 The Hayter Condor is a large ride-on cylinder mower: an easily controlled and pleasant machine to use

user. The relatively quiet life such a machine would lead in the garden, albeit a big garden, would mean that it would last a long time provided, of course, that it was properly reconditioned before starting its second life.

Rotary mowers

Having considered cylinder mowers at great length we can now turn to the very popular but often despised rotary mowers. There is a much wider choice of rotary machines than of cylinder machines. One of the reasons for this choice lies in the fact that a great many of the machines sold in the UK are imported from less grassily enlightened places, such as Europe and the USA where rotary mowers reign supreme. In those parts of the world all kinds of short green vegetation pass for lawns and such lawns are efficiently and satisfactorily cut by a rotary; it is only in the UK, where some gardeners strive to produce really fine lawns, that we require a cylinder mower.

The fact that many rotary mowers are imported can have an influence on your choice, apart from the obviously patriotic reasons. Some of these imported machines are designed to collect the drier, coarser grass of their native country but not all can cope with the finer, denser and damper grass of the UK, and attention should be paid to this matter. Mind you, there are plenty of British machines which cannot collect grass adequately either.

The virtue of a rotary mower, as mentioned earlier, is that it will cut anything, within reason. Provided you select the right machine it will cut your lawns and your rough grass too. It is also among the rotaries that you will find the cheapest power mowers of all: the very simple mains electric, plastic bodied, light rotaries of Black and Decker and others. These machines are fine for cutting small areas of lawn and will last for many years doing such work but do not expect them to tackle big jobs and do not expect to get a good finish with them either. They are a cheap, functional and reliable way of shortening grass on a small lawn but that is all. If you want more than that you will have to pay for it. Perhaps the next stage in small electric machines is the 12 in. Wolf Cadet. This has the advantage and refinement of an induction electric motor which will enable it to do tougher work than the brush type electric motors more usually used by electric rotaries.

For normal lawn cutting there are many petrol rotary motors available: some require pushing and others are self-propelled, some collect grass and others do not. For lawn cutting I think it likely that you will require a grass collecting type; there are one or two models which are grass collectors in name only so, once again, do make sure you try the things properly before buying. If you want to have a striped lawn you will need a rotary with a roller rear drive, and machines in this category are generally not such good grass collectors as the all wheel machines. This is because the grass is ejected from the back of the mower and it has to be thrown over the roller and into the grass box which does cause problems. Some machines such as the Hayter Harrier and the Mountfield M3 achieve fairly good results but if you want stripes (and therefore a roller machine) you will also have to accept less good grass collection. If grass collection is your *first* priority you will buy an all wheel machine and forego the stripes.

Achieving good grass collection is difficult and requires not only that the grass cuttings be hurled into some box or bag but also that said box or bag fills up and does not clog after a few minutes. Getting the grass flowing into the grass box in such a way that the box fills, even with wet grass, is no mean feat but if it does not do this it will be nothing more than a source of irritation to you. Furthermore, it is important that the grass box should be easily detached from the machine without spilling its hard-won contents back on the lawn. It is amazing how many grass boxes have to be tipped forward to release them from the mower, an action which usually results in half the contents spilling out. What a waste of time. The Wolf Rotondor models seem to have got the design right but the Wolf Lawnliners have not. The Honda mowers employ a bag rather than a box and this works very well as does the bag on the Snapper CV mowers. Some models such as the Landmaster Stoic, the John Deere and the Lawn-Boy have a *side* collecting bag which is adequate but awkward for manoeuvring in restricted spaces. There has been some resistance from the public to grass collecting bags on mowers and it appears that the British prefer grass boxes. However I think bags are just as good, and probably even better if well designed. They usually have a larger capacity than boxes, are no trouble to empty and are lighter.

The wheel mowers have another advantage over the roller types, in addition to better grass collection, which is that they are better able to cope with cutting long rough grass if this is occasionally required of them. If you want your mower to perform such duties it would be better if it were not the roller type. In favour of the roller models, however, is the relative ease with which they will cut over the edge of lawns. To do this perfectly they need a front and rear roller, like the Landmaster Sovereign. With just a rear roller it is possible, whereas with an all wheel model it is impossible. No model will do everything so you will have to compromise somewhere.

Whether or not you should have a self-propelled or a push model will be a matter of cost but if you possibly can I would choose the self-propelled every time. Some of these rotaries with a full grass bag are heavy to push around and you will eventually regret buying a push model I am sure. When buying a self-propelled rotary do make sure that the speed of the machine is comfortable. Some that I have tried require the operator to move at a pretty smart pace: this is uncomfortable and also makes the machine difficult to control. Of course you can slow the engine down but this also slows cutter blade speed, and rotaries do need their blades to be moving at a good speed for them to be really effective. The more expensive machines will have two or more gears, which makes life easier, and again the Snapper and some of the Hondas come into this category. In fact in a

Figure 28 This cut-away drawing of the Honda
HR21 rotary mower shows just how complicated
the modern rotary mower can become in its most
sophisticated form

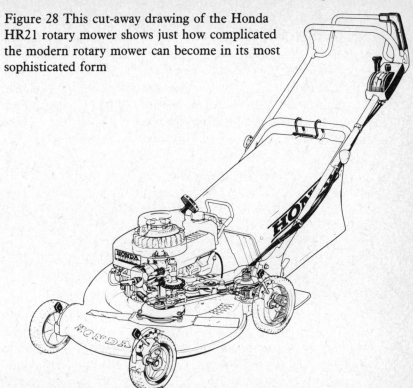

category where I generally find machines unpleasant to use these two
are the least so, and the Honda has the advantage of being reasonably
quiet too, an unusual quality among rotaries which, unlike cylinder
mowers, are mostly revving quite hard while they are working.
Unfortunately these are two of the more expensive machines offered.
The honour of the most expensive among the lawn type rotaries goes
to the Lawn-Boy but this is because it has an electric starter and that
is a disproportionately expensive item to add to a small mower. If,
like so many people, you cannot cope with the awful pull starters
fitted to most engines you have no choice but to buy a Lawn-Boy with
an electric starter. I have asked other manufacturers why they do not
fit such a device and they say 'there is no call for it' – which is just
about what you would expect them to say, I suppose.

Rotaries which have been primarily designed for the lawn can also
cope with rough grass but if you have a lot of such work it is better to
buy a machine designed for the job. There are a number of good ones

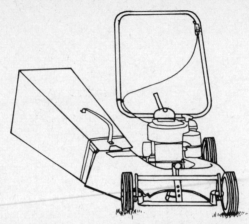

Figure 29 The Landmaster Stoic is a favourite rotary for tough conditions. The side mounted grass collector reduces the manoeuvrability of the machine but on a cutter of this type the grass collector would not normally be used

about, not the least of which is the Hayterette. This tough machine will cut anything in its path and Plate 9 shows it at work clearing a patch for cultivation in my garden. I like the Hayterette and I know from letters I have that other gardeners also find this a good machine for rough going. Unfortunately it is a push model and when the going gets really hard, pushing is the last thing you want to be doing. The Landmaster Stoic is another really tough simple machine which comes in a self-propelled version as well as a push version. Both the Hayterette and the Stoic are much favoured by the local authority users who require very rugged machines and they will easily cope with the worst garden work, despite their relatively small size.

For work in small orchards or paddocks the Hayter 21, the Osprey or the big Wolseley rotaries, all with powered wheels, are the solution. All these machines can be fitted with a trailer seat which makes them much less tiring to use and the bigger ones will cut up to half an acre of very rough long grass in an hour.

The machines used for rough work often have a different type of cutter from the normal rotary: instead of single propeller-like blades they have small swinging knives which are bolted to the edge of a large disc. The idea of these free swinging knives is that they will be easily knocked out of the way if they should strike any hard object in the course of their cutting. This has the effect of reducing the loading

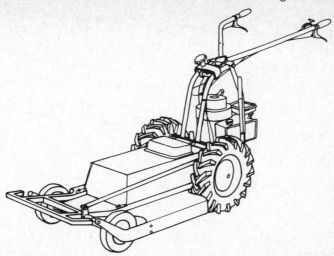

Figure 30 For heavy duty grass cutting a large self-propelled rotary, like this Wolseley, is a good idea

on the machine and preventing expensive damage; it also means that the blade continues revolving untroubled by obstructions. Such blades take a lot of stopping which is why they are so well suited to rough work. Normal bar blades tangle more easily and could stop dead if they met an immovable object in the long grass.

While on the subject of rotaries for rough cutting we should also mention the Bushwakka and the Gurkha, both made by Norlett. The Bushwakka is an old favourite and is a really efficient cutter of rough long grass, an efficiency it achieves by allowing the grass to get into the cutting blades easily and then allowing the cut grass to escape equally easily. Such design does not always make for complete safety – do not use it unless you are well away from other people and animals – but do not be deterred from using this excellent machine. Such a splendid name too, the Bushwakka.

The Gurkha is an odd looking three wheeled heavy duty rotary cutter designed for rough work and cutting grassy banks. It looks like no other grass cutter and is a good example of what is now popularly called 'lateral thinking' being applied to mower design. This is a specialist's machine which is worth investigating for use in large gardens with difficult terrain.

Before leaving rotaries the last group, the hovering mowers, must be mentioned. Flymo hovering mowers have been around for about fifteen years and Flymo has, until recently, been the only manufacturer of these mowers. Now their patents have expired and other manufacturers like Qualcast, Templar, Crown and Black and Decker are already offering Flymo stiff competition. There is no doubt that Flymo has made a great success of selling the novel idea of a hovering mower but what does this type of mower offer which other rotaries do not? I think they offer some people a great deal and they have made possible work which was hitherto either very difficult or impossible. But to other people they are a gimmick machine which offers no more than other machines.

A good hovering mower is very light to use, indeed it probably requires less effort than any other mower and that alone will make it a good machine for some people. Remember, however, that it is only a light, easy, effortless machine while it is working. When it has to be carried to and from the garden shed it can be heavy and uncomfortable to handle. So do not have one if you will need to carry it very far or, alternatively, buy a model with a wheeled trolley for transport.

If you have grassy banks or slopes, even very steep banks, or if you have grass growing well under shrubs then the hover mower is the perfect machine. Nothing copes with steep banks and slopes so well as a hover mower which can be lowered by rope down a bank, and pulled to the top again, thus allowing the operator to stand easily and safely at the top of the bank. For getting into awkward areas and for pushing under shrubs the Flymo and its kind are also perfect and Plate 16 clearly demonstrates its use in this way. Apart from one small electric Flymo none of these machines is capable of collecting grass. However, they do chop grass very finely – much finer than a normal rotary – and, therefore, it is claimed that it is less important to collect the grass anyway. Most big gardens could find a Flymo a useful part of their normal armament.

The matter of whether or not grass should be collected is the substance of another of the great grassy debates which I do not intend to take part in, although there is some information on this in Chapter 5 which may interest you.

There are some design points to consider when looking at rotary mowers which, although they do not directly affect the cutting ability of the machine, are still important. The first is the mowing deck of the machine which will be made either from cast aluminium or from pressed steel. (Plastic is only used for the hover mowers and some of the very small electric rotaries.) The cast aluminium decks are reckoned to be the best since it is possible to cast a good aerodynamic shape which is helpful in inducing the cut grass to swirl back into the grass box. The pressed steel decks appear, paradoxically, on the cheaper and the more expensive models. There is nothing wrong with a steel mowing deck that care and attention will not overcome; in fact they are very strong. If you have a steel mowing deck corrosion will be your enemy and my advice is to coat the thing first with rubber underseal, like the underside of a car. I have done this for several years and found it to be a good policy. It needs renewing every year. Obviously with the cast aluminium decks you will have no corrosion problems but remember that such decks will break if they receive a very hard knock. Some mowers, and again I mention the Snapper, have a steel lining inside a cast deck which gives some of the advantages of both worlds.

The next feature to give close attention to is height adjustment. Some mowers, like the Hayter Harrier, have a single lever which automatically raises or lowers all wheels together; others have a separate adjuster for each wheel. The advantages and disadvantages of the two systems are obvious. The important point is to make certain that the adjusters are strong enough and that the slots for holding the adjustment levers are deep. Unfortunately some makers fit very feeble and unsatisfactory height adjusters. Do not buy such mowers as they will not do your work satisfactorily.

The third feature which is necessary, particularly on rotary mowers, is some means of allowing the drive mechanism to slip if the blade should strike the proverbial 'immovable object'. If such a safety device does not exist the engine will suffer. Let me explain: if the blade, screaming round at 2000 rpm or more, should strike a stone or some other obstacle which stops it dead, it will stop the engine dead also and this will certainly result in irreparable damage being done. What is required, therefore, is some means whereby the blade, when stopped in such a fashion, does not also stop the engine. In other words it is necessary to have a means of allowing the engine to come more slowly to a stop. This is usually done by some sort of friction plate which allows normal power to be transmitted but, when overloaded, as in the case outlined, it will slip and relieve the engine of any strain. There are various ways of achieving this effect. Just make sure your mower has one of them: it is not a luxury, it is a necessity.

On power driven mowers you will need to choose between front wheel drive models and rear wheel drive models and I cannot possibly say which is better. With front wheel drive you effectively interrupt the drive by leaning on the handlebars and thus lifting the front wheels off the ground which, although it sounds daft, is quite a useful form of control. With rear wheel drive models you can tilt the front, to get the machine to cut more easily in deep rough grass, without losing traction. There is a case for both. Mountfield are among the front runners with front runners, if you see what I mean, but they do make rear drive mowers too.

Finally there are the little refinements which cost money and which are not immediately apparent, like the ball bearing wheels on the Hayters, the complex infinitely variable drive of the Honda and the general good quality of all fittings which some mowers have and others do not.

Other mowers

The *other grass* story does not begin and end with rotary mowers, however. There are the so-called sickle mowers which work like the old corn reapers, with a reciprocating blade moving over a fixed blade. Modern hedge trimmers have a similar action. The archetypal machine in this category is the famous – or infamous, depending on your experiences – Allen scythe which was made in vast numbers and is still a much used and much sought after machine. Spares are available for them and when the old Villiers engines wear out it is possible to replace them with Clintons, among others. Of course there are more modern sickle mowers available; many of them, indeed most of them, are offered as attachments to garden cultivators although some are sold as sickle mowers in their own right. (See Chapter 12 for information on cultivators.) Most of these tools are expensive pieces of equipment intended for the contractor and other professional users but Sheen offer two small sickle mowers for the gardener and it is even possible to buy a small sickle mower attachment for your Norlett Beaver Powaspade.

The German Raaspe mower is offered by Honda for attaching to the F600 cultivator. Solo Power Equipment do a particularly good looking sickle mower, although I cannot speak for its performance. Allen are carrying on the tradition of their older model by offering a

Figure 31 A cultivator fitted with a front mounted sickle blade grass cutter

small four wheel sickle mower and a much bigger attachment for their Mayfield range.

These mowers are especially good for cutting the very long grass which you cut once a year when it is more like corn than grass. If you do not have such grass you probably do not need a sickle mower unless you want to cut reeds by the edge of or even in a stream. If you do need such a tool bear it in mind when buying a cultivator and you will be able to add it as an attachment to that.

The last type of grass cutter in this chapter is the ride-on by which I do not mean the seat trailer types that are seen mowing cricket pitches but the four wheel ride-on that is like a big Go-Kart with a rotary mower slung underneath. All of these mowers are rotaries. If you do not want any truck with rotaries it automatically rules out these ride-ons; others will find them of great value. These little machines will do a very good job of lawn cutting, very quickly, very easily and provide a good deal of enjoyment at the same time. They are none of them cheap but if you want the benefits of this easy mowing you will have to pay for them. Ride-ons will not cope with very rough going but will do moderately hard work if it is required. There is no doubt that many of these machines sell, like cars, on eye appeal rather than engineering and you will have to distinguish

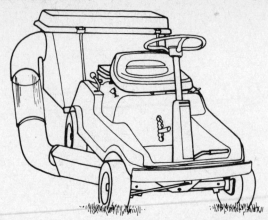

Figure 32 The usual ride-on mower with a steering wheel, enclosed engine and grass collector

between the good and the merely good looking. Once again I have to mention the Snapper which is one of the least attractive yet one of the most efficient. Its 'High Vacuum' blade and mowing deck really do pick the grass up and throw it into a hopper or trailer behind the machine. Moreover this trailer will fill even with wet grass and leaves so that it can perform two functions. The design of the Snapper makes lawn scalping almost impossible which is not true of some other designs. There are countless models available but the older ones often do not have the ability to collect the grass as well as cut it. I don't think it is worthwhile buying one that cannot collect grass, nor is it a good idea to buy one without an electric starter, particularly if it has an engine of 7 or 8 hp. Such engines require a good pull to start if there is no electric starter.

The features to look for with the ride-ons are good turning circle, wide flotation type tyres for spreading the load on the lawn, good range of cutting height to enable some rough work to be done, and an engine of sufficient power to turn a big blade and to propel the machine with you through all the conditions you are likely to encounter in your garden. You will find these mowers are mostly American but the chauvinist is saved by the English Westwood Engineering Company who make their Lawn Bug in two versions. It is also worth shopping around in this market because some imports are ridiculously expensive for no obvious reason.

Although this is the end of the section on grass cutting equipment

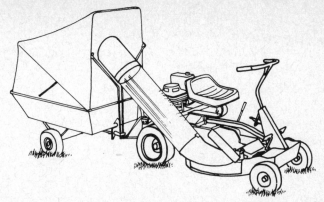

Figure 33 Snapper ride-on mower showing the grass collecting trailer. This is not an attractive machine but it is very effective, and will collect leaves as well as grass

there are further variations on the theme in Chapter 15 on Garden Tractors – if you feel you can take any more that is – and the supplementary tools for grass care are considered in the next chapter.

Grass cutting machinery: buying points

1 Lawn size: big lawns usually need big mowers, but not if there are many obstacles to negotiate. Do not buy a bigger mower than you can handle.

2 Lawn type: fine lawns need cylinder mowers. Rotaries will do for most lawns.

3 Mower type: personal preference. Rotaries are more versatile and need less precise maintenance. Cylinders give better finish but need good conditions.

4 Power: petrol is most useful but noisy. Consider battery or mains electric. Hand mowers are very useful for some small areas.

5 Cost: cheap small mowers will not do the work of bigger mowers . . . for very long. Heavy work usually means high cost. Good finish means high cost.

6 Grass collection: not all mowers are good grass collectors. Check this.

7 Grass ejection: on rotaries do you want rear or side ejection?

8 Striped lawn: mowers with rollers essential. Roller driven rotaries are not always good grass collectors.

9 Long grass: rotaries, sickle cutters or special cylinder mowers.

10 Rough grass and weeds: rotaries and sickle cutters.

11 Ride-ons: will cut a variety of grass. Easy cutting of large areas. Useful even in quite small gardens if gardener cannot use ordinary mowers. See also garden tractors (Chapter 15).

12 One machine: a good rotary will cope with grass from lawn to rough undergrowth if necessary. This is economical.

13 Special machines: for the best work in various fields special machines are necessary. This is expensive.

14 'Overbuy': it is better to buy a mower which is too good for your work rather than the other way about.

5 Supplementary Lawn Care Equipment

In the last chapter I touched briefly on the argument which goes on between those who always collect grass when they mow the lawn and those who never do. There are two reasons for doing either of these things: by which I mean you can make a positive decision to collect grass, and, equally well, a positive decision not to collect grass; or you can collect grass for no better reason than that your mower has a grass box or not collect it simply because your mower does not have a grass box. The second reasons are passive reasons I think you will agree. But none of this resolves the problem and in any case what has any of it to do with the subject of this chapter? Quite a bit is the short answer to that, as we shall see.

As to whether you should or should not collect grass I cannot say but R. B. Dawson, former Director to the Sports Turf Research Institute, in his book *Practical Lawn Craft* says that there is 'no hard and fast rule' and he conducted the experiments which make sense of this equivocality. It would seem that no harm will come to a lawn which has all cuttings returned to it and no benefit accrues to a lawn which always has cuttings removed, but there are likely to be differences between the two – in the constituent grasses, level of moss infestation and type of weed growth. But the matter is also linked to the frequency with which you mow your lawn and the condition of the lawn when it is mown. For example, leaving wet cuttings on a lawn is unsightly because they cling together in small piles and lumps whereas dry cuttings are sprayed evenly over the turf and do not show. Therefore, for aesthetic reasons alone, it is better to collect wet cuttings regardless of any other more weighty technical reasons.

The bearing which all this has on this chapter may be summed up in two words: *moss* and *thatch*. It is a favourite, though in my view unproven, argument of the grass collecting brigade that lawns which have cuttings returned to them get a thick thatch in the bottom of the grass which chokes the roots, hinders air circulation and generally reduces the health and vigour of the lawn. It is true that thatch does have this effect but whether or not the thatch is caused by not collecting grass is a point to argue. Conversely the lawn from which cuttings are always removed is supposedly more prone to invasion by moss: another point to debate, albeit not here. Read the learned Mr Dawson.

The relevant point is that once you have thatch or moss in the lawn, any lawn, how do you get rid of it? In a small lawn you rake vigorously with a scarifying rake, such as the rather good one by Wolf, mentioned in Chapter 6 on Hand Tools. With a large lawn you forget about it or try to find some mechanical means of doing the job. There are a number of motorized scarifying machines all of which are very expensive as they are all intended for professional use. It is unlikely that many gardeners will require such a machine on the permanent strength and it is one of those pieces of equipment which you will probably hire. A good scarifying will probably not need to be done every year anyway, unless your lawns are in a ghastly state, choked with moss, thatch and other rubbish. If you are intent on having your own mechanical scarifying equipment, machines are available from Bob Andrews Ltd of Sunningdale, Nickerson Turf-master and Wolf Tools; or if you have either a Landmaster Lion Cub or Norlett Beaver cultivator a scarifying attachment is available for these machines which is very efficient, I believe, not to mention inexpensive. For those people with a rotary mower there is a gadget for converting some rotaries into a temporary scarifier. This entails changing the standard blade for another special plastic blade which has a sprung wire hook in one end and a counterbalance at the other. The idea is that the hook tears the debris out of the lawn as it revolves. This little gizmo comes, once again, from Wolf Tools and how effective it is I cannot say but it is an inexpensive device which you might consider trying. Whether you use an improvised tool such as that or go for the elaborate specialist machines do not be alarmed at the awful state of your lawn after they have been at work. Despite appearances to the contrary you will actually have done your lawn much good and this will shortly become apparent to you.

One of the causes of moss in a lawn is poor drainage, we are told, and devices for improving this aspect of the lawn are also available. The simple expedient of using the tines of a garden fork to puncture holes in the lawn is frequently mentioned in the gardening press as being the way of achieving an improvement in surface drainage of a lawn, but it is a method suited only to small lawns or people with large lawns and infinite time. There are also small lawn spikers with hollow tines which remove a core of soil from the lawn and which are used in much the same way as a garden fork. One such gadget is offered by Sheen. But for lawns of any size a quicker method is required and there are some simple spikers available for attaching to a mower so that as you mow you also aerate the grass and improve the drainage. These gadgets, for fixing to many of the cylinder mowers, are made by Mow-Rite Engineering and consist of a series of star shaped wheels on an axle fixed behind the mower and designed to dig into the ground. There is also a large towed version for use with a ride-on mower or lawn tractor. E. P. Barrus also offer a version for towing. Incidentally, remember not to turn too sharply when towing one of these spikers.

Figure 34 Mow-Rite lawn aerators attached to the back of a motor mower. There are more complex versions available for bigger mowers

If you should happen to own a Merry Tiller cultivator (see Chapter 12) its set of special lawn-care tines will be of great value. The set consists of hollow tine spikes, plain spikes and slitting tines and these will provide an excellent means of aerating and draining your lawn. I cannot think why other cultivator manufacturers have not followed the Merry Tiller lead here. The same tines are available on a hand propelled machine made by Sisis and called the 'Lawnman' lawn management outfit. Other hand propelled aerators are those with the spring controlled spikes which are commonly seen in garden shops. Sheen and Tudor manufacture these. They are quite hard work to use but they do not tear the lawn too badly, because of their special design, but nor do they penetrate very deeply either. They depend for penetration on your push whereas the Mow-Rite type and another simple aerator from Bob Andrews Ltd depend on weight to press them into the ground. This second type are probably less tiring to use. But a towed or power aerator will be the thing for most medium to large lawns.

Rolling is the part of lawn keeping which seems to have lost favour in recent times and it is quite unusual to find a garden with a roller and even more unusual to find one that is used. This is odd because I would have thought that with the increasing use of rotary mowers and the consequent less frequent use of mowers with built in rollers, there would be a great need for a separate hand roller. The old high

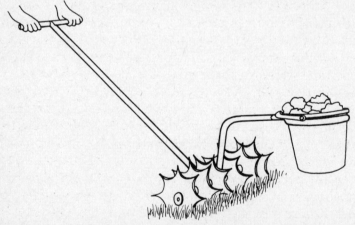

Figure 35 A simple hand push weighted lawn aerator by Andrews. Fill the bucket with weights according to the depth of cut necessary and the lawn conditions

quality cast iron rollers are rarely found, though still available, and most modern rollers are usually no more than steel cylinders variously filled with sand or water to give them weight. The only new idea has been the roller which can also serve as a spiker and as a reservoir for a double acting hand pump sprayer. Quite a good idea I think. If you do roll your lawns it is a further argument in favour of having some sort of ride-on lawn mower which is capable of pulling a heavy wide roller. Many of the garden tractor companies offer rollers as accessories; they can also be useful in the large vegetable garden too.

Whatever else you do or do not do to your lawn there is one task which is necessary on all lawns and that is edging. I have not found any good substitute for the orthodox half-moon edging spade for cutting a good sharp clean edge at the beginning of the year. There are other devices, but they are not easy to use and long hours spent with the half-moon seem to be our lot for a while yet. However, the subsequent grass trimming along the lawn edge is a job which has been successfully mechanized. The long handled shears with blades set at the appropriate angle are well known, and most of the companies making hand tools offer such a cutter. They are not a device to buy cheaply if by doing so you sacrifice quality. With the blades operating down at soil level sooner or later they are going to bite on a stone: good blades will take such setbacks in their stride while others will not. Moreover, good shears will be light and this is a vital quality in such a tool. There are a number of special edge cutting tools which are run along the top of the lawn edge and have star shaped revolving blades hanging over the edge which cut the grass. These do not work very well and I think the long handled shears are much better.

For bigger gardens, or any garden where lawn edging is a long process, there are a number of powered lawn edgers the most well known of which is the Andrews Spin Trim. This edger is electrically powered by self-contained batteries which are charged from the mains. Webb offer the 'Little Wonder' edger which has an adjustable head enabling it to cut in both the horizontal and vertical planes; it is available either as a mains version or as a 12 volt version operating by cable from a car battery. In addition to this imported machine Webb also offer their own rechargeable battery powered model.

In May of 1978 *Which?* magazine tested some of these machines and their opinion was less than favourable. But as so often happens, I find myself in complete disagreement with *Which?* and I think such tools are very worthwhile. My own machine is the Andrews Spin Trim and despite the *Which?* criticism I cannot find fault with it. It works very well, it is reliable, well made and, as far as I can see, very safe. It prefers the long edges of borders and drives to the very small circular edges around single-shrub beds in a lawn but it saves hours of work every week, is extremely easy to use and not in the least tiring. We find that a single charging of the batteries keeps the machine going for over an hour which is much more than ample time to complete our edges (which took over two hours to do with hand shears). For the really big garden a petrol version of this machine is available and there is also a petrol version model made by Victa mowers.

The only qualification which needs to be made to the foregoing eulogy on power trimmers is that you must start with a good lawn edge. These trimmers are for cutting the edge *grass*, not for cutting the edge itself. If you have poor lawn edges these machines will not improve them; that can only be done with the half-moon spade. Also you need strong edges to support the machines and on very light stony or sandy soil where lawn edges are prone to crumble easily you would do well to confirm by thorough demonstration that a power trimmer would work well for you.

Having aerated, scarified and edged it is quite likely that you will also wish to apply fertilizers and weedkillers to your pampered sward. The equipment necessary to do those things is not exclusively used on lawns but is certainly mostly used on them and, therefore, this is a good place to review said equipment.

The stuff which you apply to the grass, be it fertilizer or weed-killer, will come in three forms, liquid, granules or possibly powder and it is clear that one machine is not likely to do for all. The most common machine is the two wheeled hopper variety which spreads granules through a series of holes in the hopper bottom. Such machines are inexpensive and effective but there are some which are more effective than others. The best ones have a wide variety of delivery rates for applying various chemicals; the cheaper ones do not. It is also necessary for these machines to be made of non-corrosive material, or to be very well painted, because the fertilizers which it will be their lot to carry are very corrosive materials. That being so, I prefer the plastic type to the painted steel type. If there are

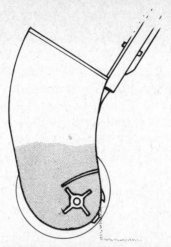

Figure 36 This cross-section through the Wolf fertilizer distributor shows how the weight of the fertilizer is kept off the star shaped agitator by a plate. This means fairly even pressure is maintained at all times, despite the amount of fertilizer being used, and results in even distribution

metal plates and grilles in plastic machines it is necessary for them to be of stainless steel so that they are also corrosion resistant. The best distributors are those sold to professional groundsmen and these will often incorporate a ground marking system which prevents you overlapping one row of material with the last, an act which is particularly damaging if you are applying herbicides. Another highly desirable quality in these machines is that they should be very stable when free standing. This is necessary so that you can safely unload a sack of fertilizer into them without their tipping over. They are not all endowed with this stable characteristic. The larger of the two Wolf models, and the one made by Al-Ko seem to be among the better small distributors, with the Wolf hopper shape incorporating a baffle plate and being a particularly sensible design.

For larger areas the spinning type of spreader is perhaps better. These work in a similar manner to the road gritting lorries seen in winter: a hopper of the material to be spread is situated above a spinning disc and as the material dribbles from the hopper on to the disc it is thrown in a wide arc around the machine. It is more difficult to deliver precise amounts by this method and too easy to overlap with a previously covered part or conversely to miss parts altogether.

Figure 37 The Parker fertilizer distributor. The fertilizer in the hopper
filters on to the revolving vanes underneath which spin it out over the lawn.
The spinning vanes are turned by the wheels as the machine is pushed along

Despite these drawbacks this is an extremely effective method for
fertilizer distribution over large areas. The Cyclone spreaders are the
well-known name in this field, but the small model offered by
T. Parker has the preferred plastic hopper whereas that of the
Cyclone is in steel.

Figure 38 A small power sprayer for towing behind a ride-on mower or
small tractor, for use with a boom as illustrated or with long lances for
spraying trees. There is a 20 gallon or 40 gallon model

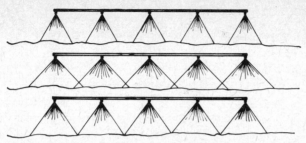

Figure 39 The right and wrong ways of adjusting a boom sprayer. The edges of the cones of spray should just meet at ground level, as in the bottom drawing. If they do not meet, or if they overlap as in the top two drawings, your fertilizing or weedkilling will be ineffective, uneven and possibly dangerous as a result

The other distributors which are necessary to anyone keeping the perfect lawn, perhaps indeed any lawn, are those for dispensing liquid feeds and herbicides. The most common of these are the pressure spray type which come in a very wide range of sizes. On small lawns your normal 1 or 2 gallon pressure sprayer will serve very well but for bigger areas bigger machines are necessary and available. Cooper Pegler, a company much mentioned in Chapter 8 on spraying equipment, have wide multi-jet spray booms which can be fitted to their sprayer tanks for use on lawns. These work well provided you make sure that the edges of the fans from each nozzle just touch at ground level. Incorrect adjustment, as Figure 39 shows, will cause the sprays either to overlap or to miss strips entirely. Time spent adjusting the boom is absolutely essential. Having once adjusted it you could leave it set but as you will see from Plate 23, the outfit is rather big to get in and out of the average shed and it will, therefore, probably be necessary to remove the boom after use.

For applying herbicides in this way it is vital that a constant pressure valve be fitted so that an even application is guaranteed. This is also important when applying fertilizers (though failure to observe the rule when using fertilizers will not be so damaging as it would with herbicide). I find the worst problem is knowing exactly where the end of the completed strip is when you turn around for the next run up the lawn. The simplest way of getting this right is to spray a path of water on some easily marked ground, for example a concrete path or drive, and measure the width of the sprayed track.

Having thus determined how wide a strip is I use stick and string markers, not to walk between, but to walk on. It is much easier to steer this way.

Cooper Pegler also make a special lawn sprayer which requires no hand pumping. Bliss. The pumping is done by the wheels of the machine as it is moved along, and it has the advantage that the long spray boom folds up vertically when not in use, thus making storage easy.

The drawback to applying liquid chemicals with any type of spray is the difficulty of preventing some of that spray drifting on to nearby flowers, vegetables, shrubs or other desirable growth. This is not a big problem, but if it does worry you there is a way of overcoming it by using the aptly named Driftmaster. This machine applies liquid in a rather novel way. A reservoir is held above a ribbed aluminium roller and the liquid is allowed to dribble on to the roller from several nozzles. It, the liquid that is, runs along the grooves of the roller which applies it evenly to the turf as it moves along. Very simple and very effective but do not use it to run across a slope, only up or down, otherwise the liquid runs to one end of the roller and gives uneven application. This machine has a little spring which scratches the turf

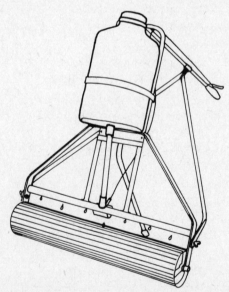

Figure 40 The Driftmaster liquid distributor. The reservoir allows liquid to drip on to the ribbed aluminium roller which then spreads it on to the turf

as it passes thus marking its progress so that you do not overlap with the next pass. So simple.

By and large I prefer to apply liquids to what I laughingly call my lawns and so I use the Driftmaster and the Cooper Pegler sprayer with a boom for all my work. Whether liquids are better than granular chemicals I do not profess to know, although I think perhaps they are less expensive. Probably we should use both.

All the distributors mentioned, apart from the Driftmaster, could also be used in the vegetable and fruit gardens and frequently are although you will need the single jet spray rather than a boom for the pressure sprayers. All, too, have a means of instantly shutting off their delivery and this is an important facility if you are to avoid trouble. On the whole I find it sensible to switch off at the end of each row and to turn round, realign the machine and set off again rather than turn at the end of each row without stopping. This can lead again to overlapping and its attendant troubles.

So now we have aerated, spiked, scarified, fertilized and weeded the lawn it ought to be in tip-top shape. If obtaining the most perfect bents and fescues is your bent, however, there are other bits and pieces which you will be interested in such as levellers, dew brooms, drag mats and bigger and better fertilizer distributors. All of these are the special field of such companies as T. Parker and H. Pattisson who supply all sorts of weird equipment to groundsmen and green-keepers and whose catalogues will have you drooling.

Supplementary lawn care equipment: buying points

Scarifying

1 Rakes: self-cleaning better than spring steel. Wheeled version of scarifiers are best.

2 Small areas: rakes.

3 Medium/large area: mechanical scarifier or attachments for cultivator if possible.

Aerating and draining

1 Small lawns: garden fork or special hollow tine aerator.

2 Larger lawns: wheel aerators. Weight type are less effort. Mower attached aerators.

3 Big lawns: towed aerators or cultivator attachment.

4 Major work: hire large hollow tine aerator.

Chemical application

1 Lawn size: all lawns benefit from *even* distribution of chemicals. Therefore use at least a spraybar on a watering can. Bigger equipment for bigger lawns.

2 Granular applicators: hopper distributors. Variety of application rates, stable, corrosion resistant.

3 Liquid applicators: pressure sprayers or gravity drip. Watering can spraybar.

4 Liquid or granular?: personal preference. Granular is less trouble, liquid less expensive. Ideally have both.

5 Large areas: need large hoppers or large tanks. Consider wheeled sprayers and towed sprayers.

6 Marking: granular easily seen. Liquid needs marking. Driftmaster marks.

6 Hand Tools

On seeing a chapter headed 'Hand Tools' you might with alarm think I am going to labour through every hand tool ever known to man but, mercifully for us all, this is not the case. Rather in this chapter I shall draw attention only to those less common or less well-known tools which are worthy of note, because we gardeners are often a rather conservative bunch who are unwilling to try some of the more unusual tools which the eager manufacturers thrust at us. Yet some of these tools are good and useful, and others are better than the more conventional tools which already fill our sheds.

There is one manufacturer which specializes in oddities and I first became interested in his range of tools many years ago in Europe. At that time they were not widely seen in the United Kingdom but I felt that they would sell well here because they seemed to offer such sensible tools which no other manufacturer was making. The manufacturer of which I speak is Wolf Tools, a company which is probably best known for the Terrex spade (which, as I said in the Introduction to this book, looks like a medieval siege catapult).

The Terrex spade has been about for many years and Wolf claim to have sold over 200,000 of them. Odd though it may seem the Terrex does work, though you must grow accustomed to it and you must not try to take too big a bite of heavy soil. Those people who are dissatisfied with their Terrex have usually not adapted to it which is a pity, because it is much easier to dig with than a conventional spade and is of particular help to people with a bad back or other weaknesses. If you want to try a Terrex spade but have doubts about it you can buy one and, if you are subsequently dissatisfied, then return it within a short period and Wolf will refund your money. Before

Figure 41 The Terrex spade with its unconventional spring lever and bicycle handlebars. Unfortunately no drawing or photograph can adequately demonstrate this tool which needs to be tested for it to prove itself

making your decision, however, write to Wolf Tools and ask for a copy of the article which appeared in the *Sunday Times* and was about a test of various spades. The Terrex was the star turn.

The rest of the Wolf range of hand tools is not as obviously unconventional as the Terrex but consists of some pretty useful looking implements nonetheless. Of particular note are the various pronged cultivators which, on close examination, you will find to be very well thought out. Notice particularly the shape of the cultivator blades. Figure 42 shows the features of the cultivator. There are also several dual purpose tool heads which are very useful and could well find a home in any garden. For breaking up or milling the soil Wolf

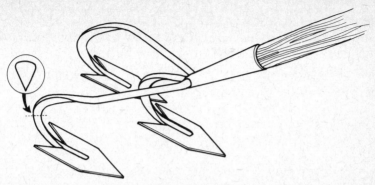

Figure 42 A three-pronged cultivator by Wolf. Notice the leading edges of the curved blade supports are shaped to allow easy soil penetration

have an ingenious two-stage tool which combines a rotary miller and a pendulum weeder in one device.

The two Wolf lawn rakes also deserve special mention; the first is the scarifying rake mentioned in Chapter 5. This really is a very good tool which has movable, stainless steel, hooked blades for clawing out the thatch and moss from the lawn. Although it rakes out prodigious quantities of rubbish it never gets clogged because, as it is moved back and forth, it is self-cleaning and it really works. The other rake is the spring tine rake, and this is so much better than other makes on the market, most of which do not have spring steel tines. Indeed before you buy such a rake bend the tines hard back and you will find that with most of these rakes the tines, once bent, stay bent. With a good rake the tine will spring back to its proper position and this is so with the Wolf. But equally important is the shape of the rake. The Wolf allows all its tines to be in contact with the ground at the same time whereas nearly all other makes have only

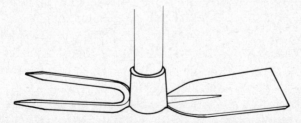

Figure 43 A small, simple double sided chopping hoe, excellent for breaking the surface of tough ground. Wolf make a version of this

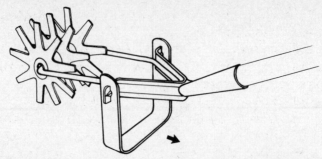

Figure 44 An example of one of the unusual hand tools available today is this Wolf soil miller. The pendulum hoe at the front frees the top surface of the soil which is subsequently pulverized by the miller's wheels. A useful tool in the right conditions

the centre tines in contact, unless a good deal of pressure is being exerted on them.

Finally, before leaving Wolf tools, the method of handle fixing should be noted because it does not depend on screws or nails or anything other than friction. The tapered handles fit exactly into the

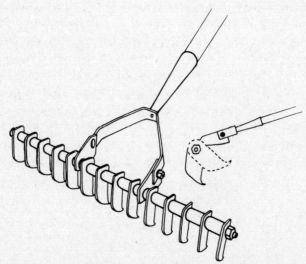

Figure 45 The Wolf scarifying rake. Notice that when the rake is pulled the teeth are down and the hooked ends tear moss and thatch from the lawn. When the rake is pushed back the teeth automatically move into the position shown by the dotted line and the rubbish, collected by the pulling stroke, is cleared off: simple and very effective

tapered sockets on the tool heads; just a light tap on the ground makes them immovable. All round, Wolf tools offer an original idea or two and if you can steel yourself to overlook their somewhat gaudy colour schemes you will find some very useful and pleasant to use equipment in their range.

Another unusual tool, but this time from a manufacturer of very orthodox tools, is the Swoe made by Wilkinson Sword. What a super hoe this is – an absolute delight to use and like all Wilkinson tools a good looking tool as well. Made of stainless steel it is easy to keep clean and being light it is not in the least tiring to use. Its particular advantage is in being able to hook around plants and thus get close to their stems, which is not always possible with the usual Dutch hoe. Actually, since acquiring a Swoe, I have not touched my Dutch hoe which seems to have the proportion of a bulldozer compared to the scalpel-like Swoe. One gardener I met has just worn out his third Swoe, a fact which I mention not as criticism but as the highest praise. He uses the thing so extensively in his very stony garden that he simply wears the blade down until it is as thin as a razor and it eventually breaks off. He thinks it is a marvellous tool and so do I.

In contrast to the delicate Swoe there is the heavy mattock which was a tool I desired for many years but could never find. Whenever there was a television film of African countries turning jungle into agricultural land it was being done by hordes of bods swinging mattocks and here we were in England too blooming civilized to be able to get our hands on such things. Finally the Chillington Hoe Company, which had been exporting all these mattocks to the rest of the world, decided to give the home market a turn. I must have been almost their first customer. They offer a range of these chopping hoes with flat or pronged heads and they are all very useful. On suitable soil it is possible, I am told, to do your digging with such a device but

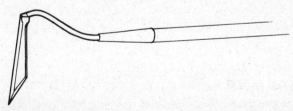

Figure 46 The Wilkinson Sword Swoe, a relative of the Dutch hoe but a better tool to use in every way

Figure 47 The head of one of the Chillington hoes. They come in various sizes and are excellent digging tools

that does not apply on my clay. However, the mattock is still very useful on the heavy soils, especially in dry conditions, as it has the ability to break ground which conventional hoes cannot tackle. It is also very useful for roughening the surface of ground which cannot be dug in the normal manner. For example, I chop away at the compacted surfaces of the clay topsoil in the flower beds before applying a mulch. These tools have particularly satisfying handles and are a generally well-made and business-like heavy duty tool which, like the Terrex, requires the user to adjust to it before it can give complete satisfaction.

Among the more conventional spades the only step forward in recent years has been in the materials used rather than in the shape of the tool. Lightweight metal shafts and stainless steel blades are now commonly used on tools which seem to be designed as much for their looks as for their digging ability. There is no doubt, however, that stainless steel tools are nice to use and very much easier to look after than the ordinary type. If you are one of those people who is a bit lax about cleaning tools before returning them to the shed it will be worthwhile your investing in stainless steel spades, or indeed any stainless steel tools, otherwise I must question whether such tools are worth so much money. But, as with machinery, it is probably worth paying for quality if only for the satisfaction which ownership of such things brings. What is not in any doubt is that to try to save money by buying the very cheap hand tools on sale in certain chain stores is folly. The cheap pressed mild steel implements often imported from Taiwan and other such places will be of no real use at all to the serious gardener, nor indeed to any gardener.

If you are looking for something original in spades a Danish version made by Lysbro is imported here and may interest you; there is an aluminium spade as well as more conventional steel ones in their range. For those who prefer the long handled pointed blade West Country shovel, these are still available from Bulldog tools of Wigan.

Before leaving the subject of digging the Dixon lever plough must be mentioned. This is a plough which is entirely hand powered and works by levering the ploughshare through the soil. The manufacturers claim that a girl can operate the thing without excessive effort and a man with an artificial leg also claims to be able to use the plough with ease. I have not been able to test this myself but if you thought ploughing was strictly for tractors it looks as if you might have been wrong.

One of the hand tools which is much advertised is the Jalo wheeled hoe which is one of the tools that I thought was something of a joke until I came to use one seriously and my eyes were opened. The Jalo is one of the things in my garden which I would not be without. The idea of a wheeled device for pushing hoes, cultivating tines and ploughs through the ground is very old and such implements have been around for generations; the Jalo is just the modern version. There are a number of different implements for attaching to the Jalo and the success or otherwise of these parts will depend on the soil and the operator. The most commonly used parts on my Jalo are the hoe blades and cultivating feet and they work very well even in our tough soil. The machine is easy to use and it is so much quicker to hoe between vegetable rows with a device like this than to use the ordinary hand hoe. Naturally, for very delicate hoeing, the ordinary hand hoe is still essential, but for between row cultivation a Jalo takes some beating. Among the other tools available for it are a lawn rake, lawn spiker, plough and ridger. The last two, of course, will work well in good soil but are not able to cope with very heavy ground; or rather the tools are undeterred by the heavy ground but I can assure you that the pusher is. The Jalo is very well made and is a step between straightforward hand tools and power tools. Even though I have a power cultivator there is still plenty of use for the Jalo, possibly because in addition to its efficiency it is also enjoyable to use.

While speaking of Jalo it is appropriate to mention the Jalo Scoop and seed drill. The Scoop is a marvellous help in the garden and like many of the best tools it is so simple. The time honoured method of picking up piles of rubbish, weeds, leaves or whatever, is to use two boards in the hands, a method which, I may say, requires wrists and fingers of steel. By fixing said boards to two long arms with handles at the top and pivoting the arms in the middle we can call that well-known gardening aid *leverage* to our assistance and this is what Jalo have done with their Scoop. It is such a simple device that you cannot imagine what a great help such a thing is until you try it. It is a help for anybody, but I should imagine it will be particularly useful to those people who suffer with back troubles. The Jalo seed drill is perhaps not such an essential item but for duffers like me, who never manage to draw out a satisfactory seed drill with a hoe, this simple device works so well. Figure 48 explains its working rather better than words and it has been a big help to me in the last two years.

For seed sowing on a larger scale I think seed drills may well become more popular as seed becomes ever more expensive and therefore a commodity not to be wasted. A simple seed sowing device is provided for the average garden by Wolf tools and for most people such a tool will be adequate. But for those with big gardens or allotments a small seed drill might be worth considering and the Drillmaster made by Richmond Gibson Ltd will be suitable. This is an application of modern materials to a very old machine and, although I have not used it, it looks to be a good tool. A machine such

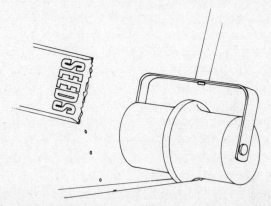

Figure 48 The Jalo seed drill. This small wooden roller shaped to make a shallow drill in a seed bed is a simple and effective tool

as this, in a single pass, opens the soil, plants the seed at the chosen spacing and depth, closes the soil over the seed, presses the soil down and marks out the next row. As seed sowing by hand is another of those bending jobs a seed sowing machine, be it the simple Wolf type or the Drillmaster seed drill, might be a very important tool for the brigade of back sufferers whose prime consideration will be a saving of agony rather than anything else.

Another job which usually has to be done by hand and involves a good deal of bending is the weeding of the flower borders. Now even this can be mechanized by using the light hand-held electric cultivator from Allen Power Equipment. Strictly, being a powered machine, this cultivator should not be in this chapter but it is nearer to a hand tool than anything else and so here it is. The idea of the machine is to provide light surface cultivation between plants. The small rotors are made of plastic and are powered by mains electricity; they are completely covered and thus there should be no danger of damaging surrounding plants. How successful the machine is will depend, as usual, on the soil conditions. If the soil is light, dry and dusty I found that this machine throws it around rather a lot; if it is glutinous and heavy it does not work too well either; but with the right soil conditions it is very effective and will save hours of effort for some people. This is definitely a tool to see demonstrated first. Ensure that it is suited to your garden and if it is you are going to benefit enormously.

For some hand tools different handle lengths are a good idea, although the English are not always keen to accept this. It is not easy finding handles of different lengths, however, and in any case it is impossible with most tools to effect a speedy change of handles even if you wanted to. For those who think this is a good idea there is a small range of implements made by Nupla. These tools are of stainless steel and the handles are of fibreglass which must make them about the most weatherproof tools in existence. Apart from the great strength of the fibreglass handles they have the advantage of being offered in ten different lengths from 10 in. to 60 in., and all are quickly fitted to or detached from all tool heads as required because they have a simple screw fitting. The tool heads are themselves of particular interest as they have the most evil looking scalloped cutting edges, which probably frighten most weeds to death before contact is made. Furthermore the hoe shapes are unconventional and

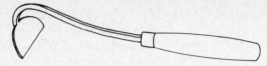

Figure 49 A small onion hoe is a marvellous hand tool for all delicate weeding jobs in the vegetable garden or the border. A nice tool to use

look very efficient too. The combination of the small double sided hoe and the short 10 in. shaft makes a fearsome tool for grubbing about in the herbaceous border and shrubbery. The handles, incidentally, are guaranteed for life and the tool heads for ten years.

The short handles make the Nupla tools into small single handed tools but there are other tools of this type which are of great value. More tool companies now appear to be recognizing the need for small hand tools in addition to the traditional trowel and hand fork. Inevitably Wolf have an extensive range of small hand tools for a variety of jobs but most other companies are also moving into this market. Beware, however, of children's toy garden tools masquerading as serious small hand tools.

Finally I would say that it is definitely worthwhile being more adventurous when buying hand tools. Some of our traditional standbys have been much improved in recent years. And whereas it can be very expensive to take a gamble on buying a new lawn mower it is not such a big risk to try a new type of hoe and by doing so you will find some real treasures. If you want to experiment but are deterred by cost or if you have a new garden and are faced with the horrendous prospect of buying all your hand tools I suggest you attend any local house auctions where you will find the garden tools often go for the proverbial song.

7 Hand Pruning and Cutting Tools

One of the paradoxical things about successful gardening is that in order to make many plants grow well it is apparently necessary to cut them at strategic points on their framework and then to call this barbarous act trimming, pruning, training or tidying up: as nice a set of euphemisms as you could wish to find. However, since we do have to spend much of our time cutting at bits and pieces of unwanted vegetation for all sorts of reasons it is a good idea to have the best equipment for the job. Indeed, cutting tools are the one section of garden equipment where it is impossible to compromise satisfactorily; you must have the best. Even if you have very little pruning to do you need a good pair of secateurs because it is the only way to achieve a good clean cut. If you do not get a good cut every time you will damage the plants: a poor cut will take a long time to heal and the chances of disease getting into the unhealed wound will be much greater. There are a number of poor quality cutting tools on the market at the moment, imported from some Iron Curtain countries and from the Far East. In some cases these imported tools are superficial copies of our well-known brands. Do not buy them. They are no good and will give you very poor results unless you are very lucky.

Secateurs

The smallest and most used of the hand cutting tools are secateurs and here we come up against another of those horticultural battles about which is the best type. There are two principal types: anvil secateurs and bypass secateurs. The first type has a single blade

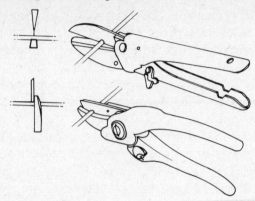

Figure 50 Two typical pruners: the Rolcut at the top and the Wilkinson Sword at the bottom. The Rolcut is an anvil pruner and the Wilkinson is a bypass pruner. The two end elevations show clearly the different blade action of each type

which cuts on to a flat surface or anvil, and the second type has two blades which slice past each other like scissors. The two types are illustrated in Figure 50. Which of these two types is best is the subject of lasting debate. I use both types and at various times I have been convinced of the arguments in favour of each. Frankly the advantages and disadvantages of both are much exaggerated in my opinion and provided you buy good examples of either you will be satisfied. The success of either has much more to do with the condition of the blades and the adjustment of the pivot than any inherent advantage of one type over the other. The biggest mistake you can make with secateurs is to ask them to cut wood which is too thick or too tough for them; nothing will destroy what qualities they have quicker than this.

Since you cannot compromise on quality when dealing with cutting tools you can save money by buying simple secateurs instead of the luxury jobs with shaped handles and other refinements. If you have very little pruning to do then small, simple secateurs will do the job very well. Even so, do not be tempted to buy secateurs which are too small. Some roses – which I suppose are the most common plants to be pruned – can have quite tough old branches and it is therefore necessary to have secateurs which can take the odd thick branch in their stride. If in doubt it is best to buy secateurs which are bigger than you think you need rather than the other way about. Wilkinson

Sword and Wolf, to name two, offer pruners of differing price: in the cheaper models blade quality is not compromised but simple handles and exposed springs are used which keep the price down.

Some secateurs have large, shaped hand grips and one of the Felco models even has a rotating hand grip which is a very good idea. These shaped or rotating handles are worth having if you have a lot of pruning to do because secateurs so equipped are far more comfortable, far less tiring and therefore much easier to use for long periods. Secateurs which may be quite comfortable for pruning a dozen roses can become mighty uncomfortable when pruning two hundred roses or several fruit trees. The constant jarring which the hand receives doing this sort of fairly heavy pruning is very painful after a time and anything which relieves it is welcome.

Another factor which affects the comfort of secateurs is the span of your hand. Obviously not all hands are the same and it is important to have secateurs which are comfortable and do not open too far for the span of your hand. Unfortunately what seems comfortable in the shop can seem very uncomfortable three apple trees later but there is little one can do about that except to buy another pair of secateurs. An expensive answer I am afraid.

When buying secateurs there are a number of design points to look for as you compare the different makes of either type. Stainless steel blades, or what Wilkinson Sword term rust resistant blades, are necessary. Ordinary steel discolours easily and a day's neglect can result in a film of rust on the blade which will begin to affect its cutting ability. Some pruners have Teflon coated blades and these are supposedly easier to cut with, are less likely to gum up and are easier to maintain. In my opinion Teflon coated blades have no advantage over uncoated blades. If your experience is different do not be put off by me. (I am sure you won't be.) Blades, being the business parts of the pruner, are the things which will wear out first and with good secateurs it should be possible to replace worn blades. In most cases it will be impossible for them to be resharpened and even if this is possible I would not recommend that you try to do it at home. The next most likely part to suffer, particularly if the secateurs have been forced through wood which is too thick for them, will be the point at which the two sides of the secateurs are bolted together. This bearing must be capable of adjustment if the cutting action of the pruners is to be retained. This is a particularly important feature on bypass secateurs where the slicing action of the two blades must be maintained.

The bypass secateurs will usually have a 'sap groove' on the bottom blade which is another measure for preventing the blades becoming sticky and therefore impairing their cutting power. Probably such a feature is worth having although I find pruners do become sticky anyway and so I carry an oily rag to clean the blades periodically. The curved blades on the bypass pruners are to prevent the branch which is being cut from being forced out of the jaws as they come together. The curve also maintains a fairly constant cutting angle between the blades. Anvil pruners cannot employ this technique and Rolcut anvil pruners have an action whereby the top blade, as it meets the anvil, is designed to have the effect of rolling the branch further back into the jaws, hence the name *Rolcut*.

Even good secateurs will often require considerable hand pressure to make a cut and as not everyone is able to exert the necessary pressure there are two special secateurs which make the cutting easier. The first is the CeKa Florian Ratchet pruner which requires only gentle pressure: its ratchet mechanism allows the cut to be made by using several small light squeezes rather than one mighty squeeze. The second machine for easy pruning is the Felco Felcomatic which is a pneumatic pruner; that is, it uses air pressure to do the work rather than hand pressure. It is small and self-contained and it also has the advantage of being able to be used on an extension for pruning tree tops.

Loppers

While most secateurs will be suitable for the light pruning of trees, heavier tools are also needed for this work as well as for handling overgrown hedges or the bigger shrubs. For this work loppers are needed. These are king-size secateurs with more robust blades and long handles capable of exerting sufficient leverage on the blades to cut thick branches. These tools come with varying handle lengths but I opt for the longer handled tools which are capable of heavier work. These will have handles of about 25–30 in. in length, while the intermediate pruners will have a length of 15–18 in. There are some interesting blade designs in this category of pruners and CeKa produces several useful types with serrated jaws or with hooked jaws to prevent the branch from slipping out of the cut. CeKa also make several ratchet models which will be a great help when cutting really thick wood. The tree loppers made by Wolf work very well and seem well designed; Wolf's claim that these loppers will cut 2 in. diameter branches I have not proved, but the ease with which I cut through a broom handle suggests they would easily cope with thick branches. Certainly all good loppers are capable of very heavy work. This can be bone-jarring work for the user, and some loppers have cushioned pads at the base of the handles which reduce the shock transmitted when the blades come through a cut. These cushion pads are a useful though not essential feature to have.

Pole pruners

One of the cutting tools which can be useful when dealing with trees is the pole pruner. The Felcomatic has been mentioned already, but the more usual types consist of lopper blades at the end of a long pole with the cutting blade operated by a cord. These pole pruners are another of those gardening gadgets which appear to be such a good and simple idea that you cannot resist buying them. Unfortunately they are not easy to use well. Directing and controlling a long pole to exactly the right spot high up in the tree is not easy and you will get a crick in the neck and put yourself in a pretty bad mood before you acquire the necessary skill to use these gadgets easily. Nonetheless, they have their place and it is worth acquiring that skill because they can save a lot of tiresome ladder work.

Pruning saws

When you get to the stage when loppers will not lop and secateurs will not 'secate' you will need a pruning saw. Indeed I prefer to use a pruning saw for certain large branches which are still within the capability of the loppers, because I find the pruning saw easier to use cleanly. They come in a variety of shapes and sizes and the Bushman range from E. P. Barrus covers just about every sort. The simple pruning saw shown in Figure 51 has a curved blade and an adjustable handle, both useful features. Notice too that the teeth of the saw are shaped to cut on the pulling stroke and not the pushing stroke as is usual with other saws. The reason for this is that when reaching through the branches of a tree it will be impossible to hold the ladder and hold the branch to be cut while at the same time sawing with your other (third?) arm at full stretch. While indulging in these arboreal acrobatics it is necessary for the saw blade to look after itself and the curved blade cutting on the pulling stroke will do just that because it is automatically forced into the cut all the time and it is unnecessary for the branch to be held rigidly while being cut. The adjustable metal handle is useful too, and notice that it can take a pole for long-range cutting, although using these saws at the end of a long pole is not easy. Some of these curved blades have a very pronounced hook at the end which prevents them from being pulled out of the cut; this is quite an asset.

There are other pruning saws but the simple curved type is capable of doing most work and is a good all-round tool. Bigger saws are available with coarser teeth and some have conventional forward cutting teeth too. There are also double-edged pruning saws but I would avoid these. It is too easy to damage the bark of branches while working in a crowded tree using a double sided blade. Bow pruning saws are another type which are widely used but do have the sharp nose model shown in Figure 52. This enables the saw to get into small spaces and the narrow angles between branches which a normal bow saw could not do. Whichever type you decide to use I would make certain that it is light and do be sure the blades are renewable: some cheap saws have fixed blades, which is no good at all.

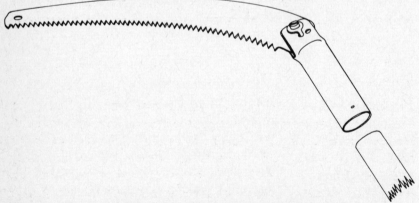

Figure 51 Sandvik pruning saw with adjustable metal handle. A pole may be screwed into the metal handle for working in tall trees or hedges. Note the curved blade and teeth for cutting on the pulling stroke

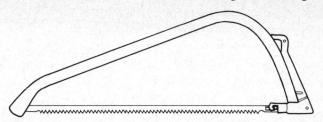

Figure 52 Narrow nosed bow saw for tree pruning. The narrow nose enables it to be used in awkward angles between branches

The temptation is to do without a pruning saw and to press any carpentry saw into action when heavy pruning is needed. Although a pruning saw is little used it is still worth having in any garden which has a few trees or large shrubs, because when it is occasionally required it is so much easier to use than any of the carpentry saws and will make a much better job of cutting live wood. A pruning saw is, in short, a much more important and useful tool than you may think.

Pruning knives

The last of the pruning tools is the pruning knife much favoured by professional gardeners and a tool which, in the right hands, is claimed to be better than secateurs for light pruning. For most of us amateur gardeners a pruning knife will not be a great deal of use as a certain amount of skill is necessary to use one well. For those determined to acquire that skill, pruning knives and budding knives are available from CeKa, Wolf and Sandvik.

Shears

In addition to the special cutting of single twigs and branches, which is roughly what pruning is, there is the general clipping and trimming of grass, hedges and shrubs to be done. For this work the traditional tool is a pair of shears and although there are many powered trimmers available (which are discussed in Chapter 9), there is a great deal of work which is still best done with hand shears. The shears of a few years ago were very heavy things and not very efficient either, but now shears are light and much more efficient. The problem with shears is that the tougher hedge shoots, which are not easily cut, tend to slide along the blades as they come together and eventually they, the shoots that is, reach the tip of the blades where the angle is such that the blades do not cut well. (This is shown in Figure 53.) There are various ways of preventing, or at least trying to prevent, this from happening. The most common idea is to have waved blades instead of straight edged blades and this is reasonably satisfactory. Another idea is to curve the blades in an effort to maintain a wide angle between the blades throughout the cutting length. Plate 20 shows this to advantage. Either method is better than nothing, and I would not buy straight edged shears for hedge cutting unless I was buying to a price.

With shears, as with secateurs, stainless steel blades are preferred if possible. Do not bother with Teflon coated blades. Also make certain that the nut and bolt holding the blades together can be tightened to maintain the true slicing action of the blades. When buying shears make certain that as you close the blades together, they make contact all the way along the edge to the very tip. If they do not do this they will not cut. This test usually shows up the cheap copies.

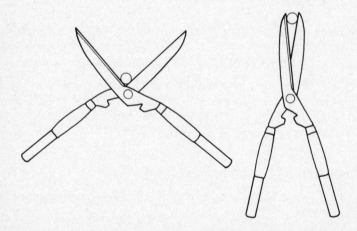

Figure 53 This diagram shows how different the cutting angle and effect is when shears are open from when they are almost closed. If it were always possible to hold the stick to be cut deep down in the jaws, as in the left hand drawing, the cutting effect would be better. Unfortunately the closing of the blades tends to force the stick out to the blade ends. Curved or wavy edged blades reduce this problem; straight edge blades are the least efficient

Shears are tiring to use, even the modern light models, so do not buy full size ones unless you can use them satisfactorily. There are smaller versions with 6 in. instead of the more usual 8 or 9 in. blades. The other feature which will make using shears less tiring are rubber buffers between the handles: they reduce the jarring effect of hedge cutting to an almost acceptable level. I think these buffers are most important. With long handled shears, such as lawn edging shears, the matter of weight is just as important and it is worth paying extra for good lightweight models. For light trimming work of all kinds there are small shears for one handed use which are very common. They are less efficient than they look and can be very tiring to use, although many people like them quite well.

Tree cutting equipment

Finally, a group of equipment which is not strictly part of this chapter, but nonetheless associated with it: ancillary tree cutting equipment. Most of this is for the professional user and will be of only very limited garden use; but if you want to go cavorting about in big trees with safety you must have the right equipment. Go to a specialist company such as Honey Brothers and in their catalogue you will find all you need – from special chemicals to safety harnesses, from cavity tools to lightweight winches. This last gadget does have some applications in the garden: a tiny lightweight Tirfor winch is capable of pulling five tons which, if you are grubbing trees, could be a useful tool.

Hand pruning and cutting tools: buying points

1 **Quality:** do not compromise on quality of blades with cutting tools. Stainless steel.

2 **Comfort:** very important if there is a lot of pruning to be done.

3 **Weak grip:** special secateurs for people with a weak grip.

4 **Secateur type:** bypass pruners/anvil pruners.

5 **Loppers:** long handles best.

6 **Knives:** for experts. Difficult to use well.

7 **Saws:** curved blade most useful.

8 Saw blades: fixed type not satisfactory.

9 Bow saw: pointed nose only.

10 Shear blades: wavy edge or curved. Not straight.

11 Weight: choose lightest shears possible. Choose short blades if necessary.

12 Shear handles: always have buffer stops if possible.

8 Spraying Equipment

I loathe spraying and it is therefore a constant source of annoyance to me that most plants seem to find it well-nigh impossible to survive from one day to the next without being sprayed with something or other. I have tried not spraying but eventually had to give in and start squirting things about again in order to save everything from destruction. One of the reasons that I loathe spraying is because the idiot chemical manufacturers often make it so difficult to mix their wretched concoctions satisfactorily and usually have totally inadequate, dare I even say inaccurate, information on their bottles and packets. The other reason I detest spraying is because, by and large, the sprayers which I have used over the years have been such an irritating and generally unsatisfactory bunch of gadgets.

The most common sprayers are the plastic pressure type which incorporate a pump in the handle with which one pressurizes the spray tank. On the whole I think these sprayers are overpriced and of unsatisfactory design although that has not stopped the Design Centre from dishing out an award to one manufacturer.

There are two basic requirements of these simple pressure sprayers and the first is that the size of the filler hole should be large: there is nothing more infuriating than filling a sprayer with a narrow neck. This can also be a dangerous thing to do because the chances of spilling chemicals is increased markedly if the sprayer is difficult to fill and if some of the more exciting weedkillers are being used you do not want to spill them in the wrong place. I would therefore buy only those sprayers with a good wide neck. Among the lower priced models (I hesitate to say cheap because none of these sprayers is cheaply priced or even reasonably priced come to that) the Hills sprayers have a good wide throat.

The second basic requirement is that the sprayer is easy to pump up, and since pumping means that you have to leap up and down on a plunger it is necessary that the sprayer be stable during these acrobatics. But are they? Not on your life. When they are full they can be pressurized quite easily but, as the cheaper ones all need two or three pumping sessions to evacuate the whole sprayer, you will be making the last pressurization when the sprayer is two-thirds empty and thus relatively light and unstable; this is when they wobble and fall over and generally cause a nuisance. This can be overcome by using the Solo sprayer which has a toe hold at the base enabling you to hold the thing steady with your foot while pumping with your arms; the Solo sprayers also have a wide neck which shows that some designers think about things before foisting them onto the public. (The Solo I

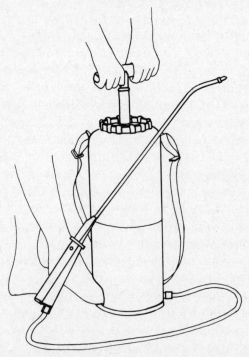

Figure 54 The Solo Power Equipment pressure sprayer has a foot hold which helps to keep it stable while it is being pumped. Notice the wide neck for easy filling

refer to in this case is Solo Power Equipment of Staffordshire and not Solo Sprayers of Essex whom we shall reach in a moment.)

Assuming that a sprayer can eventually be pressurized satisfactorily the next thing which affects its efficiency is the quality of the fitments such as the tap, spray lance and nozzle or jet. The cheapest ones use plastic taps and jets with a cheap, lightweight, easily damaged lance. These do not work well and are best avoided. Hills use plated brass fittings for their sprayers and these are unquestionably superior to most plastic types. Moreover you can buy spare parts for the Hill sprayers should they be required, so if you have another make of sprayer and you want a better quality lance, tap or nozzle then buy the parts for a Hills sprayer and fit them to the hose of your own inferior model. By doing just that I have turned one sprayer of mine, which was awful, into something which is acceptable.

If you have already used these cheaper plastic sprayers you will be aware of some of their faults. You can overcome such faults by using an electric sprayer, although I should warn you that this is an expensive alternative. Wolf Tools offer an electric sprayer which uses the rechargeable power pack from their hedge trimmer. It is a good idea and is so much easier than all the pumping which is necessary with the more conventional sprayers.

If this electrical answer is not for you but you want a good quality pressure sprayer you move into the equipment designed principally for the commercial grower – which is a move that is well worth making. These quality sprayers will not be packed in gaudy cardboard boxes and will not be on sale at every garden centre but they are worth seeking out. Such sprayers will incorporate various good design features which improve their use and performance no end. They will probably have wide fillers which will often incorporate a funnel, a pressure gauge fitted to the tank, a safety valve to prevent overpressurizing, provision for fitting a constant pressure valve which is crucial for the accurate spraying of some herbicides, filters built into their systems to prevent the spray nozzles from becoming blocked, a variety of different jets and nozzles, and last, but very important, they will probably have good quality brass fittings for long life and accuracy of manufacture. Moreover these sprayers are usually designed to evacuate completely on the initial pumping (this last being only a question of sensible design and merely requires that sufficient room be left in the tank for the air, after it takes its load of spray. In other words a 2 gallon sprayer actually needs about 3 gallons capacity; 2 gallons of spray and the remaining 1 gallon space for sufficient air. Cheap sprayers do not observe this simple rule.)

It is only among these more expensive ranges that you will find the big sprayers which can make such savings of time in some gardens. Sprayers up to 3½ gallons capacity are available and because such sprayers are very heavy when full they have trolleys which allow them to be wheeled about easily. There are also knapsack sprayers which are comfortable to use but can be awkward to put on when they are full. Nonetheless it is a very convenient way to carry 2 or 3 gallons of spray about and such tanks can also be used in conjunction with the hand pumps mentioned later, or have their own built-in pumps which the user operates continually as he is spraying.

I have a variety of sprayers but perhaps the favourite is the large 3½ gallon Cooper Pegler. It also serves as a lawn sprayer with a six nozzle boom, as can be seen in Plate 23. With this basic unit it is possible to have a hand lance for normal spraying and very long and light extension lances for tree work. The longest lance is 15 ft. If anything is likely to come close to making spraying a tolerable pastime for me it is the Cooper Pegler sprayer because it is well made

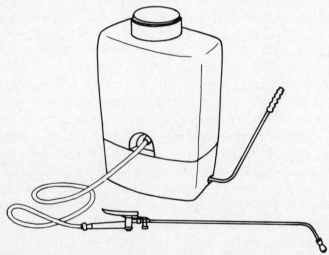

Figure 55 The Cooper Pegler knapsack sprayer. The tank is carried on the operator's back and the pump handle projects forward on the right hand side to be used by the right arm. The spray lance is held in the left hand. The pump handle is continuously, but easily, operated all the time

and so satisfying to handle. The pump unit, which is completely made of brass, and the large wooden handle make the tedium of pumping less uncomfortable than it is with inferior sprayers, and all the fittings are made of brass with leather washers in abundance. This same sprayer is made in several sizes including 1 and 2 gallon models. The tank is made either of galvanized steel or stainless steel, but copper based sprays and Bordeaux mixture should not be used in the galvanized version.

Cooper Pegler offer a wide range of jets, nozzles, lances, extensions and trigger controls to cover a variety of work and there is also a number of guards to be used when herbicides are being sprayed around crops. Two guards are illustrated in Figures 56 and 57. This song of praise to Cooper Pegler would not be complete without mention of their excellent sales literature which gives an accurate and sensible picture of the sprayer or part and a complete description with technical specification. Why do other manufacturers in the horticultural world find this so difficult to do?

But no matter how big and powerful hand pressure sprayers are there are still some jobs which require either a lot of spray or power application or both and for this work there are several options open to

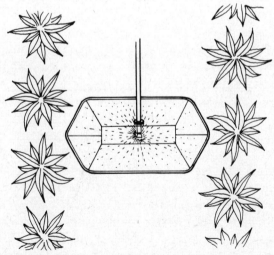

Figure 56 A plan view of a spray lance being used with a hood for weed control between crop rows. The plastic hood prevents damaging herbicides from drifting on to the crops. These hoods are available from Cooper Pegler and Solo Sprayers

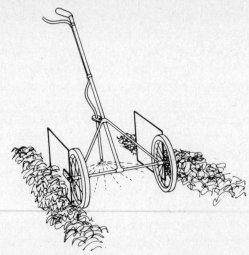

Figure 57 Side shields available from Cooper Pegler for preventing herbicides touching the crops. Useful for between row weeding or applying lawn weedkillers near flower borders

us. The simplest and cheapest is the power knapsack sprayer. This device is carried on the back, as the name implies, and the spray is powered by a small two stroke engine carried on the unit. Although this sounds heavy and awkward it is fairly easily managed after some practice. It is best used by two people, however: one to do the spraying and the other to prepare the spray and to top up the tank as required. It is possible to operate singlehanded but not recommended. Some of these machines will also spray powder chemicals and fertilizers as well as liquid, and indeed my own sprayer has this option. The advantage of sprayers of this type is that they can provide a drenching spray over a wide area and are suitable for spraying large fruit and ornamental trees because they can reach the tops of the trees with ease. (They have the extra advantage of being good leaf blowers too if used empty. The blast is very powerful and because the thing is carried on the back one can easily get to awkward places which other leaf clearing devices are too cumbersome to reach.) However, their proper role is spraying and they are very efficient sprayers, although they are not the simplest of things to use and they are expensive. They break the jump between the large hand pump sprayers and the small power wheeled sprayers which you need for big gardens.

Cooper Pegler supply a small powered sprayer for towing behind a mower or lawn tractor. There is a 20 gallon or 40 gallon model and a variety of booms and lances for different work. Some of the tractor manufacturers offer their own models but I think you will usually find them to be more expensive than the Cooper Pegler version. The Dorman Sprayer company, which manufactures specially for groundsmen and other professional users, offers a power sprayer on a hand pushed frame which is necessarily smaller than the larger towed types mentioned above; it is for the gardener with a lot of spraying to do who may not have a towing vehicle. Beyond this we come to full size agricultural sprayers and that is a different game altogether.

Even if you do require one of the big power sprayers already mentioned it is certain that you will also require smaller sprayers as well; which is another irritating thing about sprayers – you always seem to need several of the things to cover the variety of work adequately. Ones which can cope with large or small amounts of spray are useful for, after all, you do not always want to mix exactly a gallon of spray. You may require only 3 pints or perhaps 10 pints and this is awkward with a gallon sprayer – not impossible, just awkward. The *old fashioned* bucket pumps and the double action hand pump sprayers are the answer to such problems and indeed many people prefer them to the modern plastic pressure sprayers, for which

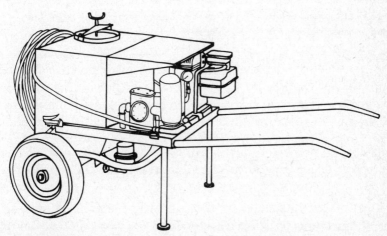

Figure 58 The Dorman wheeled power sprayer. For big jobs a wheeled spray unit such as this is invaluable; it can be used with a multi-jet boom for lawns or a lance sprayer for trees and other work

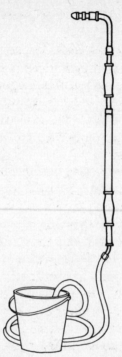

Figure 59 A double acting hand pump by Solo Sprayers. This simple type of brass hand pump is used in conjunction with a bucket or tank and is useful when large quantities of spray are needed: big tanks of spray on barrows or trolleys can be used instead of the normal 1 gallon pressure sprayer, which needs constant refilling

preference no one can blame them. Such devices are alive and well and made by Solo Sprayers of Essex, a company which, I should add, also markets a high quality range of conventional pressure sprayers and hand pumped knapsack sprayers. Their bucket pumps and double action hand sprayers are well made in brass and have a variety of nozzles for different applications. The advantage of such sprayers is that you can mix large or small quantities in a bucket and use the sprayer directly from this. If you have a very big spray job to do you can mix up several gallons at one go in a dustbin or small rainwater butt, carry it on a trailer or wheelbarrow, and spray direct from this which will overcome the irritation of constantly having to fill a small pressure sprayer. The double action hand sprayers and bucket pumps are a relatively inexpensive, though energetic, way of tackling quite big spraying jobs which might otherwise require the expensive powered machinery.

For very small jobs, on the other hand, the small hand sprayers of one or two pint capacity are extremely useful in the greenhouse or for house plants. There are several good cheap plastic models available. The best are the trigger type which work like a water pistol – they squirt when the trigger is pulled. There are small pressure sprayers in this group but I think they are ridiculously expensive and do not work particularly well either.

Sprayers are unlike most other pieces of equipment in this book in that they are likely to be essential to every gardener whereas a chainsaw, a hedge trimmer or a power cultivator is not. There really is no satisfactory alternative to spraying and if you are going to spray you will need a sprayer of some description. You are actually likely to need more than one sprayer in most gardens which is a most annoying fact of life but one which I have accepted. My present spraying armoury comprises five different gadgets ranging from a small trigger hand spray to a powered knapsack sprayer for the large fruit trees; I am sure you also will need more than one. When choosing between brands look for good quality metal fittings and for large filler holes. If possible buy a model which incorporates filters in the spray line and nozzles because there is nothing worse than using a machine which is constantly suffering from blocked jets. If you have a lot of spraying to do either obtain a big power sprayer or consider using the double action hand pump sprayer made by Solo of Essex. And remember, if you have an inferior sprayer you can improve it to some extent by adding good quality lances, nozzles and taps from Cooper Pegler, Solo of Essex or possibly Hills.

Spraying equipment: buying points

1 Design: filler holes, stable base, good pump, sufficient air space, filters, funnel neck.

2 Quality: brass fittings, good pump, metal tank, braided hose.

3 Sophistication: pressure gauges, constant pressure valves, filters.

4 Ease of use: lightweight or carrying trolley. Easy pump or power spraying. Adequate tank capacity for your needs.

5 Adaptability: range of attachments making one sprayer capable of variety of work.

6 Cost: some cheap sprayers are of doubtful value. Cheap small trigger sprayers are good.

7 Range of work: you probably need more than one sprayer. Compromise is necessary but do not carry it too far.

8 Type of tap: trigger lances are much easier to use than the normal on/off taps.

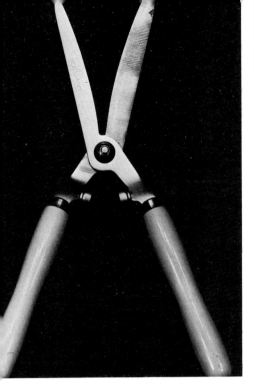
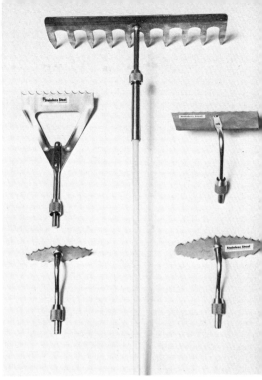

20 (*Above, left*) The curved blades on these shears make them more suitable for cutting because the angle of cut remains reasonably constant whether the shears are wide open or nearly closed

21 (*Above, right*) The range of Supersafe stainless steel tool heads and fibreglass shaft. The tools and shafts of various length are all interchangeable

22 (*Below*) The very useful Jalo wheeled hoe showing the tool frame and hoe blades. Various other attachments can be bolted to the frame and two wheels may be used instead of one

23 (*Above*) A Cooper Pegler sprayer showing the trolley and boom fitting for the application of herbicides or fertilizer to lawns and other large areas. Note the dark patch on the ground in front of the sprayer. By spraying onto a drive before use on the lawn the width of the spray pattern can be measured and you can ensure that the spray is evenly distributed. Both are most important

24 (*Left*) The Cooper Pegler tips back onto its base for pumping. Note the straps attached to the tank which enable this model to be used as a knapsack sprayer if required

25 (*Right*) A power knapsack sprayer: good machines for those with large fruit trees to spray; the oilskins and goggles are recommended wear when using these sprayers. It is useful to have a helper to refill the spray tank otherwise repeatedly getting the thing on and off can lead to frayed tempers and dislocated arm joints

26/27 Two of the bigger electric nylon line cutters, the Allen Jiffy at the top and the Black and Decker Super Strimmer below. Both are powerful and work very well. Both will cut fairly rough undergrowth including brambles and other quite tough foliage. The picture of the Allen demonstrates one of the uses of these excellent tools very well

28/29 The versatility of the chainsaw: the body of the Poulan chainsaw being used to drive a Hoffco nylon line cutter and a double bladed Carbra hedge-cutter

31 (*Below*) The Ekis Helping Hand is an attachment for use with electric hedge-cutters. As the photograph shows it greatly extends the reach of the cutter and enables tall hedge sides to be cut more easily, without using a ladder

30 (*Left*) The nylon line attachment for the chainsaw is particularly good and is easy to use. For clearing ditches and hedge bottoms as shown, all nylon line cutters and brush cutters are ideal

32 The 3·5 hp Billy Goat leaf vacuum 'hoovers' the garden of leaves and other debris. A self-propelled model is available. Our own model, photographed here, is now fitted with the optional tow-bar for use with a lawn tractor

33 A Billy Goat feeding a Donkey. Emptying the leaf bag of the Billy Goat onto the spread-out Donkey is an excellent way of coping with the leaf disposal problem

34 The wander hose attachment of the Billy Goat allows you to take the sucking power of the machine right into borders and other inaccessible spots

35 A well-designed spring steel rake. Note all prongs make contact with the ground and the curved shape contains the leaves being raked and prevents spilling round the edges

36/37 For large-scale leaf clearing the Winro blower is ideal. These two photographs require no further explanation showing on the left the 'before clearing' and 'clearing' stages while on the right is the 'after clearing' stage

38 Piles of leaves raked together or blown up with a Winro are loaded into the trailer (the early home-made model) using the simple but excellent Jalo Scoop

9 Power Hedge Trimmers, Chainsaws and Brush Cutters

You might think that this is an odd group of machinery to be covered in one chapter but as there is some overlapping of the functions of these three machines it is best that they be considered together. The most popular and widely used of the three is the power hedge trimmer and as it is also the one most likely to cause disappointment we shall discuss it first.

Power hedge trimmers

When choosing a hedge cutter it is quite easy to make a mistake by buying the wrong type and it is this which causes disappointment. So it is sensible to divide hedge trimmers into groups, according to their power source, in order to help the selection process. The two main sources of power are electricity and petrol but the electrically powered trimmers fall into four further groups and each satisfies different requirements. The four electric power groups are mains charged battery power, mains electric power, portable generator power and car battery power.

The easiest type of hedge trimmer to use, and yet the most misunderstood, is the lightweight cordless type which uses small rechargeable battery packs. These are usually among the cheapest too. Unfortunately they have earned a bad name over the last few years causing some manufacturers to withdraw from the market while many garden machinery shops will not stock the remaining makes. This is a great pity because these small light trimmers are really easy and pleasant to use *provided you use them to do the light work for which they were intended*. They were not designed for cutting tough old hedges of thick hawthorn or beech, nor were they intended for cutting back neglected and overgrown hedges of any type. They will, however, make a very good job of *trimming* box, *Lonicera nitida*, privet and yew, and of all the hedge trimmers they are the nicest, lightest and least tiring to use.

The most common hedge trimmers are the mains electric variety which have been made so popular by Black and Decker. The mains electric trimmer comes in a wide range of prices and quality and you will pay quite a bit for a good machine of this type; but if you have a lot of work for such a machine it will be false economy to buy a cheap one. Conversely do not overbuy: the cheaper ones are extremely good and will give years of service in the average small garden. Among the more expensive types the Little Wonder is very good and will cut very tough old hedges with little or no trouble. The drawback to all these cutters is the power cable, for it limits their use to hedges which are reasonably close to the house or power source. Having a cable of too great a length reduces the performance of the machine so do not imagine that you can extend the range of work simply by extending the cable indefinitely. Eventually you have to stop. What the limit of cable length is it is difficult to say, but up to about 120 ft should be satisfactory, although this may be too much for some appliances.

The alternative is to use a portable generator but this is probably only economically sensible if you have a variety of electric tools which you will wish to use in this way. Generators are very expensive items. Should you decide on this approach it will be a good idea to use a 110 volt generator and hedge trimmer and indeed this is the type mostly used by contractors. If you have an ordinary mains electric trimmer already this can easily be run from a generator; most have a 230 volt as well as a 110 volt outlet.

The last type of electrical cutter is that which runs from a 12 volt car battery. These have the advantage of being portable but the disadvantage of a high current consumption which means that the car battery runs down quite quickly. Of course if you are able to leave the battery in the vehicle and have the engine running while the hedge trimmer is in use you will prevent the battery from discharging. My own hedge trimmer is of this type and it is run from the battery on the lawn tractor but I think that although this is a cheaper method of hedge cutting it is not as good as using a 110 volt machine with a portable generator.

Apart from the light cordless battery types which were mentioned first, all these hedge trimmers will do quite heavy work. Naturally the quality of the machine matters, but I do not think you need to worry whether or not the power source will have any effect on the type of work the cutter is capable of. There are some design features which will affect the work and the worker too, however, so some thought needs to be given to them.

The length of the cutting blade is one such feature. It is very tempting to buy the trimmer with the longest blade in the belief that you will accomplish more work with such a tool, but that is not necessarily the way things work. What may seem an easy tool to handle as you try it for size in the dealer's showroom may prove to be quite a handful at the top of a step-ladder when reaching over a hedge. Most hedge trimmers are quite heavy and a very long blade makes them heavier without giving much in return except to the skilled user. I would doubt that many gardeners need the really long bladed types which are available. When standing in the dealer's showroom, as he presses ever more luxurious machines into your hands, try holding the things with your arms stretched out straight in front of you, and then hold them with one hand outstretched and you will realize just how heavy some of these little cutters are. Remember, too, that you are probably going to be using the things for a few hours at a time and after an hour most things feel heavy to those not accustomed to their use. The only way of keeping the weight down is by opting for short rather than long blades unless you are *certain* the long blade will be an advantage.

Another design feature to which much importance is attached is the doubled sided blade: that is, a blade which will cut in both directions. If you have a choice there is some advantage in having such a blade but do not worry overmuch if the blade is single sided. A more important point concerns the handles. There will always be two but their positioning can be quite a help: the type which loop over the front of the machine are usually easier to use and have the advantage of being nearer to the machine's centre of gravity which can reduce fatigue in the user.

If the idea of electricity in any of its forms does not interest you then a petrol powered hedge trimmer will have to be your choice and with such tools you need to be very careful. The instant on/off control of all the electric hedge cutters will not apply to a petrol cutter

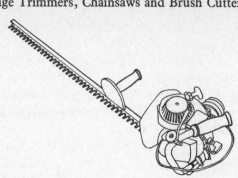

Figure 60 A petrol engine hedge cutter

which will have its engine running all the time as you climb up and down step-ladders and do all the fiddling about associated with hedge cutting. True, the blades will be stationary but nonetheless such machines need to be treated with some respect. They are, moreover, heavier to use and their noise is tiring if endured for any length of time. They usually have a small, high revving two stroke engine which is only an arm's length away from your ears so it might be a good idea to invest in 'ear defenders' if you decide on such a machine. Despite these disadvantages petrol powered machines are capable of the heaviest work and are also the most portable requiring no cables, generators, batteries or other clutter to make them work.

There are two accessories for using with electrical hedge cutters which I have found helpful. The first is the 'Ekis Helping Hand', an extension arm for attaching to most makes of electric cutter, excluding the cordless type. This device enables high hedges to be cut without the user having to clamber up and down ladders. If your high hedges are cut to a taper at the top this device is particularly useful but if you have a flat topped hedge you will still need a ladder to reach and cut the top. The important thing to remember when using the Ekis is to keep it upright, because the further the machine moves away from the vertical the greater the leverage it exerts at the end of the extension and it eventually becomes quite unmanageable. Nonetheless, used correctly, this is a valuable aid to the chore of hedge cutting: anything which reduces the amount of fiddling about with step-ladders is a good thing.

The other useful accessory which I have found is the 'Likeman Safety Harness', which holds the electric cable of a cutter away from the blade. Such a harness is a great help when using any electrical garden tool but is particularly good for hedge cutting. It means that one is completely free to concentrate on cutting, confident that at all times the power cable is well clear of the cutters. If you use this harness it is a very good idea to break the power cable and fit a plug and socket about 2 ft from the point where the cable leaves the harness. This enables you to move about free from the cable without removing the harness. The machine can be connected to another such plug at the front of the harness if you wish. If you do this you must use only proper rubber covered plugs and sockets such as Duraplugs and, most important, make *absolutely certain that the socket is on the end of the cable coming from the power source*.

Which of these hedge cutters is going to be most suited to your garden I do not know, but consider the possibility of having more than one. The heavier hedge cutters, which means most of them, are not very pleasant machines to use but they are almost a necessary evil if one is to control hedges of any size. They are unnecessary though,

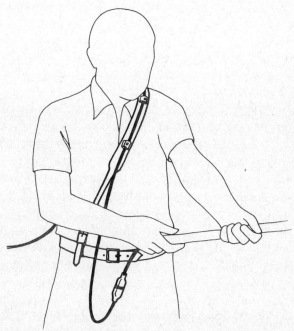

Figure 61 The Likeman safety harness which is the perfect way of keeping cables under control when using electric power tools. Note the Duraplug connection which enables the machine to be detached quickly if necessary

for the small hedges listed earlier and for the regular light trimming which some ornamental, shaped bushes require. For these duties the lightweight chargeable battery pack type are good, inexpensive and therefore worth adding to your store even if you already have a bigger cutter.

One further method of hedge cutting is open to owners of small petrol driven chainsaws, because there is a proper reciprocating blade hedge cutter attachment which can be bolted onto chainsaws in place of the normal saw bar. These hedge cutting devices are well made and extremely effective machines but they are very heavy and, when added to the weight of a chainsaw, they can be quite a handful. They will cope with really tough work and are, of course, a much cheaper way of having a powerful hedge cutter than by buying a separate petrol driven type. If you have occasional heavy hedge cutting to do this is a good economical way of accomplishing the task and extending the use of a generally under-used machine, namely your chainsaw. If heavy hedge cutting duties are more frequently your lot to perform I think you would be better advised to buy a tool specifically for the job.

Chainsaws

Having said that the chainsaw is a generally under-used machine I can also say that it is an extremely useful machine and I find my attitude to these tools very difficult to define. Of all garden machinery the chainsaw is the most anti-social there is – its piercing high pitched sound can sometimes be heard for miles – and they are aptly named buzz saws in America. Because of its noise and the frightening sight of the exposed chain screaming around, inches away from my unprotected hands, I find using such tools a most unpleasant experience. At the same time I recognize that of all garden machines the chainsaw probably makes the biggest difference between doing the job by hand and doing it by machine. Recognizing this, therefore, my relationship with the chainsaw is of the classical love-hate type.

There are more chainsaws available for you to choose from than any other single thing except lawn mowers so there should be no problem in finding one to suit. Most of the machines are powered by small two stroke petrol engines but a few small ones are electrically powered. It is unlikely that you will need any of the big chainsaws used by contractors but the smaller ones are definitely candidates for the garden, particularly if you use wood for fires.

Chainsaws are graded according to the size of the chain bar, with the smaller ones being about 10 in. and the giants going up to 3 ft and more. For garden use a 10 in., 12 in. or 14 in. bar would be adequate, and a simple saw with a 10 in. blade will be relatively inexpensive. If you decide to buy an electric saw you will find they are only made in the smaller sizes. The Black and Decker and McCulloch electric chainsaws are perhaps the cheapest available and as they are identical – McCulloch and Black and Decker being the same company – there is nothing to choose between them. For general garden use I think you will find these small electric saws hard to beat. They are light, comfortable and easy to use and will tackle quite heavy jobs if you take your time. They are not designed or intended for prolonged heavy use day in day out, and they are not meant for felling big trees, but for cutting logs and sawing timber they are practical, cheap and as pleasant to use as any such machine can be. Moreover, being electric, they are much quieter than petrol saws and therefore much less troublesome in urban and suburban areas. They make about as much noise as a big electric drill, which if not pleasant is at least tolerable. For general log sawing I would look no further than such a machine.

The specialists in the chainsaw trade seem not to have a good word to say about small electric saws. This is because they judge them against the heavyweight machines of the commercial user. Naturally they will not stand such comparison but this is a failure on the part of the chainsaw dealers to understand the gardener's relatively minor needs and his light use of chainsaws rather than a criticism of the electric saws.

The trouble with electric saws is that they are tied to their power supply cable – although there is one car battery powered model called the Minibrute – and this limits their use somewhat. Therefore if you need to use your chainsaw in a variety of positions remote from the house, which is quite likely, you are forced to have a petrol version. Here your choice is vast and when examining sales brochures you will be quite bewildered by the range. There must be a chainsaw for every tree on this island. Some of the comments made in the sales literature need qualification, however, because they are sometimes misleading.

For example, many chainsaws are advertised as having extra quiet silencers or mufflers. This is frankly hogwash. There is no such thing as a quiet chainsaw and let no one try to make you believe otherwise. Some may be a decibel or so less noisy than others, but what is a decibel among chainsaws? They are all noisy. Another bit of promotional blurb usually concerns vibration, with machines being sold as having vibration free fitments and so on; well, the small chainsaws which are likely to be of value to us do not vibrate significantly anyway, so such claims are largely irrelevant. Safety features are worth considering, however, and devices which protect the hands or act as chain brakes are of real value though not essential. Hand guards may be added to any machine.

Another good idea which is usually emphasized in the sales brochure is automatic oiling and this is a good feature. The chain does need frequent and regular oiling while in use and it is nice if the machine is looking after itself in this vital respect. A combination of automatic and manual oiling is an advantage as it allows you to increase the oiling if the going gets tough. Finally a sprocket nose chain bar will be held up as being a good thing to have and if you are going to work your saw very hard it is an asset as it makes life much easier for the chain; but it is not a necessity.

One group of machines at least, the McCulloch petrol models, incorporates an automatic chain sharpener which is quite useful but do remember this is not as efficient as a proper chain sharpener. It is only a temporary means of keeping the chain sharp and the success or failure of any chainsaw does depend solely on how well you look after the chain. It must be kept well oiled with the correct oil; it must be kept in proper adjustment and it can be both dangerous and expensive to ignore this requirement because it will damage the bar or fly off and cause you injury if it is allowed to become slack; and it must be kept sharp. This last essential can be carried out by you with a proper gadget but do not attempt to file a chain free-hand. It will not be a success.

The Poulan Micro is a simple, small, petrol driven chainsaw which I have used extensively and found to be very good. It is easy to start, fairly light and comfortable to use by chainsaw standards and capable of quite hard work. In its simplest form it has no frills but is none the worse for that and it is not expensive. The small petrol McCulloch is another small saw of which I have some experience and this has the advantage of a chain brake and the chain sharpener mentioned earlier; it is more expensive than the Poulan. Both of these saws will take the Carbra hedge cutter attachment and both will also take the nylon line weed cutter attachment which further extends the use of the basic chainsaw and takes us on to examine nylon line cutters and brush cutters.

Nylon line cutters and brush cutters

The smaller machines in this category are called trimmers and the bigger machines are called brush cutters. Both names describe the machines well: the trimmers will trim back soft green growth while the brush cutters will cut through anything from grass to thick saplings. These tools are a fairly recent introduction and in their various forms are an immense help in the garden; indeed for most people I think they are likely to be of more value than a chainsaw. The principle behind all these machines is a strip of nylon line which revolves at very high speed at the end of a long shaft or handle and cuts any soft plant growth it comes into contact with.

The versatility of these machines is amazing and they do a job which no other tool did satisfactorily before. Because the cutting medium is nylon cord it will yield when it comes into contact with tree trunks or walls or any other reasonably hard object and herein lies its value to the gardener. Now you can easily cut the grass or other growth away from the base of trees where the mower will not reach, and it is also possible to cut under the bottom of a hedge or under shrubs which were previously only accessible by crawling around on your knees with hand shears and a sickle. Grass can be cut right up to a wall and awkward mounds and banks are also cut with ease. The more powerful versions have several strips of heavy duty nylon and they will cut quite tough undergrowth, including brambles, although this does wear the nylon very quickly. An example of the efficiency of these machines will better illustrate their value: I have a small drainage ditch which runs underneath a hawthorn hedge in my garden and it used to be cleared reluctantly once a year using various hand tools. This task took the best part of a day and was hard work to boot. With a brush cutter the job is accomplished in a noisy thirty minutes. Need I say more. There are, of course, brush cutters and *brush cutters* and then there are trimmers and they are not all suited to such rough work. But it is a matter of deciding, once again, on what you will require of a machine.

The cheapest and simplest types are the mains electric trimmers which have only a single strand nylon whip. There are many different makes available and some of them are being oversold, by which I mean the makers are claiming that they are capable of work which is beyond them. As with all other things, if you buy a cheap small garden tool and ask it to do the work of bigger and more expensive equipment it will break under the strain. This has been true of some of these small electric motors. For trimming grass around trees and walls and other light duties a simple lightweight electric cutter is all you need. But do not try to cut long grass and do not try to push the thing through tough vegetation too quickly. It is also imperative that you allow the machine to build up to its maximum speed before putting it into the undergrowth otherwise you will overload the motor and damage it. If it shows signs of labouring, while it is cutting, switch off immediately.

The better electric models are fairly expensive but they will cope with much rougher handling. One which I found particularly good was the Weed Eater Jiffy which is marketed in the UK by Allen Power Equipment. This machine will cut quite rough grass and thick-stemmed weeds such as the *Umbelliferae* family. It is well made and has a simple and quick means of extending the nylon filament. This is an important point because the cord does wear quite quickly and as you will need to extend it frequently in use it is essential that this can be done easily. Do not use a longer length of filament than is necessary because this could overload the motor. Most machines have a cutter which will automatically prevent too long a piece of filament being used.

Among the other machines there is one with an adjustable head made by those thoughtful souls at Wolf Tools and an inexpensive model for most gardening duties by the ubiquitous Black and Decker. There are countless others too, so when comparing different models note the power of their motors, look for a tough waterproof case and also check the weights of the different makes. Furthermore, select a model that is double insulated and not one which is earthed as such models are not safe. Finally, choose a model with an adjustable second handle on the shaft. All these machines need two handles.

The better and more expensive electric models will be close in cost

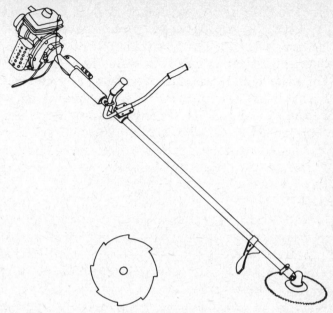

Figure 62 The typical 'Japanese Juggler' or brush cutter. The engine at one end of a long shaft drives the circular blade at the other. Various blades may be fitted for different work. (A saw tooth blade is fitted and an alternative blade is shown.) Multi-strand nylon line heads are also used for soft undergrowth

to the cheaper petrol models and in this second category the small Homelite model is unique in having its tiny petrol motor down on the cutting head of the tool. This little machine has the size, weight, appearance and performance of the best electric models but the advantage of freedom from power cables. The bigger petrol models have a different layout altogether.

The engine on these bigger machines is at one end of a long shaft while the cutting head is at the other and thus this is one of the few machines which can truly be said to be well balanced (where the word *balanced* is used in the normal way or at least in a way that I can understand). The operator holds the shaft somewhere between the engine and the cutting head and swings the outfit from side to side, scything down everything in his way. The heavier models usually have a harness so they can be carried by the shoulders, leaving the arms free for control. Time spent adjusting the harness and its point of attachment to the machine will be well spent. Most machines will

Figure 63 The brush cutter in use. Notice that the cutting stroke is made from right to left and notice too that only about half the blade is in the undergrowth. This prevents overloading, inefficient cutting and tangling. The harness supports the weight of the machine, leaving the arms free for control

have provision for adjusting the point of attachment and this will naturally have an effect on the handling and balance of the tool. Correct adjustment is important for comfort especially if you are using the machine for a long period when it can become quite tiring and hard on the back. The lighter models have no harness and are therefore both supported and controlled by the arms.

The work which these petrol driven brush cutters are capable of is amazing: the example of the drainage ditch is impressive but was a mere limbering-up exercise for the Xenoah brush cutter which I used for that job. As it did that ditch in such a short time you can imagine how much it could do in a full day or in a week: it is frightening to contemplate. Because of this work rate it is unlikely you will find enough work to keep the large machines occupied in even the biggest gardens and usually the smaller lighter machines will be adequate for the gardener's needs. But if you do have a lot of such work the big Xenoah model, again marketed by Allen Power Equipment among others, is a super machine. If you fit it with the circular steel saw blade or brush blade instead of the multi-filament nylon head you will find it devours big brambles, young saplings, bushes and really tough dense undergrowth with relish and it will go on doing so for hour after hour. One of the gardeners who wrote to me while I was researching this book referred to her Xenoah brush cutter as the Japanese Juggler which I think is a marvellous name for these tools. She goes on to say that she 'cannot speak too highly of it' and in her garden 'it saves weeks of work'. This is a recommendation which I endorse.

The option of fitting steel cutting blades is one of the advantages that the petrol driven models have over their electrical brethren, and these blades do extend the range of usefulness of the machine considerably. There is also a nylon line head which has four strands of nylon whipping round instead of the more usual one or two. If you have such a head it is necessary to wind equal amounts of nylon on to each of the four spools otherwise the head will be out of balance and the machine will shake uncontrollably when started. This will not do you or it any good at all. Even the small petrol machines, which are very light in weight and easy to use, can cope with small steel blades and will tackle really heavy undergrowth albeit more slowly than the big machines. The SRM 140D cutter is a very small model which has a tiny 13·8 cc Kioritz engine but it will do quite heavy work for all that. The secret with these little machines is to allow them to build up speed first and then to put them into the undergrowth. If this is not done they will stall or at least the machine will be overloaded. The SRM and the Homelite, already described, are both available from Trojan Ltd.

Brush cutters are such a successful tool that already a wide number of makes and models are available for you to choose from. The factor which most affects your choice is, as always, the amount and the type of work to be done. The electrics are good and inexpensive but for cutting back anything other than soft undergrowth you need the power of the petrol cutters and the versatility which their different blades and cutting lines give. But if you do buy one of these machines remember they can be extremely dangerous. To be effective their blades have to be uncovered and although some have rudimentary guards they are not very satisfactory. When using these machines I always wear goggles and several times I have been glad that I do because small twigs or chips have been thrown back to my face. For all that, these are a really useful addition to the garden and it is unfortunate that they make such a terrible noise as they do their good work. Why cannot manufacturers make them quiet?

At the beginning of this section on brush cutters I spoke of the attachment which can be added to a chainsaw to turn it into a nylon line trimmer. This gadget is the Hoffco Trimette and is available from Chain Saw Products Ltd. It will fit most of the small petrol engine saws and is really an excellent device. It can only be used with a nylon line head but it does make a very effective and powerful trimmer, quite easy and comfortable to use and with the great advantage of extending the range of work that the basic chainsaw is able to do. If you have a chainsaw and you want a nylon line trimmer this is the perfect device: it is very well made and not expensive when compared to the price of a complete machine.

It is also possible, for modest cost, to add a brush cutter to certain petrol driven hedge cutters and these are capable of using the steel cutting blades as well as the nylon line heads. The Japanese Shingu-Shik hedge trimmer is one such machine that can be modified in this way.

Unfortunately a word of warning on the fitting instructions for some of the attachments is necessary. I have found the instructions to be poor and in some cases plain wrong. In the case of the Carbra hedge cutter which I fitted to the Poulan Micro chainsaw I found no advice on how to remove the clutch from the saw. This can require a special tool or at the very least an aluminium drift otherwise permanent damage may be done to the machine.

In the case of the Hoffco Trimette an unnecessary part was included in the kit which the instructions absolutely insisted had to be fitted. This was not the case and could have been dangerous if used. It is a pity that these very well-made attachments should have such poor fitting instructions.

So where does all this motorized cutting activity leave you when deciding what equipment to buy? If you have a chainsaw already, your choice of trimmer or hedge cutter may be influenced by the fact that you can add bits to it to perform these other functions. Perhaps the big choice lies, in all cases, between electrical power and petrol power. This decision will depend on two factors, one of which is cost and the other is the unsocial noise which the little petrol engined machines make. This will be a particularly important consideration in suburban areas. Cost is, as always, an important point but it will be false economy to buy too cheaply, particularly in the hedge cutter market. Remember, you will keep a hedge cutter going steadily for several hours on a good hedge and you need a quality machine to cope with such use. Alternatively if you only need a hedge cutter for thirty minutes' work twice a year you would be very foolish to buy an expensive model. Electric chainsaws are used in short bursts as are the electric trimmers and provided you remember their weaknesses you can get away with cheaper machines for light infrequent use. When it comes to brush cutters the most important factors should be ease of use and weight; ensure that you can use the thing comfortably before you buy it and you must see it demonstrated first. With chainsaws the need to keep them well maintained is an important consideration and it is not a bad idea to buy from one of the specialist dealers because of this, although you will probably have a terrible job convincing him that you do not want a 3 ft monster cutter for forest work. If you do buy a chainsaw consider also the rather fancy sawing horse available from Dixon Gardening and Farming Aids.

Power hedge trimmers, chainsaws and brush cutters: buying points

1 **Weight:** particularly important in hedge cutters and brush cutters.

2 **Power:** electric machine cheapest but least powerful. Petrol machines more expensive, more powerful, heavier. Consider generator.

3 **Cost:** electric machines cheapest but beware of false economy. Do not buy too small for your needs just to save money.

4 **Noise:** all petrol chainsaws, brush cutters and hedge cutters are very noisy. Electric chainsaws are fairly noisy.

5 **Versatility:** attachments for a chainsaw or hedge cutter increase range of work with certain compromises.

10 Plant Supports, Ties and Clips

After the feverish, buzzing activity of the last chapter it is pleasant to turn to the silent and restful world of plant supports; another of those rare garden aids like the cloche which sit silently doing their good work with only the slightest attention or help from us. Perhaps this unobtrusiveness on their part is why plant supports are such a neglected part of gardening. Most supports are, after all, only galvanized steel wire bent into fancy shapes and as they always seem somewhat overpriced for what they are it is usually easier for us to spend money on more eye-catching garden gadgets. When the August gales flatten every plant in sight we may regret our earlier decision not to invest in plant supports, but by then it is too late. Never mind, we can resolve to have them ready for next year. But somehow next year comes and we still manage to do without them with the same awful result. Well, dull old things they may be but the plant supports which I bought many years ago have repaid their cost many times over and there is no sign of their life coming to an end yet. Most people use the traditional canes and twine for supporting plants, especially the big herbaceous plants, and this is a time honoured and proven method. For smaller herbaceous plants and garden peas the twiggy stick school has many devotees and with good reason. But there are alternatives which are well worth examining.

The plant supports which are offered for border plants have some advantages over the traditional stake and string methods not the least of which is their neatness. The plant supports made by the East Anglian Wire Working Co. are particularly good and I would recommend them to anybody. As can be seen from Figure 64 they provide support for all the stems on a plant and not just support

Figure 64 A wire support made by the East Anglian Wire Working Co. These supports are made in different shapes and sizes and become completely hidden when used with herbaceous plants rather than with these diagrammatic daisies

around the outside. This feature is of particular importance to those border plants which have a tendency to collapse outwards whether there is a strong wind or not. These East Anglian supports come in a wide variety of sizes and will cope with the biggest clumps of plants with no trouble. I find them very good. The oldest one in my collection is over ten years old and I inherited that from another gardener so it is actually much older. Yet it is still in perfect condition, despite having endured all those years of bad weather.

At first these wire supports may seem expensive but I do not suggest you buy enough to support the entire garden in one go. Rather, build a collection gradually. They are the sort of things to ask for at Christmas or birthday time instead of socks or ties: one plant support makes a very acceptable present. When you compare the cost of a permanent support such as this with the present cost of bamboo canes, which have a relatively short life, it will make the present, or your investment, seem even better.

The only thing to remember with such supports is to place them over the plants early in the year so that they can grow through the mesh easily. Trying to bend the plants through at a later date because

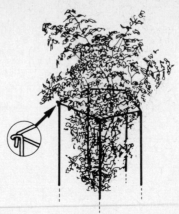

Figure 65 Westray Link Stakes join together to form a plant support of
virtually any size and shape

you forgot to put the support in position at the right time means you
will probably break the stems: if you miss the boat you miss it and
that is that. Of course some plants cannot be treated in this way: they
insist on growing in an unruly fashion and require supports of a more
adaptable kind; this is where the 'Link Stakes' of Westray Cloches
come in. These clever and simple devices link together, as the name
suggests, to form any shape desired. Moreover the shape can be
altered as the season progresses so that no matter how big or awkward the supported plant becomes the 'Link Stakes' can be adapted
to suit. These supports have only very recently become available but
I think I shall have to add some to my store. Like the East Anglian
supports they are made of galvanized steel wire and should last a
lifetime if properly looked after.

In big gardens the investment in plant supports can be high and so
it will always be necessary to have some home-made supports in
addition to the posh jobs which are bought. Rather than using
bamboo and twine I am increasingly using galvanized wire for making simple supports. A big coil of wire can be bought for a reasonable
price and lengths are then cut from it as required. These lengths are
bent into the shape shown or variations on this shape: some tall and
thin, others low and wide. Two or three of these supports are used for
each plant or clump of plants according to need and they are at once
simple, effective, cheap and long lasting though not, I admit, as good
as the bought versions. It does not need a great deal of imagination to

Figure 66 A simple home-made wire support which can be very useful in the herbaceous border. It may be made short and wide for low growing plants, or tall and narrow for other plants. Simple to make and cheap too

see that by using a combination of galvanized wire for the legs and wire netting for the top a fairly decent home-made support could be made for low cost and I have used such contraptions with great success myself.

Netlon, the netting company, has a range of plastic plant supports which attach to a wooden stick or cane. Unfortunately these require the cane to be stuck into the middle of the plant root on a big plant or, at the very least, right beside the main stem and I suspect this would not do the plant any good at all. Nonetheless these 'Circa Rings', as they are called, are inexpensive and this alone will recommend them for some uses. Where there is no possibility of damaging the roots of a plant they will provide an effective support but are not as durable or versatile as the other supports.

There are special supports for such plants as tuberous begonias and carnations which I have no doubt will already be known to those gardeners who specialize in those plants. These special supports are also useful for other plants too. The adjustable begonia supports are particularly useful for holding any heavy headed bloom which wants to fall face down into the mud. Of course such supports are made for begonias and if you do grow these plants but do not yet use these supports I suggest you try a few straight away. They will make life much easier for you and the begonias. Mine come from Blackmore and Langdon but they are also available from East Anglian Wire.

Figure 67 The simple adjustable begonia support of Blackmore and Langdon is useful for supporting all kinds of heavy blooms

The fruit cage companies have, in recent years, been offering ready made metal and netting supports for runner beans and peas. These come in various shapes and sizes and will be particularly useful in town where it is much less easy to lay your hands on the odd bits of wood which might serve as bean supports. There are the normal ridge tent type of support in various lengths available from Agriframes and C. Sutton while a plain upright version is sold by Tortube. Both Agriframes and C. Sutton also offer versions for use in restricted spaces and the maypole type of C. Sutton is particularly useful for this work. Lower supports for peas are available too and these consist of tubular metal hoops about 3 ft high which are draped with an appropriate netting.

Whether you think such supports are better than the home-made wood, string and netting types which most of us erect each year is a moot point. Certainly they are simply erected, will last for many years and remove the need to find suitable materials for supports each spring. They also make a very neat job whereas some of the home-made contraptions one sees are, to put it mildly, a little bit tatty.

The rigid or semi-rigid structures which we use to support various plants are very important but equally important are the means by which we tie or clip plants to stakes, wires or other supports. It is worth spending some time hunting through the accessory stands in garden shops to find good plant ties or clips. There are many on the market, some of which are good and some bad, but there are two which I have found particularly useful for a variety of jobs and which seem to me to be better than most. Even so it must be said that, for certain work with tender plants, there is still nothing, in my opinion, to beat raffia.

The two things which I find very useful are both illustrated. One is a plastic plant tie which comes in various lengths and is very versatile. All the raspberries are tied to their wires with these chaps, the climbing roses are tied to their wires and they are also good for tying plants to stakes. It is possible to join them together if a very long tie is needed and they will do for many other jobs in the garden too. I have used them for tying up rolls of netting, bundles of canes, fixing netting to poles for bean supports and they are the ideal means of tying the netting to wires when making a fruit cage (see Chapter 11). Most garden shops sell these things but if you cannot find them they are obtainable by post from Westray.

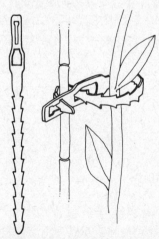

Figure 68 The marvellous plastic ties which are invaluable for all tying in and training

The second useful thing is a small wire clip made of spring steel which clips to a bamboo cane and holds a plant stem quite firmly. These clips are so quickly and easily used that I find them an indispensable aid in the garden, but care must be taken when putting them on otherwise it is possible to damage the plant's stem.

The last type of support to consider has only become necessary since the use of peat growing bags has become so widespread. It is not possible to drive supports into the growing bag, or at least it is not possible to do this with any hope of success, so an alternative has had to be found to support plants such as tomatoes when they are grown in this way. The answer comes from ASL, the sprayer company, which makes metal supports designed specifically for supporting plants growing in peat bags.

When buying plant supports or the materials for making your own the most important consideration is long life, because unless these things last a very long time they are uneconomic. Once it is accepted that you are buying these supports for life they appear to be a bargain. And this attitude could with advantage extend to the normal purchase of plant canes and stakes because no matter what fancy gadgets the garden industry provides for us we shall still need canes and stakes as well. On the basis that long life is desirable in such things I, several years ago, decided to use stout chestnut fencing stakes to support outdoor tomatoes, dahlias and chrysanthemums instead of the slimmer and weaker canes or stakes usually used for this work. It is a decision which I have not regretted.

Figure 69 The simple spring steel clip which is so useful for holding plant stems to bamboo stakes

Plant supports are not the first thing you think of when spending money on the garden and like so many good products they do not display well and are therefore ignored by garden centres. Yet they will repay you many times over if you can persuade yourself to buy good ones. They do make the tedious job of tying in and looking after border plants and cane fruit so much easier and more pleasant – and this alone makes them a worthwhile investment.

11 Fruit Cages

Fruit cage is the generic name given to any frame and net structure used to keep birds and animals away from crops. Whether the crop in question is fruit or vegetable is immaterial; if it needs protection from birds a fruit cage of some description is necessary. There was a time when protecting soft fruit against bird attack meant draping rather unsightly old net curtains over the bushes which, in the absence of anything else, was better than nothing. Now a number of firms offer fruit cage kits at reasonable prices which make it possible for most of us to give our crops the protection they need.

If you are one of those fortunate people whose gardens are not troubled by greedy, malevolent birds you will wonder why the rest of us bother to go to great lengths to keep our crops covered with such an assortment of nets, wires, bird scarers and cotton. If, on the other hand, you are familiar with the damage which a couple of bullfinches or pigeons can do when given the opportunity, you will realize the value of a fruit cage. I long ago came to the conclusion that the only way I was going to grow soft fruit satisfactorily was by buying a fruit cage and thus it was that I came to own a 36 ft × 16 ft Agriframes cage as my defence against bird attack. You may wish to protect your crops against other predatory examples of our wildlife such as rabbits or even deer but whatever the reason, if you have not already done so, I urge you to give up the unequal struggle against nature and invest in a cage. If you do there are two courses open to you: one is to make your own cage and the other is to buy a kit.

Buying a kit is probably the more likely course. Although there are several makes to choose from the problem is that large and cumbersome fruit cages are almost impossible to display satisfactorily in a garden centre and it is therefore unlikely that you will easily be able to see examples erected before you buy. Fruit cages are one of those things which it is more usual to buy by post when you are, in a sense, buying blind. If it is possible, therefore, I suggest that you visit one of the agricultural shows, the Chelsea Flower Show or a garden such as that of the Royal Horticultural Society at Wisley, where you may have the opportunity to see some of the different makes erected and displayed for comparison. The reason that I suggest you see them is not because one is better at keeping out wildlife than another but because each of the various makes does have a distinctly different appearance. This is largely due to the colour of the netting and poles used by the various manufacturers.

You might reasonably think that fruit cages are judged only by their ability to keep the marauding, piratical British wildlife away from crops and that any concern for the look of the thing is rather unnecessary. But I assure you this is not the case. A fruit cage, you see, is a large item in any garden and it is vital, therefore, that it does not offend the eye. However, what offends the eye is a very subjective thing as I have found in my talks with gardeners and manufacturers. Some people demand that their fruit cages be green while others insist they be black and it is a good idea to find out which camp you are in *before* ordering.

In the important matter of crop protection I think there is little to choose between the various makes, all of which have a metal

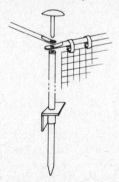

Figure 70 Detail of the Sutton Masterframe showing how the top tubes are joined to the upright. The base plate ensures that the upright is held securely in the ground. A similar method is used in the assembly of Knowle Fruit Cages. The smooth mushroom peg offers no rough edges to snag the roof netting when this is being placed in position or removed

framework supporting a fine mesh netting. Since there is little difference in this respect it is likely, therefore, that you will make your decision on such things as colour, construction or materials and in these matters there is sometimes considerable difference.

If you do favour green then it is quite likely that you will be interested in the 'Masterframe' made by C. Sutton Ltd. This cage has a steel tube frame which is coated in green plastic to prevent corrosion and give weather protection, and it uses green plastic netting. The method of joining the frame tubes is shown in Figure 70 and you can see that this arrangement allows corners of any angle to be used, should this suit your garden; you are not restricted to right-angle corners. On the other hand there is perhaps less inherent rigidity in this method than in the Agriframes' joints.

The Knowle Nets cages overcome the problem of corrosion of the metal frame by using aluminium tube instead of steel. This sounds to me like a very good idea. The method of joining the framework is similar to that of the Sutton Masterframe but the netting used is black. Knowle offer a choice of height which the others do not: you may order your cage 6 ft or 6 ft 6 in. high. If you grow raspberries or small fruit trees in your cage I think it wise to have the 6 ft 6 in. versions as the saving in buying the 6 ft version is very small and hardly seems worthwhile.

The Agriframes cage uses black Netlon plastic netting for the sides and Lobrene knitted netting for the roof. The steel tube frame gets its weather protection from being galvanized. After several years there are the faintest signs of rust on some of the welded joints of my Agriframes cage but it is still in excellent condition. The welded frame joints of the Agriframes cage are very different from the cap and pin method of the other makes and do have an inherent rigidity which is good in one sense but does, of course, mean that the corners of your cage can only be right-angled. This will not matter to most people who will probably want a right-angled cage in any case. If you do decide to buy an Agriframes cage there are two tips which I can pass on to you. The first is to grease the joints lightly before assembly because this will enable you to dismantle the cage easily in several years time if you want to take the thing with you when you move house or if you want to move it to another part of the garden. The second tip is to brace the structure with extra wire if it is big; this is to prevent the greased joints sliding apart when the frame is rocked by gale force winds, and believe me a gale force wind imposes great strains on any fruit cage, particularly large ones. This is very simply done by tying a wire from one side member across to another.

There are two further points to make about buying a fruit cage of any make. The first is to make sure that you have at least one door incorporated in the frame. Although a door is usually a few pounds extra it is worth every penny of its cost. The second point is to buy the biggest fruit cage possible, subject to certain qualifications mentioned later. The larger the cage the lower the cost per sq. ft of covered ground; for example a cage 12 ft × 12 ft costs about 17p per sq ft at 1979 prices while a 48 ft × 24 ft costs about 9p per sq. ft. Of course there are many other factors to be taken into account when deciding the size of the cage but where possible the bigger it is the better the value for money. There are, however, complications to this 'big is best' policy and it is necessary to study carefully the manufacturers' price lists so that you choose the optimum size fruit cage.

Another example will better illustrate this point: fruit cages come in units, as Figure 71 shows, and when choosing a frame it is desirable to choose the largest size compatible with your needs without going to a bigger unit. Thus a cage 12 ft × 12 ft will be the largest size cage on frame TYPE 1 and should you decide you want a cage 12 ft × 13 ft you will go to frame TYPE 2 which is considerably more expensive because of the extra tubes needed. Your gain in area

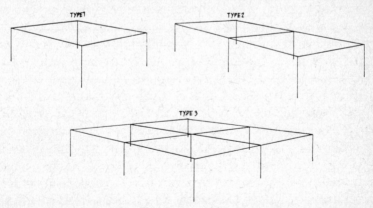

Figure 71 Diagram showing the configuration of the frame of fruit cages. The largest available size within each frame class represents the best value for money

covered would be about 8 per cent while the increased cost would be about 25 per cent. So in this case the 'big is best' argument needs to be qualified: it would be much cheaper for you to have the slightly smaller frame, namely 12 ft × 12 ft. The largest size cage in each frame category gives the best value for money.

The shape of the cage can have an influence on cost too and it is very worthwhile considering this point before buying. Two more examples will illustrate this: a cage 12 ft × 12 ft covers an area of 144 sq. ft, and a cage 18 ft × 6 ft also covers an area of 144 sq. ft, but the second cage, the rectangular one, will cost about 35 per cent more than the square one. With a bigger cage the difference is less but it is still important: a cage 24 ft × 24 ft covers an area of 576 sq. ft, while a cage 48 ft × 12 ft also covers 576 sq. ft, but again the rectangular cage costs more. In this example it is about 20 per cent more, although it varies from make to make. The moral of this story is, therefore, where possible to buy a square cage rather than a rectangular one of the same area. Many of us unfortunately do not have this choice because the site chosen for the fruit cage dictates its shape. In my own case I bought an uneconomical 36 ft × 16 ft cage, which cost 22 per cent more than the 24 ft × 24 ft cage of equal area, because I sadly had no alternative.

You will avoid all the fuss of choosing between the different makes by building your own cage from wood, wire and netting and you will save money at the same time. Buying one of the well-known makes of fruit cage could be as much as 50 per cent more expensive than making a simple fruit cage of the type shown in Figure 72.

The uprights used for the framework are chestnut fencing stakes which are obtainable from fencing contractors. You should choose your own if possible and try to get them straight in length and round in section. Avoid the thick stakes which have been split into two thinner ones. You may also be able to buy the galvanized straining bolts and wire from the same place but, if not, any hardware store will stock them. Buying wire is, incidentally, one of those times in life when 'those in the know' can make the rest of us feel complete idiots and 'those in the know' savour and relish such moments as I am sure you are well aware. The reason in this case is because wire is sold not by length, as any sensible person might imagine, but by weight. This means that if you breeze into a shop and announce your clear intention to buy 30 yd of wire, blank stares are what you will be met

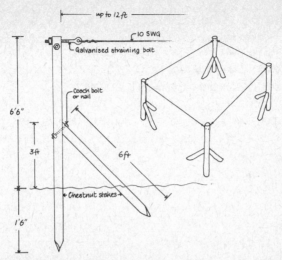

Figure 72 Details of construction of a home-made fruit cage. Extra uprights needed to support the wire between the corner posts on big cages do not usually need the 6 ft bracing stakes. The netting is hung from the wires and pegged to the ground

with. 'We only sell it by weight, mate, here's a kilo' – and you will ask in vain how long a kilo of wire is because no one knows. I asked at several shops and got answers which differed considerably. To save you such embarrassment I can tell you that 1 kilo of 12 swg (2·5 mm) wire is about 28 yd long and 1 kilo of 10 swg (3·15 mm) wire is about 18 yd long. For the purpose of the home-constructed fruit cage I think 10 swg wire is the more suitable. You could, if you wish, buy galvanized stranded steel wire which is much stronger, a good deal more expensive and, I think, unnecessary unless you are intending to do a Rolls Royce job.

Figure 72 shows the method of construction which is quite straightforward. The side netting is held to the wires by the simple plastic ties shown in Figure 68, and the roof netting – which must overhang the sides all round – is held to the side netting by the same ties.

I think it advisable to use an upright at least every 12 ft although only the corner posts need to have the 45° support posts as it is only the corner posts which have to take the strain of the wire. The posts must be treated with a wood preservative and I have not included this in the cost as it is likely you will have some of this in your garden shed already. The various nails and staples have not been included in the cost for the same reason.

Materials and cost for 12 ft × 12 ft fruit cage	(1979)
4 × 8 ft chestnut stakes	£3.89
8 × 6 ft chestnut stakes	4.67
8 galvanized straining bolts	2.40
2 kilos 10 swg (3·15 mm) galvanized steel wire	1.71
100 plastic ties	1.00
Netting (Knowles) for side 16 yd × 6½ ft	4.84
for roof 5 yd × 13 ft	3.02
Cord (Knowles) 17 yd	.55
Total	£22.08

Materials and cost for 36 ft × 12 ft fruit cage	(1979)
8 × 8 ft chestnut stakes	£7.78
8 × 6 ft chestnut stakes	4.67
8 galvanized straining bolts	2.40
4 kilos 10 swg (3·15 mm) galvanized steel wire	3.42
200 plastic ties	2.00
Netting (Knowles) for side 33 yd × 6½ ft	9.98
for roof 13 yd × 13 ft	7.86
Cord (Knowles) 33 yd	1.07
Total	£39.18

The wire which is not used for the framework is cut into short lengths of about 6 in. and used to peg the side netting to the ground. There is no door in this cage and entry is gained by untying the side netting at a corner post and drawing it aside like a curtain. (Easier said than done.)

Whether you buy or make your fruit cage it is quite likely that you will also need small temporary structures to keep birds away from strawberries, various of the brassica family and peas and also to keep birds and animals away from seedlings and seed beds. Making such structures has been greatly helped by the Netlon company which makes a wide variety of plastic netting for all sorts of jobs. The two nets most suited to our needs are Netlon Garden Netting which is green and has a ¾ in. (19 mm) diamond mesh and Netlon Fruit Cage

Net which has a ¾ in. square mesh and is black. The Fruit Cage Net is much stiffer than the Garden Netting and is easier to handle, but if you are draping net directly over plants the very lightweight Garden Netting is probably better.

Draping nets directly over the foliage of plants is a reasonably satisfactory temporary measure but if possible it is better to make a small framework to support the netting. The 'Hortiball' system is perfect for this work. Using bamboo canes or ½ in. aluminium rods, which can be obtained from Knowle Nets, you can easily build a simple, strong support for the netting. Hortiballs can be bought in shops or by post from Knowle Nets or C. Sutton. (Figure 73.)

For these small temporary structures which are needed to protect various plants at certain times of the year, you will have no choice but to make your own, with or without Hortiballs. But for the big permanent fruit cages making the choice between buying and doing-it-yourself is more difficult. It is cheaper to make your own but with small cages the difference in cost is small: as I write the 12 ft × 12 ft home-made frame without a door is less than £3 cheaper than the Sutton 12 ft × 12 ft without a door. However, the savings on a bigger cage are greater: the home-made 12 ft × 36 ft cage costs less than £40 at 1979 prices whereas some of the commercial makes cost over 50 per cent more.

If you decide to buy you may be sure that all the cages keep birds out provided you maintain the nets in good condition. Persistent squirrels can eat their way through the nets and wrens can even squeeze through ¾ in. mesh netting (and quite frequently do when the red currants are ripe), so your choice will depend on looks and price. The eye appeal of fruit cages has already been discussed and is, as I have said, a subjective judgment, but price is not. Of the three widely advertised makes Knowle Nets cages are the most expensive with the small extra cost being accounted for by the aluminium frame which will, of course, be totally corrosion free for life.

Whether you make or buy I am sure you will find a fruit cage a very worthwhile addition to the kitchen garden; there is only one vitally important thing you have to do with your cage and that is to remove the roof netting before the winter snow comes. None of the fruit cages mentioned here is built to withstand the weight of snow on the roof. The fine mesh nets used do not allow snow to pass through so it

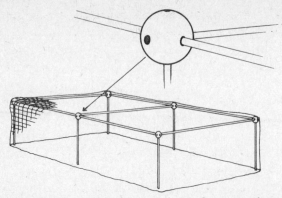

Figure 73 A simple low cost small cage suitable for protecting a few strawberries, brassicas or peas may be made from bamboo, netting and Hortiballs. Hortiballs are perfect for these improvised structures

very quickly builds up and its weight can cause the frames to buckle or break or the nets to tear. If, like me, you have ventured out in the middle of the night to save a fruit cage from a snowy death you will realize the importance of removing the roof net. In my case the late and heavy snow of 10 April 1978 caught me on the hop. The roof net had been removed over the winter months but had been replaced at the end of March, as usual, in the belief that winter was over. Then, two weeks later, we had heavy snow and I, returning home at about midnight in my best party dudes, had to don wellingtons and other snowproof gear and venture out Oats-like into the blizzard to inspect the damage. I was confronted by the sight of the roof netting, normally a taut and springy 6 ft 6 in. above ground, sagging to within 3 ft of the ground and looking decidedly seedy. I shook the snow down and retired, somewhat the worse for wear, only to return at about 5 am to shake a fresh fall of snow down. Fortunately in daylight I was able to see that no damage had been done to either the net or the frame – which I think says a great deal for the strength of the Agriframes cages – but it might have been a very different story. It must be admitted, however, that removal of the roof netting is an extremely irritating business and you may be tempted not to do it. You must resist that temptation. I find removing the roof net is good occupational therapy for visiting corpulent relatives seeking light post-Christmas exercise on Boxing Day, and if you are particularly clever you will be able to adopt the role of supervisor and foreman while the aforementioned corpulents do the work. But however you do it– do it.

If you need protection in winter because you are growing brassicas in the cage, which appeal to pigeons, then a coarse mesh, 3 in. × 6 in., pigeon net should be used. This will allow snow to pass through and no damage will be done. All manufacturers offer this as an extra and Netlon sell it separately for the do-it-yourself brigade. However, those of you who are plagued by bullfinches draw no comfort from knowing that pigeon netting is the stuff for winter. Bullfinches do their worst damage in winter when they eat the buds of soft fruit, particularly gooseberries, and pigeon net will not keep them out. I cover my bushes, after removal of the roof net, by draping Netlon Garden Netting directly over them until the roof is replaced. This is at once untidy and unsightly and is exactly where we came in with our old net curtains.

Fruit cages: buying points

1 Bought in/DIY: cost difference is small on the small cages.

2 Shape: square is better value than rectangle.

3 Size: usually the bigger it is the better the value but do not go unnecessarily to a bigger frame type.

4 Door: doors are extra but very worthwhile.

5 Colour: a subjective judgment; green or black.

6 Frame: galvanized steel, plastic-coated steel, aluminium.

7 Joints: mushroom type, rigid tube.

8 Pigeon netting: usually only necessary when growing brassicas in winter.

9 Rabbit protection: Agriframes offer rabbit protection, but easily added to others by using wire netting.

10 Small cages: temporary protection easily moved, use Hortiballs and aluminium or bamboo canes with Netlon. Small cages such as this may be all you need.

11 Extension: it is relatively easy to extend the well-known makes of fruit cage.

12 Permanent/movable: all fruit cages are in theory movable but in practice this is a lengthy and inconvenient process which is best avoided.

12 Power Cultivators

If you have come to this chapter fresh from the comparative simplicity of the fruit cage chapter prepare to ease the mind into a higher gear, for you are about to be faced with a bewildering array of makes, models and options which will, I suggest, make even the most blasé admit that they do not know it all. Just to put you into the right frame of mind let me tell you that when I counted the different number of powered cultivators which I had on file I found the total was eighty-seven and it is certain that there are others available of which I am not aware. However, I think you will agree that somewhere among the eighty-seven there is likely to be one to suit your particular need.

First it is meet that we consider a few of the reasons for buying a cultivator in the first place, in case you are one of those who consider that you can do quite well without one. Cultivators are one of those tools which satisfy all the classical reasons for buying garden equipment outlined in Chapter 1: a cultivator will save you time, it will save you effort and it will enable you to do jobs which are impossible by hand but, above all, in my opinion, cultivators are fun to use and that is also a good reason for having one. I greatly enjoy using my cultivator and always welcome the opportunity to try some of the many other cultivators on the market. Whatever your reasons for deciding to buy a cultivator I am quite sure it is a decision you will not regret. I have met people in my research, otherwise sane and normal men, who develop a great affinity for their cultivators much as they might their cars: indeed one gentleman spoke with equal reverence of his Rolls Royce car and his old Howard Bantam Rotavator. You have probably all heard of, or perhaps know of, ancient gardeners who will not be parted from a favourite spade or hoe handed on to them by their father and his father before that – well a good cultivator engenders that same feeling in me and others whereas, inexplicably, a chainsaw does not. However, if the romance of the cultivator leaves you cold consider it only as a ruthlessly efficient machine and treat it thus, you will still find it a great asset in the garden, whatever size your garden may be. Size of garden is, of course, an important factor in deciding which cultivator to buy and we shall cover this point later; but be quite sure that, no matter how small or large your garden, there is something amongst those eighty-seven or more cultivators to satisfy you.

It is obviously neither sensible nor practicable to discuss the merits of all eighty-seven cultivators in one book; moreover it is not necessary. Rather, in this chapter, I shall explain what can and cannot be done with each type so that you are equipped to make a decision yourself. And before going on it is a good idea to get the terminology straight: a powered cultivator is also known as a tiller, a rotary cultivator or a rotavator. The last name is actually the trade name of the Howard Rotavator company and correctly used applies only to their products but it is such a good name that it has become the generic term for all garden cultivators. A sort of horticultural Hoover.

Types of cultivator

There are two basic types of cultivator and the differences between them are shown in Figure 74. The boom type is a small but nonetheless very important section which will be dealt with later. One thing which all cultivators have in common is a system of rotary digging where rotating tines (rotors) bite through the soil as the machine moves along. The thing which distinguishes one type from the other is the means by which each maintains forward motion. The machine on the left of Figure 74 has powered wheels which take it forward while the rotating tines are trailed behind. The machine on the right has no wheels and it moves forward by the action of the tines clawing at the soil and pulling it along as they dig. This obvious difference affects the work the two machines are capable of and the ease or otherwise with which they can be operated. There is also an important effect on price. The wheel driven machine is usually more expensive as it is a more complicated piece of machinery and is

Figure 74 Two basic cultivator types. On the left the wheel driven type with the rotary tines at the back, and on the right the forward tine type which has no drive wheels. This exaggerated diagram shows how the wheel driven type digs shallow and fine while the forward tine type digs deeper and rougher

generally made to the high standard which commercial growers require. It also needs a more powerful engine because it not only has to drive its rotors but its wheels as well.

The important differences, however, are in the type of work which each machine will do. As the exaggerated drawing shows the speciality of the wheel driven cultivator is its ability to prepare a good tilth suitable for a seed bed and for shallow between row cultivation or weeding. Such machines are generally not good for the deep rough digging of autumn and winter because they leave the soil too finely broken and the depth of cultivation is too shallow to be of real value for winter digging. However, the control of depth of dig with wheel driven cultivators is usually more precise. This is a great asset, and because of the hoods which cover the spinning tines it is possible to work very close to growing plants without any great risk of damaging them. There is no better way of spinning in weeds, green manure and compost and if, like me, you garden on heavy soil, a wheel driven cultivator is the only successful way of obtaining a decent seed bed early in the spring when the ground can still be wet. Because the wheels drive the machine along the operator is required only to guide it and to operate the clutch, throttle and gears (if any). This means that almost anybody is physically capable of using at least the smaller types of wheel driven machine.

The forward tine cultivators (illustrated on the right of Figure 74) are probably more popular among gardeners because they are generally cheaper to buy and simpler to maintain. They will dig much deeper than their wheeled cousins and can be made to leave the ground rough enough for autumn digging, although this will depend on soil type. Using these machines effectively requires practice and sometimes a bit of effort. This is because of the method of forward movement which relies on the tines clawing their way forward through the soil. In very soft dry soil it is possible for such machines to dig *down* rather than *forward*, while on very hard soil they try to walk over the top of the ground rather than bite into it. The technique necessary is to make the rear stabilizing skid or feet stick into the ground by pressing on the handlebars and then the tines are made to pull against the restraint of the skid. In other words the front of the machine is pulling against the back and in ideal conditions the operator merely guides the show and has a relatively easy time. With a big machine in less good conditions with an operator who has lost his rhythm things can get out of hand, as I well know, and what should be a relatively simple and painless exercise can turn into an all-in wrestling match where the wise money will back the cultivator to win.

If the rear skid exercises too much restraint the tines will not be able to pull the machine forward and so it will try to dig down. The technique here is for the driver to lift the handlebars thus relieving the restraining effect of the rear skid and allowing the tines to claw forward. Until this apparently simple sounding technique is mastered the tendency will be to release the machine too much whereupon the tines will claw themselves forward and up, allowing the whole issue to jump out of the ground causing the operator to drag it back. These difficulties will largely be overcome as the operator becomes more skilled but even so the forward tine machine will never be as easy to control as the wheel driven machine and for this reason a forward tine type is not so suitable for the precise work of between row surface cultivation: not only is it difficult to steer with great precision but it is not easy to control the depth of dig with any great accuracy either. The ability of such machines to create a good seed bed varies greatly according to soil type and condition, make of machine and rotor blade type, but generally forward tine cultivators are less good at preparing a seed bed than wheel driven machines.

This is because to prepare a good seed bed you need a relatively fast rotor speed and a shallow dig and both are difficult to achieve with a forward tine machine. On good loam, where it is relatively easy to work a good tilth, most cultivators of any type will create a good seed bed but on heavy soil the forward tine model will be at a disadvantage, although there are ways of minimizing the disadvantages which we shall come to later.

It is perhaps a good moment to give the lie to a widely held misconception about cultivators which is that the weight of the machine affects the depth of cut, with the heavier machines being capable of deeper digging. In my experience this is not true: the depth of dig is more influenced by the skill or otherwise of the operator and by the design of the machine rather than by its weight. To illustrate my point I quote one example: I was trying to break in some new ground which had been rough grass and weeds for many years, perhaps thirty years or more, and the heavy cultivator singled out for duty would not do the job. It had the power but it had an inefficient rear skid which could not be persuaded to restrain the machine sufficiently to force the tines to bite into the soil; consequently the machine walked away over the surface with me trying to dig my heels in to restrain it – to no avail I might add. The machine which easily conquered the job was the comparatively light Templar 5 hp tiller. This machine has a very efficient twin rear skid which stuck in the ground and forced the tines to bite and pull against the skid. The Templar weighs much, much less than the originally selected cultivator which shows that while weight may be a factor it is far from being the most important factor in making a forward tine cultivator dig deep or, indeed, dig at all.

The Japanese companies of Honda, Iseki and Kubota make machines which can, by adding or removing accessories, be made to perform either as forward tine machines or as wheel driven machines. This sounds like the perfect compromise if one is able to disregard cost. However, cost is the one thing which it is impossible to disregard and for this reason you will probably not be able to make your decision on what to buy solely on the grounds of the method of the cultivator's drive.

Which of the two basic types is best for you and your garden is a matter for discussion. Certainly the wheel driven machines are easier to handle and are generally less physically demanding, but they are likely to be the more expensive too. They are ideal for between row work in the vegetable garden because of their precise control and shielded tines but not very good for deep digging; they are usually less versatile than the forward tine machines.

The forward tine machines on the other hand are capable of most garden jobs and are likely to be cheaper. They can sometimes require some considerable effort from the operator although there are ways of minimizing this. However, it is not sensible to base your choice on this one aspect of the machines without taking into account the other factors in this chapter and also considering the third and very important class of cultivator, the boom type.

I call this group the boom type because they carry the work head forward of the machine on a boom, as the drawing shows. This group is small in number but very important for all that because the machines in this category are designed specifically for the gardener, not for the nurseryman or smallholder. These machines, the Norlett Beaver Powaspade, the Landmaster L88 and the Landmaster Lion Cub are very versatile and can dig in a variety of ways. They can do the normal forward rotary digging such as the bigger machines can but they can also be used for reverse rotary digging and for working sideways across a plot in the manner of spade digging. Both the last two methods remove the need for the operator to walk on freshly dug ground which is an important point to some people. These machines also prove the point about weight being relatively unimportant in

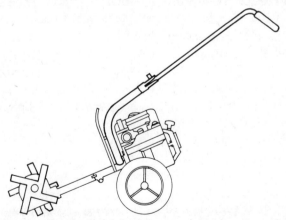

Figure 75 The boom cultivator: smallest, lightest and easiest of all cultivators to use

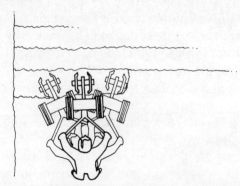

Figure 76 Diagram of the Norlett Powaspade being used to dig sideways across the plot, like conventional spade digging. This method leaves no footmarks on dug ground. Only the boom cultivators can be used in this way

rotary digging because although they are all very light they will all dig very deep if it is required. These machines do work extremely well, are easily managed by anyone and are perfectly suited to the small garden. They are also capable of work which bigger machines cannot tackle such as light surface cultivation in flower borders and perhaps even work in small garden greenhouses.

If your prime requirement of a cultivator is quick digging of large areas, however, these boom type machines are not ideal. Although lightning fast compared to hand digging, when compared to the more orthodox cultivators they are relatively slow. Their other qualities will outweigh such considerations for many people, of course.

You have, then, a choice of three distinct types of machine and a few Japanese models which manage to combine two types in one machine. Since digging is the basic function of all cultivators it is important to ensure you get the right machine for your digging needs and there is no substitute for trying out equipment before you buy. Trials should preferably be on your land but this is not always possible. Do not buy an untried machine.

Attachments

Man, being an ingenious animal, has really allowed his imagination and inventive capacity to run riot when dreaming up attachments which can be hung on the average garden cultivator. If you are so inclined you can have water pumps, circular saws, sickle mowers, rotary mowers, compost shredders, ploughs, ridgers, trailers, snow ploughs, bulldozer blades, tipping buckets and for all I know a thing for getting stones out of Boy Scouts' feet. You can, if you are really keen on self-sufficiency, even have a threshing machine for your Landmaster Lion. How about that?

I realize that such arcane gadgets are not likely to figure prominently in your plans but the range of attachments which it is possible to hitch up to your tiller is important and could influence your choice of model. The most common attachments are different rotor types for different jobs. These rotors are mostly used on the forward tine machines to make them more suitable for jobs to which they are otherwise unsuited. For example, some companies offer the finger rotors which are designed to facilitate the preparation of seed beds and there are special hoeing tines for light surface work and pick rotors for hard or heavy ground. The Japanese companies offer special rotors called drum rotors which have the tines bolted to a large central drum. I have found these particularly good on my own Honda FS 50. They are beneficial in several ways as they make the machine more stable and controllable as well as making it easier for shallow cultivation when this is necessary. The only drawback to drum rotors is their very high price. Most machines will come with slasher rotors as standard and these will prove good enough for most jobs; as with hand tools you can often compromise by using one tool to do the work of another, although it is better if possible to have the tool for the job. The widest range of rotors or tines is offered for the Merry Tiller which not only has a variety of digging rotors but also special aerating, spiking and slitting tines for lawn maintenance, as mentioned in Chapter 5. Among the cheaper cultivators the Qualcast has a good range of strong and inexpensive attachments which I have found useful in my garden.

Earlier I said that the wheel cultivators were ideal for between row work because their covered tines did not damage plants on either side. The forward tine machines answer this by having steel discs fitted to the outside of their rotors to prevent damage to plants. These work reasonably well and most manufacturers offer them as extras.

Different rotors are popular extra attachments which do not exceed the capability of the machine as it is usually a case of changing one set of rotors for another. However, some cultivator attachments

Figure 77 Side discs on the end of the rotors of a forward tine cultivator protect crops on either side of the machine

are very different and can stress the machines considerably: such things as ridgers, trailers and ploughs fall into this category. The most common of these is the ridger which is an invaluable aid to people like me who grow a lot of potatoes. (Is there any worse job than earthing up potatoes?) But pulling a ridger through the ground is a demanding task for some of the lighter machines and just because the manufacturer offers a ridger among his equipment does not necessarily mean all his machines can cope with it under all conditions. The photograph of the Qualcast cultimatic ridging in my garden (Plate 39) shows that a relatively small, light machine can cope very well with such work under dry conditions; but on the same ground in the wet the wheels would not be capable of giving sufficient grip, so a pair of digging rotors instead of wheels would be used to drag the outfit along, and this is not always a satisfactory answer. The amount of soil which a ridger is pushing aside as it is dragged along is surprising and the resistance is great, so if this is going to be work which you will do fairly often make sure your machine can cope with it easily. If, however, ridging is likely to be an infrequent activity you can afford the compromise of a smaller, less powerful machine.

Compromise is not possible when ploughing, however: either the machine can cope with the task properly or it cannot. There can be no half measures. You may think that ploughing with a garden cultivator is a bit of a joke and that you are unlikely to be so silly as to attempt it anyway so the whole discussion is of academic interest only. But if you do think that you will be making a mistake. A plough is a very useful attachment for a cultivator which I thoroughly recommend you consider seriously. For a machine to be able to cope with a plough I think it needs to have a 5 hp engine, a reverse gear and at least two forward gears. Having said that, I note that Kubota offer the T320, a small cultivator having only a 98 cc engine which can be equipped with a proper single furrow plough. Moreover, Kubota also offer the necessary extras such as weights and big wheels which make it likely that this little machine is up to the job. If you want a small machine which is capable of ploughing this could be worth investigation. Generally, however, a machine used for ploughing will be a bigger machine.

The advantage of ploughing is that the ground can be left in the ideal state to benefit from the winter frosts and winds. One of the criticisms which old gardeners level at the rotary cultivator is that the action of the rotating tines leaves the ground too finely chopped for proper drainage, aeration and weathering to take place over the winter and that the only satisfactory way of doing this is to leave the ground rough-dug by spade. There is much in what they say. It is true that rotary digging does not leave the best overwinter soil surface but if time and effort saved are more important to you than a hand-dug vegetable garden, then a rotary cultivator is an excellent tool for you – though a plough would be even better. With a plough the criticisms of the aforementioned old gardeners become irrelevant because the plough leaves an excellent surface for overwintering; the plough is, after all, the tool which has been much favoured by farmers for the past several hundred years and their achievements with it are notable, I think you will agree. Be warned, though, that if you decide to buy a plough you will also need the extras to make it work. You will need wheel weights, front weights and possibly bigger wheels with good tractor grip pneumatic tyres or spade lug wheels. The investment in such equipment is high and therefore *insist* on a demonstration before parting with your money. This will ensure that the machine can cope with your ground and, just as

Figure 78 Spade lug wheel. These special wheels are for extra grip in muddy or difficult ground for ploughing or ridging

important, you can cope with the machine. Do not attempt to plough without extra weights on the machine; these are essential and I should point out that adding such weights to the machine presents a golden opportunity to strain backs, pinch fingers and generally do harm to your person. Be careful until you have grown accustomed to the process and then still be careful.

Why, you may reasonably ask, have I gone on at such length about ploughs when they are likely to be little used by most people? To which I answer that I am trying to persuade you to use this device and not to consider it as being unsuitable for the garden. I use my plough on two small plots one of which is 30 ft square while the other is 30 ft × 60 ft. These two plots can easily be ploughed in ninety minutes whereas digging by hand would take several weekends. Those people with good soil or plenty of time or both cannot imagine how the thought of the autumn dig casts a shadow over the whole year for those of us on less satisfactory ground. Will the weather remain good enough for long enough to complete the digging? Will the back stand the strain? Will all the crops be out of the ground before winter comes and makes the ground impossible to dig? All these questions are asked and worried about. With a plough all such worries are removed: you can 'dig' the garden when it suits you without difficulty; indeed, if necessary, you can 'dig' it several times during the winter and you could not do that with a spade on anything but the best ground. But the most potent reason I know for ploughing is quite simply that I like doing it; it gives me more pleasure than any other single gardening job and I therefore urge you to consider buying a plough for your cultivator too.

What I said about insisting on a demonstration of the plough applies equally to some of the more expensive attachments, such as the big sickle grass cutters which are offered for the bigger machines. These attachments are very expensive and you must be certain they work well in your garden before you buy.

There are countless other attachments available, one of which is a trailer and these are dealt with in Chapter 13. Whether or not you need some of the more bizarre bits and pieces which manufacturers put in their catalogues I do not know but the pull of these accessories catalogues does wane after a few months (I am sorry to say) and you will find that the special gizmo which once seemed essential to the well-maintained garden does not hold quite the same fascination after a time. If you still find yourself irresistibly drawn to a particular item after several months, though, my advice would be to give in and get it. I do.

There is sometimes a big difference in price between the bits offered by one manufacturer and the bits offered by another. Quite often the simple bolt-on bits are interchangeable so that you may find that the hoes or ridger made for make A also fit make B. If this is the case you can sometimes save yourself a bit of money. A good example of this is the plough of my Honda: when I wanted a plough Honda had none in stock but I discovered that the Merry Tiller plough was identical, except for the hitch box. So I bought the plough from a Merry Tiller agent and for thirty shillings a local blacksmith adapted the hitch box to fit the Honda. This manoeuvre saved me time and money because Merry Tiller were selling the plough cheaper than Honda. The moral of which tale is to explore every avenue to make sure you could neither buy better and cheaper elsewhere nor adapt one make to fit another.

The final point to make about attachments is that they do have to be attached. This truism is often completely overlooked in the enthusiasm to amass a shed full of tools for the machine. Some bits are easily added and some are not and it can be a pain in the neck if you spend all weekend bolting and unbolting bits and pieces so that you can do a variety of jobs. A more important fact is that some bits do need a good deal of strength to cope with and it is wise to find this out before you buy. Remember that on a big forward tine machine there will be no transport wheels because the machine will be too heavy to push and therefore it will need to be driven from the shed to the garden. Once there the drive wheels will be removed and the rotors put in their place. When the digging is over the reverse process is necessary and on a big machine such work requires real effort. The lighter forward tine machines nearly all have transport wheels for pushing them around but even so you do not need to push them too far up an incline to realize just how heavy even they can become.

As you will have seen the attachments can vastly improve the basic cultivator and serious thought needs to be given to this aspect of the choice between the makes. Certainly it will be sensible to shop around and to check on prices and the possibility of buying cheaper parts from different manufacturers.

Quality and sophistication

Among the vast array of machines on offer there are some very sophisticated ones and some very very simple ones, some of outstanding quality and others which are only just about good enough for the job. As in most things you get what you pay for and as a general rule I would tell you to buy the best you can. If you do this you will, in many cases, be paying for quality, engineering and strength which you are not likely to test in the garden. Nonetheless, it is always a pleasure to own good machinery and if you can afford to indulge yourself by buying a Rolls Royce, when a Mini would probably do, then why not.

As this subheading implies, there are two good reasons for paying more for one machine than another – quality and sophistication – by which I mean the quality of workmanship and materials and the degree of mechanical complexity of the machine. The cheapest machines are very simple and are of a quality good enough to stand hard use in the garden but they would probably not endure the prolonged bashing which a commercial grower would give them. This is where the gardener gets caught. If he decides he would like one of the posher machines he finds himself paying a very high price for a piece of equipment designed for commercial use. That, unfortunately, is life.

The very simple garden machines invariably have the drive from the engine by a belt and the final drive by chain (see Figure 79). The chaincase will be completely welded and therefore sealed for life. This practice makes for simple, quick, cheap manufacture and is

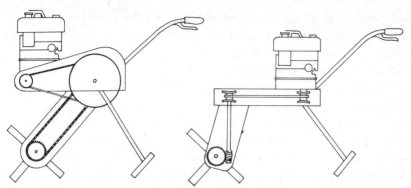

Figure 79 Two alternative drive systems for cultivators. On the left the drive from the engine is by rubber belt and then by chain to the rotors. This is by far the most common type. On the right the drive from the engine is also by belt, but operating in the horizontal plane, while the final drive is by a shaft and worm gears. The rubber belt in both cases provides a measure of safety because if the rotors get stuck the belts will slip and prevent damage being done to the engine, chain or gears

perfectly adequate for all garden use, but it is obviously not as good as having a bolted up chaincase which can be split open for mainte-nance and replacement of parts if necessary. However, if you want such 'refinements' you must pay for them, though I wonder if you would ever look at the drive chain even if you could. I doubt it. I have not looked at the drive chain on my machine in four years and I do not intend to in the next four either. Such facilities are important to the professional user but not to the average gardener.

The simple garden machines usually have one fixed single forward gear or speed and the addition of extra forward gears or reverse can be expensive but such refinements as these have a more readily under-stood benefit. A reverse gear is almost an essential, in my opinion, particularly on a big machine or where the operator may be less physically agile than the average Adonis. The thing which takes the fun out of using a cultivator is too much manhandling of the thing. It's a bit like a motorbike in this respect; you know how marvellous it can be swooping along the road but what a difference when you have to heave the ghastly thing onto its stand or push it about the garage. With a cultivator you churn merrily down the garden and then you are faced with turning around at the end or pulling it out of a corner and, like the motorbike, its character changes completely as it becomes a horrible, sulky, dead lump of metal. This is when a reverse gear is really appreciated. Unless the machine you buy is very light or cost is the most important factor to be considered I would recommend having a machine with reverse.

Whether more than one forward speed is important depends on the jobs you intend to do. Certainly if you intend pulling a plough at least two gears are necessary. It is also very useful to have a slow crawler gear for some between row cultivation, but this is a matter of choice. The advantage of having several gears is that you are more likely to have the right gear for a variety of cultivating jobs under varying conditions; with only one gear you will have to compromise. There are two principal ways of changing gear: one is by using a conventional gear lever and gearbox like a car and the other is by the simple expedient of manually changing the drive belt to a different set of pulleys. Some machines fall midway between the two by using a lever controlled belt change system. The more gears the higher the cost and generally the more pleasant the machine is to use. This is particularly true of trailer pulling. With a variety of gears it is possible to get a reasonably fast gear for this work, whereas with a fixed gear machine you crawl about at a snail's pace.

One extra which you will pay for and which is much mentioned in catalogues is the facility to swing the handlebars from side to side so that the operator does not have to walk immediately behind the machine and thus does not walk on the newly dug ground. Sounds like a brilliant idea and there is always some smart Aleck pictured in the catalogue doing just this with a nonchalance which makes you loathe him from the start. Controlling a machine while walking to one side of it with the handlebars turned accordingly may look easy but it is actually quite difficult and not to be recommended if you are doing precision between row hoeing and cultivation. *Between* rows can very quickly become *through* rows. From which you will deduce that a swivelling handlebar seems like a good idea but it does not work out so well in practice – unless you do enough work to become very adept at using it.

There is one rather nifty device which, as far as I know, is peculiar to the Japanese machines and that is the steering clutch or clutches. If you are buying a big machine these devices are well worth serious consideration because they make turning so easy and simple. The drive to either axle can be disengaged at will by levers on the handlebars and the machine can therefore be made to turn on six-pence with no effort on the operator's part at all. This makes turning at the end of rows, manoeuvring in confined corners or backing a trailer an absolutely effortless doddle. If you have never used a machine thus equipped you cannot imagine what a help such devices are. Unfortunately these are only fitted to a few of the bigger machines and they cannot be added to the others.

In general the sophisticated machines look better designed and thought out when you see them standing beside some of their more primitive brethren, and their quality is equally obvious. It is easy to recognize well-finished paintwork and fittings, and good welding is another easily recognized feature which not all machines can boast. Some of the cheaper machines I have seen have been welded up badly out of alignment and even if you are buying at this end of the market that is no reason to accept such things as bent or twisted frames and poor welding. On the other hand you cannot expect to pay rock bottom prices and get the quality of a Howard.

When you examine machines in showrooms you will notice distinct differences in quality which are not apparent from brochures but are immediately obvious when you see the real thing. The Japanese machines are all very well finished and their attention to detail is remarkable. The controls on the new Honda F600 operate so smoothly it's more like driving a car than a cultivator. Such machines are expensive but they do give a lot for the money. The Howard machines, too, are very well made but have a quite different character from the Japanese machines. The Howards are very functional and robust with no pretensions to style: they have the same feel about them that a good agricultural tractor has and they are obviously of the highest quality – which their price reflects and which you have to pay if you want to share that quality and sophistication. It must be admitted that for garden use such machines are a luxury and the cheaper machines do a job which is nearly as good for much less money. Quality, technical sophistication and mechanical complexity have to be paid for but, for we gardeners, they are things which are not always essential therefore you must distinguish between what is essential for you and what is merely desirable. But do not make false economies in this area: do not, for example, decide that you do not need a reverse gear if you know that because of age or ill health you will not be able to manhandle a machine backwards. Unless you are fit and strong it is worth buying the help a reverse gear can give you. In other words, what is only an expensive luxury for some may be essential for others. At the other extreme it is tempting to buy a big sophisticated machine which is altogether too big, heavy and complex for your needs, and this is just as big a mistake.

Which make?

Having decided which type of machine and what accessories you are likely to want, the problem of which make comes next and it is a problem of some magnitude. The best thing to do is to ask for brochures, and the name of the nearest dealer, from the manufacturers listed in the appendix who are offering machines of the type you think you require. Then try to inspect the machines in the flesh, so to speak, and finally have a demonstration of the machines which you have put on your short list. Do not be cajoled or pressured into buying a particular make when you feel it to be, in any way, the wrong one.

Not having tried all the machines available in all the gardens in the country it would be an arrogance on my part to tell you which brands are best but I do have some experiences which it is worthwhile my passing on.

The boom type cultivators probably have a wider appeal than any others and yet it is their category in which there is less choice than any other. The three well-known machines are the Landmaster L88, the smaller Landmaster Lion Cub and the Norlett Beaver Powaspade. I am familiar with both the Lion Cub and the Beaver Powaspade and find it difficult to choose between the two. There are differences: the Landmaster has a more powerful engine and a handlebar throttle control while the Norlett has an arrester which helps digging and a system of tommy-bar nuts which makes changing its configuration very easy. They both have an excellent range of attachments which are all reasonably priced and they do work exceedingly well. I like them both. (The Norlett company, incidentally, have a very good short sales film of their machines which they will make available for showing to garden societies and it demonstrates the capabilities of this small machine rather well.)

Two cultivators which are actually forward tine machines but are so much smaller than the others in that category that they deserve a mention here, are the Flymo GM and the Westwood Gemini. Plate 40 shows how small the Flymo is compared to the Honda F600. It is very light, well made and powerful although its Ducati two stroke engine is rather noisy. The machine comes with a tool kit which would do justice to a Rolls Royce, and even includes feeler gauges. The Flymo is so small and light it can be used for shallow row cultivation and it can even be manipulated through the rose beds with care, although I did this once as a test rather than as a regular habit. However, it gives an indication of the machine's manoeuvrability. It can be made to dig quite deeply and it has the advantage of folding easily for stowing in a car boot for transport to the allotment. Unfortunately there are no attachments or transport wheels yet available for this machine.

The Gemini uses the delightful Suffolk four stroke engine which has powered thousands of mowers over millions of miles of lawn since its introduction and is a very good and relatively quiet motor. There are several attachments for the Gemini not least of which is a hopper that attaches to the front, giving you a powered wheelbarrow.

Among the larger cultivators the cheaper ones are all simple forward tine types. At this end of the market there are two machines which I have used extensively and like: the Templar Tiller is just about the best value on the market at the moment for a basic single speed cultivator and it works extremely well. It is one of the

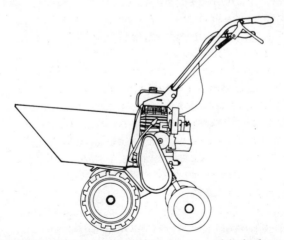

Figure 80 The tiny Westwood Gemini cultivator with the barrow front attached

machines fitted with a twin restraining skid and this contributes in no small way to its success, making it dig very deep if necessary and at the same time keeping the machine steady, stable and easily managed. A 5 hp forward tine tiller working hard can be a handful for some ladies but my wife found the Templar easy and pleasant to use. Although these machines can only be bought by post it is possible to visit the garden of a Templar owner for demonstration before you commit yourself. Details of this scheme are available from the manufacturer.

The Qualcast also represents very good value for money, as you would expect from this company. The machine is very similar to the Templar and works well too. The less powerful of the two Cultimatics has two gears and is remarkably inexpensive for a machine offering this facility, while the more powerful 4 hp version has a single forward speed and a reverse; it is just about the cheapest reverse gear machine there is, I think. There are a number of attachments for the Qualcast all of which are quite inexpensive, although I would like to see them offer heavier wheels as an extra item. However, I strongly suspect that the heavier wheels of a rival manufacturer could well fit the Cultimatic so that that problem could be overcome. These machines, like the others at the economy end of the market, have very simple belt tension clutches and an all welded chaincase.

The Norlett Tillers take us into a more refined world where reverse gear is offered on nearly all models and the top of the range machine has a 5 hp engine with five forward gears and one reverse which should make it capable of a variety of work. The 3 hp Tiller-

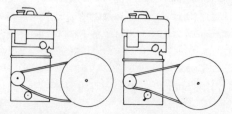

Figure 81 Diagram showing the simple belt tensioning clutch much used on cultivators and other machinery. On the left the belt is slack and no drive is transmitted from the engine. On the right the small jockey wheel has been moved up, the belt is tightened and can therefore transmit the drive from the engine to the flywheel

mate with which I am familiar is a good machine and although it has only a single rear skid it is one of the better ones of its type. The machine is not too heavy, is easily managed and digs well. It also has the advantage of having the huge range of Norlett attachments behind it which must be a considerable attraction. These machines have a bolted chaincase which means the mechanic in you can be let loose on an oily chain periodically if that is your fancy.

The Landmaster and Merry Tiller ranges take us into the world of the commercial grower and if you are contemplating working machines very hard on a variety of jobs throughout the year the 7 hp giants which both companies offer might be of interest. Furthermore, both companies offer an extensive range of attachments including, as I have mentioned earlier, a threshing machine. If you grow your own corn– good luck! At the prices which you will have to pay for such machines you expect a good deal and I think you get it. The machines are well made and very strong as examination of their slasher rotors will confirm. One point here in favour of the Landmaster is that the slasher blades are *bolted* to a hub which means they can be replaced if, as can happen, they become damaged. This is an idea which I think could be more widely adopted. Before leaving the forward tine machines there is one which I have not used but which has a specification and pedigree which appeals to me and I think warrants attention: this is the Terratiller, which is made in small numbers in Bedfordshire and which can only be bought direct from the makers. The machine has a proper clutch, gear drive and a Clinton iron engine and, moreover, it comes from the same stable as the well-known Monrotiller.

The wheel driven machines are much fewer in number than the forward tine type. This is because it is not possible to make them cheaply and therefore, because of their prices, their appeal is limited. The wheel driven machines are much favoured by commercial growers and, particularly in the less agriculturally advanced countries of Europe, they serve as small farm tractors. The already much mentioned Howard company is synonymous with rotary digging and the Howard 350 is a particularly good machine which I greatly enjoy using. Although a big powerful machine which is capable of very hard work it is nonetheless easy to use and was much liked by my wife who is pictured with this machine in Plate 42. The picture demonstrates clearly the ease with which such a machine can negotiate narrow rows. One point of warning, which also applies to other wheel driven machines, is that they can overbalance if you are not careful and what was once an easily managed rather pleasant sort of cultivator can instantly become a hernia-inducing, crop-damaging monster. The reason for this relative instability lies in the narrow track of the machine – width from wheel centre to wheel centre – and the relatively high centre of gravity. If allowed to lean too much these machines will tip over. Not allowing them to lean too far seems to be the solution. Mention of this facet of their behaviour does tend to exaggerate it and I do not want you to think that wheel driven machines go falling about the garden like a lot of cultivating drunks. Far from it. They are usually easily managed and the Howard 350 is a particularly good example; it is also one of those machines with an indefinable quality which makes you *like* it, besides appreciating its working value. There is also a smaller Howard, the 220, which is suited to smaller gardens.

One of the continental machines in this category which is imported here is the BCS distributed by Westwood. Rather a smart looking machine this, which I suppose we might expect from Italy, and one which works well too. In my fairly brief tests I have been impressed by it and, bearing in mind that it is imported, it is reasonably priced.

For both the BCS and the Howard there is a useful range of attachments and the advantage of not having to remove the wheels every time you wish to add a new attachment is yet another reason for these wheel driven machines being particularly suited to the lazy or the less physical types among us.

The Japanese machines are the ones which fit into either category: wheel driven or forward tine. Mostly they will be used as forward tine machines but the addition of an expensive attachment allows them to perform à la Howard, and Plates 40 and 41 show the Honda in both guises. As you may by now have gathered I am much impressed by the Japanese machines, and indeed my own machine is a Honda, although I must admit it was bought by accident rather than design. A happy accident as it has turned out. The trouble with the Japanese machines is that at the moment they do not have the extensive dealer network which some of their competitors have. However, I am confident that they will improve this position quickly because the products are deserving of attention. The machines are used as agricultural machines in the East and come here well tried and proven. I have been impressed by my own machine over the years, also by the Honda F600 which I tested extensively and by the F400 which I have used too. The Iseki range which is distributed here by Chain Saw Products Ltd appears to be very good – not dissimilar to the Honda– and there is a huge range of attachments for this brand. For sheer versatility I think the Japanese makes have it over all the others but there is a drawback: the price of their parts and attachments is generally higher than the home-grown makes. Nonetheless, before deciding on your machine, I think that you should look at the Japanese machines.

When comparing prices between makes it is easy to become confused because some machines come completely equipped for digging with a set of standard rotors while others do not and you will therefore need to add the cost of rotors to the price. In some cases you get neither rotors nor wheels which I think is a bit of trickery to make the price appear lower than it really is.

The last thing to say about cultivators of any type or make is that, in order to derive the maximum possible benefit from them, you must arrange your garden to suit them. By this I do not mean wholesale landscaping and general upheaval but sensible arrangement of crops to suit mechanical cultivation. It may say on a seed packet, for example, that the seeds inside are to be sown in drills 9 in. apart. When you have a cultivator ignore such directions because your row widths will need to be spaced according to your machine's capability. It will also be sensible, if possible, to arrange longer rows and if you have a fruit cage make sure there is sufficient room to get the machine between the side netting and the posts supporting the raspberries or cordon fruit trees. This sounds obvious but it did not stop me from making the mistake of not being able to get my machine into the fruit cage.

Before listing the buying points it is worth pointing out that second hand cultivators are frequently advertised and can be a good way of obtaining the better makes which otherwise might be thought too expensive for the garden. It is probably not a good idea to buy the cheap cultivators second hand, unless the price is very low, but the best makes will certainly be a good buy. It is still possible to obtain spares for old machines either from the manufacturers or from specialists such as Chester Hudson of Horam in East Sussex. Mr Hudson keeps spares for old Howards, Simars, Cliffords, Barfords,

Autocultos, Shays and other cultivators. He will sell you complete reconditioned machines too, if you so desire.

Whether your cultivator is new or old I am certain it will give you much pleasure and satisfaction and by observing the simple rules on garden layout you will derive the maximum benefit from it. Indeed, you will wonder how you ever managed without a cultivator and will probably consider expanding your vegetable garden when you realize how easily you can cope with it.

Power cultivators: buying points

1 Type: forward tine, wheel driven, boom.

2 Ease of handling: wheel driven easiest; forward tine more difficult.

3 Garden size: consider only the area to be cultivated. Small gardens can still have large vegetable plots.

4 Cultivator size: soil conditions and amount of work are as important as garden size when deciding how big the cultivator should be.

5 Range of work: the more powerful machines are usually the most versatile. Consider range of accessories.

6 Gears: necessary for heavy work, e.g. ploughing and heavy trailer pulling.

7 Reverse gear: almost essential except on lightweight machines.

8 Engine size: 2 to 3 hp for ordinary rotary digging; 5 hp or more for ploughing and power driven attachments.

9 Cost: simple low cost tillers are good value in the garden. Sophisticated machines are expensive but may be easier for ladies or older people to handle.

10 Second hand: second hand cultivators of the better makes are worth trying. Spares are available for many old and obsolete machines.

13 Barrows and Trailers

Sooner or later while working in the garden one is required to carry bulky loads from point A to point B and, possibly thereafter, on to points C, D, E and F. Grass cuttings, compost, leaves, fertilizer, peat, plants and goodness knows what else are constantly on the move in most gardens and the means by which nearly all these things are carried is the wheelbarrow. Indeed, it will not surprise me when historians eventually discover that the stones for the Pyramids and Stonehenge were lugged countless miles on ancient wheelbarrows. What is surprising is that the one-wheel monstrosity which is the common wheelbarrow is still so popular when it seems to do little else except fall over.

Barrows

From the chapter introduction you may conclude that I do not care for the ordinary wheelbarrow and you would be right. The standard wheelbarrow with a galvanized steel body, tubular steel frame and single front wheel is a masterpiece of poor design. The body or hopper is usually too small and too shallow, the legs at the back are too close together and the wheel at the front is usually of too narrow a section for the wheelbarrow to be of any real use. The limitations of the small body are obvious. The problem caused by the narrow spacing of the legs is one of stability or rather instability; the wheelbarrow when loaded has a very high centre of gravity and should have widely spaced legs to make it stable. Mostly this is not the case, which results in the wretched things falling over when they are left unattended on slightly uneven ground with a full load. You have all experienced this I am sure and there is nothing you can do about it except kick the thing – which accounts for the dents in my barrow. The wheel being of a narrow section makes the loaded wheelbarrow a fearsomely difficult thing to push because the infernal wheel, being so thin, insists on cutting into moist ground and therefore requiring superhuman pushing from the driver. This tendency for the wheel to sink into the ground is, of course, particularly annoying on lawns.

If, despite these faults, you still feel the desire to buy a traditional wheelbarrow I can at least advise you to invest in the old wooden wheelbarrows which are always pictured in photographs of old gardeners working at *the big house*. These wheelbarrowing juggernauts do carry substantial amounts, are completely stable and mostly have a large puddingy pneumatic tyre to prevent marking the turf. They are also very heavy, even when empty, and are not a vehicle for the memsahib to use or indeed for most sahibs come to that. If you do not see these barrows in shops try writing to T. Parker and Son.

While three-quarters of the world has been soldiering on with the conventional wheelbarrow a number of enlightened companies have been selling more sensible solutions to our transport problems. The most recent is the Ballbarrow which, although basically the same as a traditional barrow, is made entirely of plastic and is therefore light. Furthermore it has a huge ball at the front instead of a wheel which makes it much easier to push over rough ground and it has big feet which help to keep it stable. Yet despite these good features I do not warm to it because it is rather an odd looking thing; however, that is a very subjective and largely irrelevant judgment.

The other wheelbarrows which overcome the design faults of the usual barrow are the two wheel types. These have a large body which is carried close to the ground on two wheels, one on each side, and this layout gives them a number of inherent advantages. First, the load is spread on to two wheels which in theory reduces the load per wheel and therefore reduces the tendency of the wheels to dig in and mark the lawn or grass paths. I say 'in theory' because in practice some manufacturers fit small narrow wheels which do sink in and leave two marks instead of one, thus turning a potential advantage into a disadvantage. Look for big wheels, therefore, and look for wide wheels if and when you buy. The second advantage comes from the low body which can, by tipping forward, be used for unloading rubbish very simply, because the body pivots on its axle very easily.

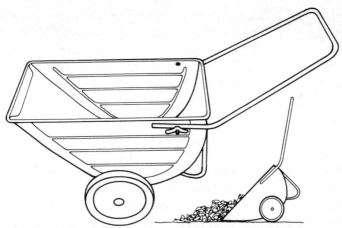

Figure 82 A small two wheel barrow. Notice that by tipping it forward
rubbish is easily unloaded while conversely leaves and other rubbish may be
swept directly into the barrow like a large dustpan

More important, it is easier to load because rubbish such as leaves can
be swept straight into it like a glorified dustpan. The third advantage is
that these two wheel barrows are much more easily pulled than an
ordinary barrow and pulling is a better way to handle big loads than
pushing. Last, the two wheel barrow places much less strain on the
operator because almost the whole weight of the barrow and its load is
taken by the wheels and not the arms of the gardener as is the case with
the old barrows.

There are a number of these barrows available in different sizes.
Corrie of Petersfield make one with a shallow pan and a bigger, deeper
model called the Trundler. A much less well-known model is the
High-Hoe Barrow from Highlight Engineering which also has a deep
body and big wheels, which is a good point. Moreover this barrow is
not expensive. Almost inevitably Wolf tools also make a rather good
two wheel barrow. Two bigger versions of the same thing are made by
Link-Hampson and Vulcan Trucks Ltd. These two are both of about
5 cwt capacity and adaptable for towing or pushing. They both have
large pneumatic tyres and ball bearing wheels are an optional extra
which will be worth having if you are going to do much pushing with
these barrows-cum-trailers.

A stage between the push or pull barrow and the towed trailer is the
Packhorse self-propelled barrow offered by Bob Andrews Ltd of

Sunningdale. This machine, which is supposed to carry up to 3 cwt, is propelled by its own battery powered electric motor and the battery can of course be recharged. This will be the perfect answer to those people who have need of something bigger than a barrow yet do not have a towing vehicle for a trailer.

Trailers

In Chapter 15 on tractors I mention that the single most useful accessory you could buy for your tractor would be a trailer. This also applies if you have a ride-on mower which has a draw bar for trailer pulling. If you have a garden which is big enough for a ride-on the chances are you could also use a trailer with advantage. Most of the tractor companies offer metal two wheeled trailers among their accessory lists but some are expensive. The Al-Ko looks to be one of the least expensive and it is also one of the bigger ones. The best trailers are the wood and metal type, again made by Link and Vulcan. These trailers are very versatile, as Plates 51, 52, 54 and 55 and Figure 83 show, and will be of great value in the garden. The tipping action of some of these trailers is useful, particularly when unloading manure, leaves and other bulk commodities. Tipping saves time and back-breaking effort.

I find my Link 10 cwt trailer is a particularly useful size for the garden and even fully loaded it will be well within the capability of most tractors to pull it. This particular trailer can be adapted to a four wheel hand-pulled trolley, and it can also have side gates which make it very useful for collecting grass, leaves and straw. Furthermore it can, by the addition of a special hitch supplied by Link, be made to attach to most of the popular cultivators and this is an advantage. If you have either a tractor or cultivator you can use this trailer. Vulcan make a similar model but they also do a smaller version which will perhaps have a wider appeal: it can be used as a small three wheeled hand barrow as well as a towed trailer. Vulcan will also be prepared to make barrows or trailers to order for special tasks if you require this and their experience in this field would obviously be valuable if you were designing a truck for your own use.

A cheaper but slightly more risky way of obtaining a special barrow or trailer is to make your own or to have one made by a local blacksmith, garage or engineering firm. My first trailer was such a

Figure 83 A Vulcan truck cum barrow. As shown this is a very large, stable three wheel barrow. By fitting the tow-bar and moving the castor wheel into the position shown by the dotted line this hand cart becomes a trailer for a cultivator or garden tractor

model, built like the brick out-house of proverb (solidly that is), but it had a number of faults which I pass on so that you may profit by them. The track was much too wide and I would suggest that the maximum width should be no greater than 3 ft, with 2 ft 9 in. probably being better, which would make the track a little less. Width is really determined by your paths and gates. To achieve narrowness it is obvious that the wheels must be under the floor of the trailer, which makes it high, but this is a necessary compromise. It is also essential to have pneumatic tyres and pretty squidgy pneumatic tyres at that, in order to reduce the possibility of damaging the lawn in wet weather. A four wheel trailer would be even better for soft going as its load is distributed lightly on four wheels instead of more heavily on two. It is also, I think, quite important to make the trailer as light as is possible without sacrificing its strength. Removable or drop sides are not necessary, though they are useful, but a removable tailboard is essential. My first trailer was very heavy and had no tailboard which limited its use somewhat.

Plate 53, showing the Templar Tiller and trailer, proves what a good job the local blacksmith can do. This trailer was made to special order for a Templar Tiller and, after some early teething troubles, it is now working well and is beautifully made. The problem of making a trailer for a cultivator is the difficulty of achieving a strong and fairly rigid coupling between the two: the coupling must have no vertical movement which would allow the outfit to sag in the middle and yet must be completely free in the horizontal plane to allow the coupling to hinge and thus make turning possible. You might consider buying the special couplings from Link and making the rest of the trailer to fit.

If you approach Link-Hampson they might, and I emphasize might, be prepared to sell their barrows and trailers as parts, and without the wood, which means the difficult metalwork would be completed and the wood could easily be added by you at home. This would also make the trailer cheaper. When I asked Link-Hampson about this they said they would be very pleased to hear from anyone interested and might be able to help them. But all this supposes that you need or want a trailer in the first place and perhaps you think that you do not. I ask you to read on.

At the beginning of this chapter I said that gardeners always seem to be heaving materials X and Y between points A and B and that some form of carrying implement was therefore crucial to our way of gardening. Well, a wheelbarrow of some kind is vital to most people but, in moderately big gardens, bigger barrows or a trailer are an immense help and their uses are infinite– and not even imagined until you have used one. Our trailer has variously been used to shift 10 tons of gravel, 7 tons of manure, several thousand gallons of water and countless bundles of hedge cuttings, leaves, weeds, rubble, compost, bonfire ash, logs and anything else you can think of, at different times in its life. For example, the 30 gallons of waste water which we were able to take, in a drum on the trailer, from the house to the vegetable garden and other beds every night for five months in 1976, saved the garden from dying in the drought of that year. The 7 tons of manure were left in the drive and had to be moved quickly to another site 150 yards away uphill. Think of doing either of those jobs with a wheelbarrow. I could go on but by now you will have caught the drift– do lay your hands on a trailer for your cultivator or tractor if you possibly can.

In Chapter 12 on cultivators and Chapter 15 on tractors it is emphasized that certain qualities are necessary in the pulling vehicle if satisfactory working is to be achieved. These points are worth re-emphasizing here. Tractor towing is relatively easy unless very heavy loads are anticipated in which case you will need wheel weights and possibly tractor grip tyres. Remember, too, that big drive-wheels give the best grip. There should be no problem about having enough power, only having enough grip to use that power on hills and in mud.

The driving technique with cultivators when hitched to a trailer can be awkward and requires some getting used to. Do not be put off if early steering attempts are less than precise. The cultivators with several gears will be the best hauliers of heavy loads. Fixed single gear machines will pull well but will be less able to cope with hills or mud. This is because of having too high a gear for such conditions when pulling heavy loads. If possible use big tractor grip wheels and wheel weights for best pulling performance in rough going and remember that steering clutches will improve handling and steering immeasurably. A very important point to remember in hilly gardens is that cultivators have no brakes and machines can run away with you on a hill if you de-clutch. Both Link and Vulcan offer brakes as extras for their trailers and these are worth having where you have to negotiate hills. Lastly I would recommend having a cultivator with an easily engaged reverse gear if you are using it with a trailer as this makes manoeuvring so much easier.

Finally I must mention the very original approach to the problem of moving loads about a large garden which was shown by two gentlemen I met. They both use small dumper trucks for this purpose, of the type often seen on building and other construction sites. One of these men even cuts his grass with his machine by towing a small set of gang mowers behind it, which means the machine is giving very good value for its cost. These dumper trucks can be bought cheaply second hand, often in a pretty poor state it must be admitted, but probably good enough for the comparatively light duties of a garden. A new machine is about the same price as a garden tractor and for special applications might just be worth considering (although I mention this really to show that, in order to arrive at a solution to certain problems, sometimes a bit of what is fashionably called lateral thinking is required).

Now whether or not a beaten up second hand dumper or a large wheelbarrow or a super trailer is the load carrier for you I cannot know. But when so much of our time is spent carrying various bulky materials about I do know that it makes good sense to use the best available tools for the job – and the orthodox wheelbarrow is not often one of those tools.

Barrows: buying points

1 **Stability:** two wheeled barrows, large wooden barrows.

2 **Tyres:** as wide as possible, or pneumatic, or both. Ballbarrow.

3 Lightweight: plastic barrows or small Corrie.

4 Size: big two wheel barrows also serve as trailers. 5 cwt capacity.

5 Self-propelled: 'Packhorse' 3 cwt capacity.

6 Wheel bearings: usually plain bearings but ball bearing wheels a great help when pushing.

Trailers: buying points

1 Size: small trailers can also be used as wheelbarrows. Consider width of your paths.

2 Versatility: for tractor or cultivator towing; drop sides; gate sides; four wheel or two; tipping or fixed.

3 Loads: for bulk loads buy a tipper; for leaves, grass, straw have gates.

4 Brakes: necessary on cultivator pulled trailers in hilly gardens.

5 Materials: wood and metal or all metal. Wood and metal probably best. All metal can be smaller and cheaper.

6 DIY: home-made or local made trailers and barrows can be good and inexpensive. Cultivator hitch is difficult. Buy this part from Link if possible.

7 Price: as all trailers are interchangeable check the prices of trailer offered by each tractor manufacturer; there could be big differences for similar products. This type is usually all metal and small.

39 (*Left*) Rear view of the good value Qualcast Cultimatic fitted with a ridger blade. The worth of a ridger blade to those who grow potatoes, celery and brassicas cannot be overemphasized. Driving a machine fitted with a ridger is not easy and requires some practice before a good job results

40 (*Right*) The good finish and car-type gear controls of the Honda F600 are shown here

41 (*Below*) David and Goliath: the contrast between the small easily handled Flymo cultivator and the large Honda F600 demonstrates more clearly than words the range of choice open to gardeners and also makes obvious the fact that some machines will be capable of work which others cannot do

43 The ability of the Howard 350 to make a seed bed where forward tine cultivators had failed is shown here. On the left is the clay rubble left by the forward tine machines. On the right is the fine tilth left by the Howard

42 The excellent Howard 350 here being used by my wife for cultivating between rows of young brassicas and gladioli. The fact that she is easily able to control such a large powerful machine in such restricted conditions demonstrates the ease of control which is a feature of rear tine cultivators

44/45 These two photographs show the value of the rear tine cultivator for 'spinning in' weeds and green fertilizer. The picture on the left is the 'before' and on the right the 'after'. The clean ground on the right was achieved with two passes of the Howard 350

46 Two sets of slasher rotors which show the difference between the expensive cultivators and the cheaper models. On the left the massive forged blades of a big Honda and on the right the obviously lighter and flimsier blades of a cheaper machine. One is designed for heavy commercial use and one for the lighter duties of the garden. Both work well

47 Slasher rotors for a Merry Tiller. Notice that the tines of the left rotor all turn down, or in, while those on the right go in both directions. The right hand type is usually used but for close inter-row work the left hand type is best because with all blades turned in towards the machine no damage will be done to crop rows on either side

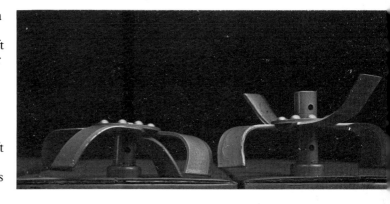

48 These are special pick rotors for a Merry Tiller and are used for breaking very rough hard ground

49/50 The unique versatility of the Japanese machines here demonstrated by a Honda. Top, the machine is fitted as a normal forward tine type with the slasher rotors replacing the drive wheels. Below, the special attachment is shown fitted which converts the machine into a rear tine type like a Howard

51 The versatile Link 5 cwt trailer cum barrow. Here used as a trailer but easily converted to a large two wheeled barrow which has the advantage of a sloping back for easy loading and unloading

52 The advantage of a trailer over a barrow, although obvious, is under-lined here

53 A special trailer made to order by a village blacksmith for fitting to the very good Templar Tiller

54 One face of the Link 10 cwt trailer. Here my trailer is attached to a cultivator. Driving an outfit like this is not easy and requires much practice before it is mastered. This trailer can be used with high sides and will also convert to a four wheel hand trolley. The tractor linkage is shown in photograph 55

55 Two excellent British products together – the very good value Westwood Gazelle lawn tractor pulling the Link 10 cwt trailer. The trailer
contains two rakes, a bale of peat, two watering cans, a Swoe, a fork, a
garden line, a bag of fertilizer and several trays of seed potatoes, all of which
would take a lot of carrying in a wheelbarrow

56/57 The X300 Sheen flame gun. This is a heavy tool to handle and where possible it is best to use the trolley shown in the second photograph. The hood may be detached if required

14 Leaf Clearing

Interest in leaf clearing is obviously directly proportional to the number of trees in your garden, or perhaps in your neighbours' gardens. It would appear, from people who have written to me and from others that I have spoken to, that for those people to whom leaf clearing is a problem it is always a *big* problem which takes time and effort to solve satisfactorily. Time and effort will solve many problems, of course, but there are more constructive things to do with both of these commodities than to run around after millions of leaves when there is equipment which will do that job for you.

The simplest method of gathering leaves is to rake them into a pile and carry them off for composting, mulching or burning according to your taste and all that is required for such work is a good rake. I have found the large wooden hay rakes to be good for this work, and the spring steel lawn rakes will also serve. If you have only a few leaves to pick up many of the modern grass collecting rotary mowers will suck leaves up and throw them into the grass box. Mower manufacturers sometimes make a point of this in their sales literature and it is a satisfactory method of doing the job. The Snapper High Vacuum mowers do a particularly good job of picking up leaves and grass. Other people I know run the mower over the leaves, chopping them very fine and leaving them on the lawn. But there are also a variety of machines designed specifically for clearing leaves and it is these which we shall discuss here.

Leaf sweepers
The simplest and most common machine is the leaf sweeper which comes in a range of sizes and works by having a stiff brush rotating in

front of a collecting bag: the brush rotates and flicks leaves into the collecting bag. What, you may ask, could possibly be simpler or better? Well not much could be simpler but many things could be better. The leaf sweeper looks like the perfect answer to leaf clearance but, unfortunately, it has a number of faults which detract from its usefulness. This is not to say that leaf sweepers do not work but rather that they will only work in the right conditions. As you will see from Figure 85 a leaf sweeper has to be very close to the ground for the brush to be able to pick up the leaves; however, this will also mean that the front bar of the leaf sweeper digs into the ground and catches on bumps, lumps, mounds or other slight irregularities in the lawn. This problem is reduced by having a narrow leaf sweeper but as that reduces carrying capacity it is not the perfect answer. Many leaf sweepers are also badly designed and made, which does not help them overcome their other faults. You should look for one with a rigid frame and strongly welded joints. There is one particular brand widely available in this country which has a complex tubular frame bolted to the brush assembly and it is, quite simply, far too weak to work properly.

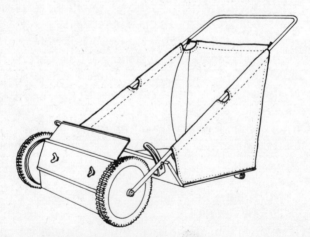

Figure 84 A simple brush leaf sweeper. The brush at the front is driven by the wheels and the leaves are thrown back into the canvas bag by the spinning action of the brush. Notice the rigid metal floor of the leaf bag, the rear supporting wheels under the leaf bag and the handlebar which attaches directly to the wheel spindles. This last feature means that the pushing effort is directed straight to the wheels and there is no complex sub-frame to buckle, bend or twist under strain. Not all leaf sweepers are so well designed

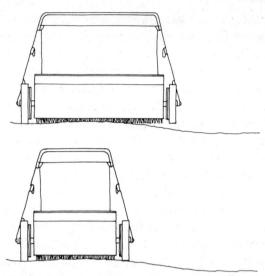

Figure 85 These two head-on views of conventional revolving brush leaf sweepers show one of the disadvantages of the type, namely their inability to cope satisfactorily with uneven ground. This fault is worse in the wider models as this exaggerated diagram shows. Small models are better but, of course, are less capacious

Another area of weakness in leaf sweepers is in the collecting bag or box. This must have a hard floor if the machine is to be satisfactory. The soft floor or semi-rigid plastic floors are not good enough and with a full load of wet leaves such bags distort and drag on the ground or interfere with the wheels and generally make life miserable. Good machines will have a galvanized steel floor. The bag should be of a good quality canvas or nylon and not some easily torn flimsy plastic. If your conditions are suited to a leaf sweeper, namely, you should have a flat, smooth lawn, it will pick up a considerable weight of leaves and it is necessary therefore that the bag is supported by wheels at the back. At least one machine does not have these wheels.

A further problem with such machines is that the brush only revolves when the wheels revolve and therefore the optimum efficiency of the machine is related to walking pace. However, not all places are accessible at walking pace which means the machine will not work with a consistent efficiency.

None of this sounds like much of a recommendation for leaf sweepers but, as I have said, if your conditions are right and you get a machine with the right features it is a fairly good and reasonably inexpensive method of picking up leaves. The Wolf model appears to have the right design for a small leaf sweeper.

There are several large leaf sweepers for towing behind ride-on mowers and garden tractors which suffer the same faults as the hand push machines. You should look for the same good design points but place even more importance on rigidity because of the bigger loads and greater stresses which a towed leaf sweeper has to contend with. The Case leaf sweeper which uses two brushes and has the tractor supporting the heavy end of the bag seems to be a better design than most in this category.

As with all things there is a leaf-sweeping 'Rolls Royce' which is manufactured by Nickerson Turfmaster Ltd and this comes in three versions. Two versions are for towing and the third is self-propelled. In all cases the brushes are power driven by a petrol engine and so they work regardless of forward speed; this overcomes the problem of the cheaper models. All have strong collecting boxes of steel or fibreglass and are models of what a good leaf sweeper should be. Their price once again shows that good design and good materials do not come cheap.

There are hidden advantages to using a leaf sweeper which also need to be considered. The beneficial movement of the brushes on the

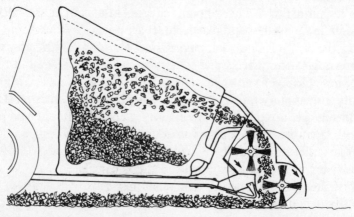

Figure 86 The Casc leaf sweeper for towing behind a small tractor or ride-on mower. This sweeper uses two contra-rotating brushes and has the brushes at the back instead of the front where they usually are. The other good point to notice is that the weight of the bag is borne by the tractor hitch rather than fiddly little castor wheels or rollers

grass cannot be discounted having as they do a light scarifying effect. Good leaf sweepers will also pick up grass cuttings which are left behind after using certain rotary lawn mowers. Thus if you can buy a good machine and use it in the right conditions a leaf sweeper is a good way of picking up leaves. Big smooth lawns are home for such as the Nickerson Turfmaster where their capacity for fast work can really be used to advantage.

Vacuum leaf clearers

The next category of leaf collectors are the vacuum type which are in effect colossal garden 'Hoovers'. There are several to choose from. The simplest really are like a house floor-cleaner because they have a motor, albeit a petrol one, which creates the suction and an enormous dust bag at the back for the leaves and other debris which are sucked up. The cheapest of these machines is pushed along but there is a self-propelled version and an optional tow bar which allows the thing to fit behind a small tractor if required. These machines work very well, as Plate 32 shows, and my own machine has been a great help in our garden.

There are drawbacks, however. Sucking up leaves is another of those ideas which seem too good to be true but where the reality is different from the contemplation. The vacuum leaf clearers do have faults. They will not pick leaves out of long grass (about 4 in.) very satisfactorily and they work less well with wet leaves, which is obvious I suppose. On large areas they require frequent emptying and this is a nuisance (the emptying process is shown in Plate 33). Initially we were disappointed with ours but we have grown to appreciate it and would not now be without it. It will even pick up leaves off a loose gravel drive without picking up the gravel and owners of loose gravel drives will know how difficult it is to keep such areas clear normally; the only way is slowly with a rake and patience unless you have a vacuum.

The big advantage of the vacuum clearer is that it can be used little and often, keeping things under control and never letting them get out of hand. Use it much as you would your carpet cleaner: a quick whistle round every day or so and the leaf problem is solved. Continuing the analogy with the carpet cleaner, the leaf vacuums have a wander hose attachment for sucking leaves out of flower borders and other awk-ward places. This is a real boon and worth having – except when it

Figure 87 The ultimate in bulk grass and leaf collection is the E-Z Vac. The flexible hose fits to the outlet of the rotary mower underneath the lawn tractor and an engine situated on the tow-bar of the tractor drives a fan which sucks grass and leaves up the hose and into the trailer. These machines are made to fit most makes of tractor

clogs. (This can happen when the greedy thing slurps up a small stick which then lodges in its neck causing a blockage.) There have been several makes available at different times but the most common is the appropriately named 'Billy Goat' distributed by Bob Andrews Ltd of Sunningdale. There are several versions of the basic machine but our 3·5 hp model, which is the smallest and simplest, has proved good enough for our needs. If you do have a Billy Goat remember not to leave the bags full of wet leaves in the shed for a few days; and if you take my advice you will protect the neck of the bag against the sharp edges of the machine. We did this by sewing a leather collar inside the bag's neck. I wonder why the makers do not do this in the first place because for the price I think they should.

An even bigger version of the vacuum leaf clearer is offered for attaching to many of the garden tractors which are presently available. These cleaners have an enormous hose attached to the outlet of the mowing deck and leading away to a trailer behind the tractor. The suction is provided by an engine situated on the trailer. Such machines are obviously capable of handling vast quantities of leaves and grass but you need the tractor in the first place. If you have such a tractor this could be the answer to your leaf collecting problem.

Leaf blowers

The last mechanical method of leaf collection is, in my view, by far the best, particularly for large areas or lots of leaves or both. With this method you blow instead of sucking, which sounds quite daft until you think about it. The wind is a real nuisance in the autumn when you are trying to collect leaves and I must confess that I thought that any machine which blew leaves about was doomed to failure from the start; we have enough wind without making more, thought I. With some reluctance, therefore, I tried the Winro Blower and my expectations were not high. Within minutes I realized that this was the perfect answer to leaf collection. The great thing about the Winro Blower is that it gives an extremely powerful air blast but it is a blast which you can control and herein lies the secret of its success. Throughout the autumn months we used the machine and we were very sorry to have to return it to Andrews at Sunningdale.

The idea of the blower is to blow leaves into a pile which can then easily be carted away or burnt. The range of the blow is quite incredible and it is possible to clear large areas of leaves literally in minutes. If you have rough wooded areas beside your formal gardens you simply blow the leaves from the formal part to the wild part and there you leave them. If this is not possible you blow the leaves into a pile for dispersal as mentioned. Either way is quick, easy and relatively effortless because the machine is quite light and easy to use. It will even tear wet leaves off the ground when they have become stuck. Such is

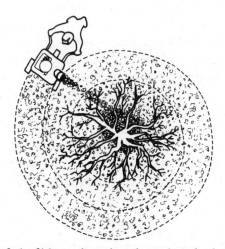

Figure 88 Plan of a leaf blower in action. A good method of using these machines is to move in decreasing circles round a large tree blowing the leaves against the tree as you go. The leaves pile against the trunk and are easy to collect for disposal

my enthusiasm for this machine that it will be the very next thing added to our garden armoury. Used in combination with the Billy Goat vacuum clearer all our leaf problems will be solved.

I understand that leaf blowers have not sold very well in this country, although they have in the USA and I think this is because people misunderstand them and, like me, cannot at first appreciate the concept of blowing leaves as readily as they can the principle of sucking them. I am sure this will change and leaf blowers will make their mark because, for large areas, they are unbeatable.

While dealing with leaf collection it is a good time to mention the 'Donkey' which is used throughout the year but which is particularly useful at leaf collecting time. The Donkey is a square of strong material, such as canvas, with handles at each corner so that it can be gathered up and whatever rubbish is on it can be carried to the compost, bonfire, trailer or wheelbarrow. It is particularly useful for emptying the Billy Goat bag on, as Plate 33 shows. The Donkey is made from various materials by various companies and goes under different names but no matter where it comes from it must represent just about the best value in garden equipment of any type or kind. Whatever else you need for leaf collecting, I think a Donkey is particularly useful and worthwhile.

Choosing from the more complex equipment is relatively easy in this field unlike some others. If you want to clear small areas, or large areas with few leaves, an ordinary leaf sweeper will do the job provided the ground is smooth. That is most important. Buy only the best push models. For large smooth areas the superb Nickerson power machines are the thing but the price is high. For a tidy garden and the ability to clean flower beds and other awkward places a vacuum clearer is the answer with a wander hose; there is a model called the 'Huff 'n' Puff' now available which is smaller than the 'Billy Goat' models. For big areas the Winro Blower is the very best tool.

Leaf clearing: buying points

1 **Few leaves:** if smooth ground a leaf sweeper will do or a lawn mower.

2 **Low cost:** the only low cost leaf collector is a leaf sweeper.

3 **Speed:** a blower, or if leaves must be collected a power or towed sweeper.

4 Flower borders: vacuum and wander hose.

5 Gravel drives: vacuum only.

6 Manoeuvrability: depends on size of sweeper. Vacuum models are manoeuvrable. Winro is manoeuvrable.

7 Lightweight: only the Winro, or use self-propelled sweepers and vacuums, or towed sweeper and vacuums.

8 Large areas: trailer vacuum, blower or power sweeper according to conditions.

9 Quality: beware of some of the leaf sweepers.

15 Garden Tractors

In the first chapter of this book I said that one of the reasons for buying garden machinery which is often overlooked is the enjoyment or fun which it will give you. This applies to some machines more than others, but perhaps the one which is most fun to use is the garden tractor. Surprisingly for such an expensive item there are about sixty models to choose from, almost every one of which is imported from America or Europe. Precisely what constitutes a garden tractor is difficult to define but for the purpose of this chapter I include anything which has the appearance of a miniature agricultural tractor rather than the Go-Kart look of the ride-on mowers covered in an earlier chapter.

People's fascination with models and things miniature may well account for the interest in this section of garden machinery yet you should not imagine that these little tractors are toys: they are capable of a great deal of hard work all the year round if you exploit them fully (see Plate 1). The smallest, simplest and cheapest of these tractors are called lawn tractors and they are obviously the least versatile. The other tractors are usually called garden tractors and the biggest of them are at once complex, powerful and mighty expensive. The lawn tractors, as their name implies, are invariably equipped as standard with a rotary mowing deck which is slung under the tractor. This mowing deck will have two or three blades and will have a cutting width which can be over 3 ft and herein lies the first practical reason for having such a machine: their ability to cut very large areas of lawn very quickly. If you can imagine taking a 3 ft wide cut every time you go up the lawn, and also taking that cut while moving at 6–8 mph, you can see how speedily you will be able to accomplish your mowing. Whether or not you pick the grass cuttings up is for you to decide. Some models are able to collect grass cuttings and others are not. Personally I do not collect the cuttings left by my tractor unless the cut is long or wet or both. If you want to collect the cuttings you can buy the sort of machine with its own built-in collector, or you can trail a leaf sweeper behind the tractor, or you can attach one of the large vacuum trailers which some tractor manufacturers offer and which are described under leaf clearing in Chapter 14.

Now if these machines only cut grass they would need a steady hand on the pen at cheque signing time as you tried to justify such an expensive mower, but they actually do much more and the range of attachments for them is often quite extensive. Most of the attachments require pulling and include such things as rollers, lawn aerators, spray tanks, gang mowers and, most important of all, trailers. This last item can make such an enormous difference to working in bigger gardens that I would recommend a small tractor and trailer to anyone with more than half an acre of ground, especially if that someone was in any way handicapped. Trailers, trolleys and barrows are dealt with in detail in Chapter 13; suffice to say here that the trailer is certainly going to be the single most useful thing you can buy for your tractor. The other simple towed equipment will appeal mostly to those people who have to maintain large areas of lawn for which the more normal pedestrian lawn equipment is just too small and therefore too time-consuming to use effectively.

Lawns, however, are not the only areas of grass which have to be cut. Many gardens have rough grass or other undergrowth to be kept under control and you can push your lawn tractor into these jungles with no qualms. There are, of course, many special machines for cutting long, rough grass – machines like the sickle cutters or the big rotaries of Hayter and Wolseley – but if you have a wide variety of grass to cut and you want to do it all easily, quickly and with the same machine, you need a lawn tractor. My own tractor is a small John Deere, bought second hand, which has served me well for several years and despite terrible abuse it is going magnificently. When I bought it there was no oil in the engine, one tyre had been run flat for some time by the previous owner, the cutter blades looked as if they had been used to chop nails and the whole machine was generally rather sad. New blades, some oil and a repaired puncture put everything right and I have had no trouble from this machine since. It is used to cut all our grass including formal lawns, orchard and very long rough grass as Plate 6 shows. It copes with all these things very well and is even used to cut low growing brambles and other undergrowth in a wooded part of the garden.

Although these small tractors will do this variety of work I am not suggesting they are the best thing for each particular job. They are not. However, with one machine you can cut virtually everything you will ever need to and that is a great asset. The alternative is to have a special tool for each job and apart from the expense of having several machines to do different work, you also have the problems of storage and maintenance which go with having several little-used machines rather than one which is frequently used – even though the one machine may be a compromise. Because of its ability to do the work of several special machines the price of the tractor, which at first seems pretty steep, now seems altogether more reasonable. Nonetheless if you do have a great deal of one particular kind of work a special machine might still be the better bet.

In my own garden there is an area of grass, weeds and wild flowers which, because of the wild flowers, we leave uncut until early September when it is so long it is more like a field of poor corn than anything else. This sort of territory is usually the ideal place for a sickle cutter but the John Deere copes well although it is not designed for such work; and this makes a point that I wish to emphasize. If I had more work of this kind I would certainly need a special machine or a bigger tractor but because I only have to do this job once a year I am prepared to compromise by using the small tractor which is, after all, having to cut this grass, pull me and itself uphill, all on 8 hp. That is a tall order, which might damage this small tractor if it was called upon to do such work too often.

For gardens which do require a more powerful tractor there are garden tractors which do not appear to be vastly different from lawn tractors, except in name, but which are actually quite different technically, and consequently different in performance. Garden tractors are likely to have a more sophisticated technical specification which will often be similar to an agricultural tractor. They will probably have hydrostatic drive, a hydraulic system for accessories, a power take-off, and a much more robust construction.

All of that sounds nice but what benefits will it bring you? The more robust chassis and axles will mean the vehicle will be capable of taking the roughest ground and the roughest treatment in its stride without bending or flexing and without breaking. It will also be able to carry heavier loads. The hydro-static drive will make the thing much simpler to drive because forward and backward motion are very simply controlled by one foot: press the toe on a rocking pedal for forward and press the heel down for reverse. This leaves the hands free to fiddle with other controls as necessary and if you use a number of gadgets you will appreciate having your hands free to manipulate them properly, believe me. A hydraulic system will be an optional extra available on many of the bigger tractors enabling you to have hydraulically operated lifts for the mowing deck, front loaders, rear cultivators and the other attachments which make big jobs easier.

The mini-tractor market is very competitive in America and most of the tractor manufacturers offer a similar range of tools: I am sure that if manufacturer *A* brought out an oil drilling attachment all the other makers would have introduced their own version within a week. Whether they would all work is quite another matter. When looking through the different brochures it will be very difficult to distinguish between the good tools and the gimmicks; it can only be done by demonstration. An example came up while I was researching this book: I asked the UK distributor of a popular tractor if I could try the rear rotary cultivator attachment which was offered for his tractors and he referred me to his local dealer, for the demonstration and trial to be arranged. The local dealer, sad to say, would not demonstrate the cultivator attachment because he said that it did not work and he therefore did not sell it. But he pointed out that a rival make did work quite well and perhaps I ought to see that instead! I also came across other people who had bought things for their tractors which did not work well and who had had great difficulty on some occasions even convincing their so-called dealers that certain of the attachments in the brochures were available to be bought. So beware of duff attachments and duff dealers, and hope that your dealer would be honest enough not to show you something which he knew was no good. Among the bad fittings there are also many superb fittings and if you make certain you see them working before you buy you will not make a mistake.

Assuming that you do get the right equipment there is no end to the work which you can do with a garden tractor. Most will pull a single furrow plough and nearly all offer rear rotary cultivators which perform in a similar way to the wheel driven cultivators described in the cultivator chapter, which is to say that they are good for shallow cultivation (up to 7 in. deep) and preparation of a good tilth. Deep digging is better done by plough. Not all of these rear cultivators work, as I have said, but some do. The better ones will be hydraulically raised and lowered and are likely to bite into the ground better when the going is hard. The simple ones are belt driven and will usually be less useful on hard ground as they rely on their weight to make them dig in. Some cultivators have an auxiliary engine and this will be necessary for use on low powered tractors of only 8 or 10 hp which do not have the surplus power necessary to drive a separate cultivator in difficult conditions. If you have a big garden, or if you are unable to do heavy work because of ill health, a tractor driven cultivator could be very useful to you. In the second case, even in a relatively small garden, you could justify using such a tool if it saved you strenuous work. Whatever your reason for having a cultivator do make certain that you buy one which is offset behind the tractor so that all wheel marks are removed from the soil as you go along.

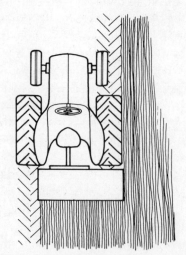

Figure 89 A plan of a small tractor and cultivator showing how the cultivator being offset to the right removes the tractor's right hand wheel track. The left track will be removed on the next pass. Some cultivators can be offset on either side

There are other implements for garden cultivation such as disc harrows, spiked harrows and hoes, some of which are towed and others of which can be fixed to the hydraulic three-point hitch at the back of the tractor.

The front of the tractor can also be used to take attachments and the most commonly offered tool here is a bulldozer blade for a variety of uses. For a bulldozer blade to work effectively it needs to be properly designed and angled and for the tractor to be capable of pushing it, it will probably need wheel weights and special grip tyres or chains. Virtually all manufacturers offer wheel chains as an extra. Other front mounted items include a revolving brush, a special rotary mower for the Case tractors, a special cylinder mower for the Ariens tractors and snow ploughs for most makes. These last implements may be more useful in parts of this country than we might think if winters like 1978–9 are to be repeated. The snow ploughs work by pulling the snow into a blower by means of an augur and then blowing it out to one side, clear of the path or track. The better ones are hydraulically controlled and shaft driven, while the simpler types are belt driven and mechanically raised and lowered.

The ultimate front attachment is a hydraulic loader which can be extremely useful in the right garden. One gardener I met uses his front end loader for lifting big logs on to the circular saw table, for lifting his chicken houses onto blocks, for loading hay bales for his horses, for loading manure from his stables and a variety of other jobs too. If you have the work for this attachment it will save much backache but it is not an easily removed accessory; once on the machine it is best left there. For the gardener of whom I speak, this is no problem as he has two more small tractors to do other work, although it should be pointed out that his garden is fourteen acres in size. Some machines when rigged up with an hydraulic front end loader are rather ungainly beasts. Others, which have been designed from the outset as a front loader, are better balanced and in this category the Case 646 Loader looks like a good design. Certainly it is less cumbersome than the tractors which have had a loader added to them; moreover it can continue to do duty as a rotary mower or whatever else you require whereas most others cannot mow when equipped with the loader.

Finally, having added things to the back and to the front, you can also add things to the top and the side of your tractor. To the top you can add an all weather cab while to the side, and probably more useful, you can add a sickle mower for very long grass. All of which means that a small tractor is a pretty useful machine and is not just a plaything. Well, they are great fun to play with but that is a bonus, because their capacity for work is enormous.

When you come to look at the various models currently available there will be startling price differences some of which are justified and can therefore be explained and others which cannot. Once again you must carefully decide exactly what you intend to try and do with a tractor, apart, that is, from sailing round the lawn grinning like a Cheshire cat. There are, as always, horses for courses. For grass cutting, other grass maintenance, trailer towing and similar duties a lawn tractor will do adequately, with an 8–10 hp engine being quite good enough for the job. Whether the thing has an ordinary manual gearbox like a car or one of the various fancy automatics or infinitely variable gear systems is not crucial. The variable speed drive of some of the John Deere models is rather good in that it allows infinite control of the forward speed of the tractor without altering the engine speed and therefore the cutter speed. This means you can always achieve exactly the right combinations of forward speed and cutter speed for the conditions. This is not always possible with an ordinary gearbox and you have to compromise but it is no worse than the compromise of driving a manual gear car.

For heavier work, where you will require your basic tractor to *power* attachments rather than tow them, you will need the bigger engines of the garden tractors – 12–20 hp, depending on the work (not only on the sort of work, but also the amount of work). Are you, for example, going to use the machine a few hours per week in the summer or several times each week throughout the year? If the second category is the more likely you will do well to have a big engine and the surplus power which will allow that engine to cope easily with its work and therefore to last a long time. Where you require a rugged tractor but do not need a lot of power the 8 hp garden tractors such as the Wheel Horse Commandos might be suitable.

While on the subject of power remember that power is only any good if you can use it and therefore you need to pay attention to wheel size. If you require your tractor to do heavy pulling – and some are capable of very heavy pulling if necessary – then large wheels are important. Some machines have relatively small rear wheels which would not help them to grip. The Case tractors have by far the largest drive wheels but others, such as the MTD 990 by Barrus, also have good big wheels. The grip will be helped by changing the usual smooth lawn tread tyres for deep tractor grip tyres where necessary. The grip of special tyres and large wheels will not normally be that crucial but for hard work on hills or muddy terrain they should be considered.

With most tractors the auxiliary equipment is driven by a system of pulleys and rubber belts, a system which is simple (if primitive) and works well. The better engineered machines, on the other hand, use shaft drive or hydraulic drive for their fittings. The Graveley tractors, for example, have all their fittings including the rotary mowers shaft driven and this is naturally more expensive than belts, while Case use hydraulic drive as do some John Deere and Bolens models. The simple lawn tractors will almost certainly have belt driven mowers and probably belt drive to the rear axle. This system works well but make sure that you always have a spare main drive belt and spare mower drive belt in your shed; and do whatever you can to find a local supplier of belts to the motor trade who will probably have belts of the size you require. If you cannot do this you will have to buy belts from your tractor distributor and for those with a weak heart this will be a risky business. The price of these glorified fan-belts, when they are stamped as official spare parts by some tractor manufacturer, is beyond belief. A bucketful of diamonds would come cheaper.

If you are intending to use the heavy front end attachments such as the loader or the forward mounted rotary mowers or the bigger bulldozer blades you will need to ensure that the tractor has sufficient strength to cope with them. The front axle, wheels, bearings and king pins must be especially strong. The strain imposed by an extended and full loader is very great and only the best equipment can cope. Look, for example, for an axle beam of cast iron rather than the box section steel of the cheaper makes. But if you are only going to use a tractor for grass cutting and trailer work you will not need to pay the price for extra strength and technical refinement unless, of course, you want to.

Among the least expensive tractors available is the British Westwood Gazelle in its various forms. This simple and useful machine has a large twin bladed rotary mower with a rear discharge, manual gearbox, headlights and fairly smooth 11 hp Briggs and Stratton engine. It is a comfortable machine and reasonably quiet too. There are also two 8 hp versions, one of which has an electric starter and the other a recoil starter. This alternative is sometimes offered on the smaller tractors but despite the extra cost of an electric starter I would always choose to have it. A recoil starter on small engines is not too bad but the bigger engines fitted to tractors are not easy to start by the traditional pull-a-rope-and-hope method. Some engines have an electric starter with a rope start as well, which is a very useful emergency standby.

Before finishing this chapter on tractors there is one design to be mentioned which looks like the tractors but which might perhaps be more at home in the lawn mower chapter. It is the Nickerson Turfmaster which comes in two sizes and is that rare animal a *cylinder* mowing tractor. The smaller of the two machines, the Turfmaster 70, is the one most likely to have a use in the garden and a pretty good machine it is too. As Plate 7 shows this machine has three separate cylinder mowers which hang from its sides and back giving it a cutting width of almost 6 ft, which is quite impressive. For large formal lawns this is a good machine and it is quite versatile too: it can be used with all three mowers working or with just the rear one, if this is necessary for close work. Apart from the usual towing work this machine is not as versatile as the tractors but it does offer this special ability to cut grass with the cylinder mowers which many people demand. Doing this with the other tractors means towing small gang mowers and they will therefore lack the manoeuvrability of the Nickerson. The Nickerson is a machine which was originally intended for use by the professional and the bigger Nickerson will probably still appeal mostly to people in that group, but the smaller Turfmaster 70 is already well used by gardeners and for good reason. Like the Westwood, the Nickerson is British made, a fact which alone will win it many customers.

This appraisal of the qualities of small tractors does not take into account their greatest attraction which is their ability to turn drudgery into fun. So many of the hard jobs done by a tractor are made enjoyable when they would otherwise not be. It is easy to understand and recognize the normal pleasures of gardening, the growing of plants, but very often the sheer hard work which is necessary to achieve a good harvest or an attractive border is over-looked or endured in the belief that the means justify the ends. Well so they do, but how much better when the means by which we can achieve our ends are every bit as enjoyable as the end itself. How much better to find as much enjoyment and satisfaction in the hard, mundane garden maintenance work as in the skilled and pleasant gardening tasks. With a small tractor many ghastly jobs become enjoyable and that alone is a good recommendation for having one, apart from its proven capacity for work. Nothing would induce us to part with our tractor, even if we lived in a flat.

A letter which I received from a lady sums up the value of a small tractor in the garden '. . . we have been absolutely delighted with its performance. It cuts marvellously. We have about an acre of rough grass in three separate areas of the garden. Previously we have cut this twice a year with an Allenscythe which I have found too heavy and difficult to manage. But now I can do the whole thing quickly and easily myself and the resulting finish is far better. It goes very well even over roughish ground . . .'

Tractors: buying points

1 Garden size: mostly for larger gardens but handicapped people could with advantage, use one in a smaller garden.

2 Mowing: principal use: will cut virtually any grass and some rough undergrowth. Consider also extra mowing attachments apart from the standard rotary, e.g. sickle bar, gang mowers, front rotary.

3 Use: for most garden use a lawn tractor; for heavy work and power attachments a garden tractor.

4 Sophistication: for most help buy a machine with hydraulic implements. Good gear range or automatic.

5 Strength: make certain machine is strong enough for your work, check chassis, axles, engine power.

6 Pulling: if pulling is of prime importance check wheel size and gearing.

7 Rotary mower: do you want front or rear discharge; leaf collector or not?

8 Manoeuvrability: good turning circle is very important.

9 Electric start/manual: if possible only buy electric start models.

10 Cost: all are expensive. Simple lawn tractors are least expensive. Compare prices carefully.

11 Demonstration: have a thorough demonstration in your garden.

12 Service: check on service availability, especially on more complex machines.

13 Dealers: small dealers will probably not stock these machines. Many dealers do not understand the accessories fully.

16 Miscellaneous

In every library there is a shelf for the large and odd shaped books which cannot be fitted into the normal library sections, and similarly in this survey of garden equipment there are some things which I just cannot fit into any of the other chapters. So, grouped here under the meaningless heading miscellaneous, is garden equipment's answer to odd-shaped books.

Flame guns

Flame guns are generally used as a method of weeding and for clearing overgrown ground as a first step in preparing it for cultivation. How good they are at such work is a matter of opinion, and also of expectation. Most people expect a flame gun to devour everything in its path and of course it does not do this – which means it disappoints many people. But if you understand what it is doing you will appreciate it more readily. There is much to be said for flame guns and I have been very glad of the Sheen X 300 which I bought second hand many years ago for the outrageous sum of £4. As a means of killing weeds on paths and drives a flame gun is fairly quick and fairly cheap and quite effective. It is not so effective as putting down one of the modern weedkillers such as simazine, but it is cheaper. Weedkilling with a flame gun will never be as effective as chemical weedkilling because the flame gun kills only the top growth; it does not kill the roots. Therefore if you have a crop of some easily killed annual weeds invading your drive a flame gun will kill them but if perennial weeds are your problem a flame gun is only going to give you a temporary clean up.

The flame gun is good for clearing thick undergrowth and tall weeds on a neglected plot, but at first it appears not to work. I had imagined that any reasonable weed would instantly disappear in a puff of smoke when confronted with a 2000°C flame gun but this does not happen. Weeds seem to survive the fiery blast, albeit looking somewhat groggy, but standing nevertheless. They are in fact dead and another pass with the flame gun two or three days after the first will clear the lot. In other words patience is required. The advantage of this method of clearing is that the ash is returned to the soil to do some good and you are spared the trouble of disposing of the rubbish you have cleared.

A use which has only recently occurred to me is in the vegetable garden where for the last two years I have been using the flame gun to kill the weed seeds lying in the surface soil prior to sowing the vegetables. I find this very effective and it gives the vegetables time to establish before any competing weeds germinate. Another use is starting the bonfire when it is mainly composed of greenery which is otherwise reluctant to ignite.

Flame guns can be alarming tools because of the roar which they make but used sensibly they are quite safe. Most of them work on paraffin but some now use propane gas. The propane type is perhaps easier to handle as the gas cylinder is carried on the back leaving the hands free to carry the flame wand. The paraffin types have a two wheeled trolley and this is very necessary because they are heavy tools to carry, particularly when the steel flame hood is in place which will usually be the case. Small stick flame guns are also available for light duties and these are, of course, much more easily used but have a smaller flame. On the whole a flame gun could not be considered an essential item in the garden but I am glad that I have one, although that feeling is influenced by the low price I paid for mine.

Sheen make a complete range of flame guns and also publish an excellent booklet on flame-gunning. You should read this if you are contemplating buying one of these tools; and if you do have stone or gravel paths and drives you will find them a particular help.

Generators

In one of the earlier chapters it was suggested that electric tools could be powered by a small portable generator. This gives complete mobility to tools which are otherwise tied, almost literally, by their power cables to the house. However, portable generators are expensive items to buy just to give your electric hedge cutter mobility. But if you are able to use a generator to power other tools, such as an electric chainsaw, electric nylon line trimmers and possibly for camping and caravanning activities as well, the cost of the machine will be spread over these other activities and the purchase of a generator will make economic sense.

There are several models made by Honda which can be carried from place to place while Preci-Tarpen and Andrews make wheeled generators. These latter are obviously more suited to garden use but will perhaps be too bulky for the caravanning brigade who will find the smaller Hondas more suitable.

Perhaps the best reason for buying a generator will be if you already have a number of good electrical tools all of which will be able to work farther afield when coupled to a generator.

Compost shredders

Every garden book ever written exhorts the gardener to make a compost heap, and I imagine most of us do. However, not all garden waste is suitable for composting – because of its bulk or reluctance to decompose quickly – and things like rose prunings, hedge cuttings and other twiggy material are notoriously difficult to cope with and are usually burned. This is regarded as wasteful by many people. There have been a number of compost shredders over the years, although some seem to have been withdrawn from the market because they have not always been entirely successful. One which does remain is marketed by Merrittstyle and is called the Mighty Mac.

This machine does not produce compost but it does reduce difficult woody waste to fine chips which, when added to an ordinary compost heap, will more easily rot down. The idea is that you feed into the mouth of the machine cardboard, small logs, brussels sprouts stalks, brambles, bones – indeed anything organic – and it is all reduced to easily handled chippings which may be used directly as a mulch or composted in the usual way. In a big garden which generates a lot of difficult-to-compost waste a machine like this could do some powerful good.

When using this machine it is a good idea to wear goggles because it is possible for it to throw stones out which might inadvertently have been loaded in with the other rubbish. Also remember to feed material in at a reasonable rate otherwise it is possible to clog the machine, particularly if too much wet matter is being put through.

This is an expensive device and one which could only be justified where there is enough work for it. It is also another of those machines to see very fully demonstrated before any attempts at autographing cheques are made.

Hole borers

Hole borers are, I realize, an item not likely to be high on anyone's list of *garden tools I must have* but as it is quite probable that at some time in a gardening lifetime you will erect a fence it is useful to know that such things exist and are available for hire.

Some of the garden tractor companies offer hole borers as an attachment for their machines and E. P. Barrus and Solo Power Equipment have hand-held petrol driven models available which, it is claimed, will bore a hole of 2 ft depth, suitable for a large stake, in ten seconds. That sounds very quick to me and should make fencing a fairly easy task.

Hire equipment

Many of the items mentioned in this book will be of only occasional interest or use to some people – like the hole borers of the previous section – and yet when they are required they can save an immense amount of work. When odd machinery is required for a single job it is sensible to hire equipment, provided you realize the limitations of this method of using machines. The cost of hiring some equipment is very high. Easily damaged tools such as chainsaws are often very expensive to hire. The cost of hiring is also affected by the period of hire and hiring for one day costs more per hour than hiring for a week. That does not mean you should hire for a week to do a day's work but if you have a lot of work to do it is worth considering long-term hire as this can be much less expensive than you might think. It is also worth comparing prices if you have the chance; I have found wide differences in price between different hire shops.

The big drawback to hiring garden equipment is the weather. If you have ordered a machine, for example a cultivator to be delivered on a particular day, it will be very annoying if the day chosen is enjoying torrential rain and hail. There is little you can do about this except pay up and get on with the work. I once hired a mammoth Howard Gem cultivator for two days and during those two days the only other person I saw was Noah in his Ark: it rained as it has not rained before or since but I still had to use the machine or waste the hire charge and lose my place in the booking queue.

Some decent hire shops will allow the hiring to be cancelled if the weather is bad and even refund your deposit too. Others will not. The weather is part of the risk you take when hiring garden machinery and that is all one can say about it.

When hiring you must insist that the machine is properly explained to you before you take it away and also *insist* that if it has an engine, that engine is started before you remove it from the shop.

Apart from the difficulties with engines the other difficulties can come when you use the machine. You will obviously be unfamiliar with it and some things, especially forward tine cultivators, take some getting used to. Do not be put off if at first it does not seem to be performing in the way you think it should. This is probably your fault, not that of the machine; but if it is the machine at fault do not hesitate to contact the shop and make certain that you do not pay for work not done.

Hiring equipment can be a good way of trying something which you might subsequently buy. Some garden machinery dealers also operate a hire service and they naturally tend to hire the same makes which they sell. Therefore if you know that you are thinking of buying model X it can be a good idea to hire a similar machine for half a day to confirm that your choice is right – or possibly to discover it is wrong.

It is also a good idea to combine with neighbours when hiring. Most mechanical equipment will cope with a great deal of work in one day so by doing work for a neighbour or two you will keep your cost down and use the machine to its full extent. However, if you are the person responsible for the hire it will be your deposit that is sacrificed if your neighbour, and former friend, damages the machine.

An alternative method of hiring is to pay a friend a reasonable sum for borrowing his machine. The dangers in this are obvious but so are the advantages. If you feel your friendships can stand the strain of this sort of deal there is much to be gained: you will not be restricted by time or weather and you will have expert advice on hand all the time.

On balance I think hiring is a good idea as long as you are aware of the pitfalls and are prepared to take the weather risk in your stride.

17 Maintenance

It is almost obligatory for books on machinery to have a chapter on maintenance because it is supposed that people want to maintain their machinery. In my experience most people want to do no such thing. They expect their machines to work well at all times in spite of neglect. It is therefore pointless setting down planned programmes of maintenance which everyone will ignore and which are virtually impossible to follow even for the enthusiast. Six of the tools in my garden shed have petrol engines and two more will be added shortly which means I shall spend all my time fiddling and adjusting if I follow all the maintenance advice that has come my way over the years. But, having said that, there are a few things which are worth attending to because of their special importance.

Perhaps the most important is changing the oil in four stroke engines. Because of the appalling conditions in which our garden machinery engines operate and because, good though they are, many are built to a price rather than for quality, it is necessary to change their oil rather frequently. Remember the oil in most of these engines is not pumped around and filtered as in a car; instead it lies in the engine crankcase collecting all the muck and rubbish which finds its way into the engine. This turns the oil into a passable imitation of grinding paste which does the moving parts no good at all. Change oil frequently, particularly on high revving engines in rotary mowers and other machines where prolonged high speed running is called for. Lloyds of Letchworth did some tests on oil in garden machinery engines and found that oil which had been in an engine for 100 hours was allowing an engine wear rate eight times greater than oil which had been used for 50 hours. For the spasmodically used garden machines I think an oil change every 25 hours of use is worthwhile or yearly if this is sooner. Since the rubbish which gets into an engine does so through the carburettor, it is also necessary to keep the carburettor air filter clean and efficient. This applies particularly to mowers and cultivators working in dry dusty conditions. If you look after nothing else but the engine oil and the air filter you will be doing a great deal.

Engine starting is often a problem, especially with two stroke engines, but I find a new spark plug works wonders and new points too if necessary, though this is unlikely to be so on our relatively little used machinery. However, a simple piece of test equipment for sparking plugs and magnetos is the Tri-Max ignition tester available from Ledger Selby. This enables the electrics of engines to be tested simply and easily which could save you a great deal of time. It is always infuriating having to fiddle about trying to check the strength of the spark or, indeed, to check if there is any spark to check the strength of. The Tri-Max should be a help. Ledger Selby also sell a nifty portable rev counter, which determines the revolutions of an

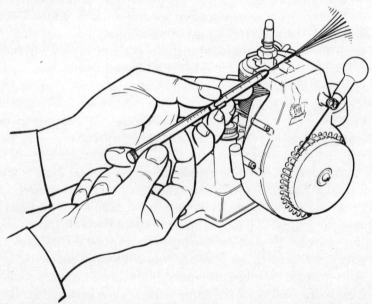

Figure 90 This is the useful Vibra Tak which is a simple and effective means of measuring engine speed in rpm for any maintenance work which may be necessary

engine by the vibrations of that engine. Both or either of these gadgets would help with home maintenance.

If you are intent on maintaining your engines completely it is wise to obtain, if you can, proper workshop manuals from Briggs and Stratton, Tecumseh, Kohler, Honda and so on. Honda workshop manuals for their machines are usually excellent, while the good spare parts diagrams in the handbooks of Howard and Qualcast machines will be a help when dismantling or assembling engines and gearboxes. For most people, however, I suggest engine repairs are best done by the service agent.

Looking after the rest of the machinery is usually a matter of keeping rust at bay. Garden machinery is often not very well painted at the start of its life and after a couple of seasons kicking around the average garden it can look pretty tatty. It does pay to keep machines reasonably clean, by which I mean knock the mud and grass off at the end of each session and wipe the mower blade with an oily rag before returning the mower to the shed. It is absolutely essential to keep digging blades clean and shiny otherwise their efficiency is not just reduced, it can be almost destroyed. Cultivator rotors, plough shares, ridgers, hoes, spades, edging tools, forks and all similar tools must be cleaned and given a protective oil coating if they are to be of any lasting value. This is particularly true of a plough share which should be greased when it is stored from one year to the next.

If rust does get a taste for any of your tools it can be removed with an electric drill and wire brush or emery cloth and oil or wire wool and oil or all three and patience. If the rust is too bad try using a rust remover such as D-Rust. I have found this to be fairly effective; even so, it is better to try to prevent rust rather than having to cure it.

Rust on mowers is a big problem caused chiefly by wet grass clinging to various parts. The undersides of rotary decks are particularly vulnerable as are the grass deflectors and grass boxes on cylinder mowers. Modern plastic grass boxes are a complete answer to rust but the old sheet steel types are badly affected. For the underside of steel rotary decks and for the inside of steel grass boxes I use Holts rubber underseal and this works very well indeed. It will need renewing every spring on rotaries used in rough conditions, where sticks and stones have been allowed to chip the underseal, but it is a very good protection which takes no time to apply.

While you have the mower upside down to apply the underseal it is a good idea to file any burrs off the rotary blades. If you wish to have a proper edge restored, however, the blades will need grinding and this should be done by an expert. The blades of a cylinder mower also need to be ground by an expert: grinding and resetting of the cylinder blades cannot be done at home but if there are any nicks or burrs in the blades, caused by stones, it is safe to remove them with a few strokes of a fine file. Some other cutting tools may also be improved by the careful use of a file. Some of the blades on reciprocating hedge cutters are quite soft and these can be improved with a file if any damage has been done to them but in normal use they will not need much attention. The chain of a chainsaw, on the other hand, will need regular attention if it is to retain its cutting power. Do not, however, attempt to sharpen a chain without a proper jig for doing the job. To try to sharpen a saw chain without a jig or guide is quite simply a waste of time. The guides are available from tool shops or if you cannot obtain one locally apply direct to Chain Saw Products or Glanfield Lawrence.

My final comment on maintenance concerns wheels and wheel bearings. As a great many of the machines we use are pushed about on wheels it makes very good sense to keep wheel bearings well greased and clean. So often I have found people struggling with push machines of one kind or another just because the wheel bearings have virtually seized. The plain bearings, which are most commonly used, become dry and stiff quite quickly. A few drops of oil or some grease can make an amazing difference to the ease with which some machines can be pushed. Since saving of effort is the *raison d'être* of much garden machinery it is sensible to do the simple maintenance which allows it to save the most effort.

There is obviously a great deal one could write about the maintenance of garden equipment – indeed it could fill several books – but my belief that most people will not maintain their machinery very well no matter how much is written plus my belief that most equipment does not need the constant attention which some would have us give our machines, have kept this chapter brief. The single most important point is to remember to squirt a good deal of oil about the place and keep equipment reasonably clean and dry. If you do that most machinery will last a very long time in most gardens.

If you strike major trouble take it to your dealer where you will get good treatment if you have given him good treatment. If you buy your machinery from him he will be keen to keep it in good order, but if you buy complex garden equipment from a department store or from one of the multiples you cannot expect your nearest dealer to lay the red carpet down for you when you strike trouble. Try taking it back to the department store and see what they say. (Nothing helpful will be my bet.) My advice would be to buy your sheets and blankets from the department store, your buckets and brushes from the corner hardware shop and all your garden machinery from a garden machinery dealer. But take your time in finding a good one. They do exist.

18 The Last Chapter

The trouble— I have frequently been told— with writing a book about garden equipment is that it will be out of date before it is finished. Well that is in some part true: some new lawn mowers will doubtless be introduced and others will be discontinued in the life of this book. But no matter what manufacturers and importers decide to do the *advice* in these chapters will hold good. It is worth remembering that, despite one or two fairly recent introductions such as brush cutters, there is little new in the equipment market. Indeed some designs have been around since the last war and before.

In the first chapter the point was made that there was an abundance of riches in most categories of garden equipment and having now read the book I think perhaps you will agree with this. The choice confronting the prospective buyer is usually vast and it is not always the most obvious tool which is the right one. Some tools and machines which are made by big marketing orientated companies are widely advertised and easily found in all shops ranging from Woolworths to Harrods while other products from smaller companies frequently go unnoticed. The most easily found are not always the best, although they often are, and sometimes the obscure deserve their obscurity. However, when you come to buy equipment for the first time, or perhaps to replace worn out machinery, I hope after reading this you will explore the market thoroughly before making your choice. You can only benefit by doing so. The addresses contained in the appendix should help your market research and they include a number of companies not normally associated with serving the gardener and who you will therefore not normally encounter in your meanderings through the gardening press or garden machinery shops.

Just as the most obviously advertised equipment may not necessarily be the best so the most obviously engineered products may not necessarily be the best. By which I mean that sometimes the less obvious approach to a problem may be the right one, or at least one of the right ones. The leaf blower is a classic example of this: conventional wisdom tells us to sweep leaves or vacuum them, both of which methods are successful, but for large areas the leaf blower is the unlikely but perfect tool.

Which leads me to make another point about choosing garden equipment: do not necessarily do what you have done before. Just because you have not used a cultivator for digging do not suppose that you could not benefit from using one, or if you have always used a cylinder mower do not hesitate to try a rotary mower – it may be more suited to your grass. On the other hand for those weaned on rotary mowers a change to cylinder mowers could well improve your lawn, if improvement you desire. In the hand tool category there is most scope for the adventurous and there are some very useful, if unconventional, gardening weapons now on sale which are worth trying.

A point frequently made in this book is the need to see equipment, particularly the more expensive equipment, demonstrated thoroughly before buying. This is so important that I think it is worth re-emphasizing here. Very often machinery disappoints because the expectations of the buyer differ from the intentions of the designer. This leads to dissatisfaction and, in extreme cases, to common assault. One good piece of equipment, for example, which has a bad name that is partly due to being misunderstood by the consumer (a result of over claiming by the advertising possibly) is the cordless electric hedge trimmer. This is a good tool for the relatively light work for which it was intended, but unfortunately more was expected of it than it was designed to give. Such misunderstandings will be avoided if you insist on seeing all equipment properly demonstrated either by the dealer. or by a friend or neighbour who may already own the model in which you are interested.

Finally, whether you are buying a humble onion hoe or an all singing, all dancing garden tractor I hope you will remember that gardening is supposed to be a pleasurable pursuit and, therefore, tools and machinery which give you some enjoyment as well as utility will be the best buys.

Appendix

The information in the various appendices is intended to show quickly what equipment exists and who makes it. The company names can be linked to the address list at the back of the book. Comparison tables are used where appropriate, but in some cases the subject matter of the chapters is too diverse for such tables to be of value. In other cases the number of products or companies in a category is too small to warrant anything more than a simple list. Where possible a guide to price has been used but in some cases information on prices was not easily obtained. This was due to the reluctance by some manufacturers to supply information and in some cases the price of products was about to change at the time of writing. Where, for whatever reasons, prices were not known I have thought it best to make no indication rather than to guess wrongly.

The terms *high*, *medium*, *low* appear in the tables or in the lists after a company's product list, and these broad price groups are meant to convey that the manufacturer in question makes equipment which is, for example, *high*, in price compared to other equipment in the same category. Remember, however, that *high* prices do not always mean poor value for money; often the reverse is the case. Conversely *low* price goods are not necessarily good value.

The section on cloches has a price index which makes precise comparisons between different makes. I felt this was the only section which lent itself to this treatment.

In some cases there may only be *medium* or *high* listings and this is because the equipment in that category which is *low* priced has not been included because it is not, in my subjective opinion, worthy of inclusion.

The appendices and address list will help greatly when choosing garden equipment but there is a three dimensional appendix in the form of The Institute of Groundsmanship Exhibition held every September at Motspur Park near London, and at Windsor Racecourse from 1981 onwards. This exhibition is really a trade exhibition but if you are contemplating major expenditure on garden equipment of any kind it is *the* best place to go to see what's what.

Cloches appendix

The table over lists various types of cloches and the features which each has. Certain terms should be qualified before you use this table.

Handle only those cloches which are capable of being lifted easily in one hand are listed as having a handle. Thus the Novolux cloches and the Rumsey clip do not qualify.

Access those cloches where it is possible to remove a roof panel for access to crops qualify in this category. It must be noted that in the Westray the bird netting must be removed first if the cloche is to be used in this way.

Stable in winds most cloches are stable most of the time but only the heavy glass type resist high winds.

Ventilation by adjustment of a roof panel good ventilation is possible.

Cost index this index shows the relative cost of different cloches, e.g. the cheapest cloche is the Rumsey which has an index of 100 while the Chase High Barn has an index of 402 which means it costs 302 per cent more than the Rumsey or it will cost about four times as much.

Cost/sq. ft index this index shows the relative cost efficiency of the different cloches, in other words the cost of each sq. ft of ground covered. Again the Rumsey covers the ground most cheaply and has an index of 100 while the Chase High Barn has an index of 294 which means that it costs nearly three times more to cover each square foot with the Chase than with the Rumsey. This index shows, however, that the most expensive cloches are nonetheless good value for money. Note that where this index is the same or lower than the cost index you are getting relatively good value for money.

Cloches

Cloche type	Height (in.)	Width (in.)	Area covered 30 ft row (sq. ft)	Handle	Ventilation	Access	Transparent roof	Bird netting	Stable in winds	Cost index	Cost per sq. ft index
Chase High Barn All glass	19	23	57·5	Yes	Yes	Yes	Yes	No	Yes	402	294
Chase High Barn Glass roof/Correx sides	19	23	57·5	Yes	Yes	Yes	Yes	No	Yes	371	272
Chase High Barn All Correx	19	23	57·5	Yes	Yes	Yes	No	No	No	340	250
Westray High Barn Polythene roof/Correx sides	21	27	67·5	Yes	No	No	Yes	Yes	No	425	266
Westray High Barn Glass roof/Correx sides	21	27	67·5	Yes	Yes	Yes	Yes	Yes	Yes	531	331
Chase Low Barn All glass	12	23	57·5	Yes	Yes	Yes	Yes	No	Yes	330	241
Chase Low Barn Glass roof/Correx sides	12	23	57·5	Yes	Yes	Yes	Yes	No	Yes	314	231
Chase Low Barn All Correx	12	23	57·5	Yes	Yes	Yes	No	No	No	283	206
Westray Low Barn Polythene roof/Correx sides	13	24	60	Yes	No	No	Yes	Yes	No	330	231

	13	24	60							436	306
Westray Low Barn Glass roof/Correx sides	13	24	60	Yes	Yes	Yes	Yes	Yes	Yes	436	306
Chase Tent Glass roof	10	14	35	Yes	No	Yes	No	Yes	Yes	196	234
Chase Tent Correx roof	10	14	35	Yes	No	No	No	Yes	Yes	164	197
Westray Tent Polythene roof	10	14	35	Yes	Yes	Yes	No	No	Yes	199	241
Westray Tent Glass roof	10	14	35	Yes	Yes	Yes	No	Yes	Yes	305	366
Rumsey Clip Correx roof	8·5	17	42·5	No	No	No	No	No	No	100	100
Calvert Clip Correx roof	7·5	19·5	48·75	Yes	No	No	No	No	Yes	106	106
Chase Clip 24 in. × 12 in. glass roof	10	14	35	Yes	No	Yes	No	Yes	Yes	156	188
Chase Clip 24 in. × 18 in. glass roof	15	20	50	Yes	No	Yes	No	Yes	Yes	208	175
ICI Novolux 6 ft cloches	11	18	45	No	No	Yes	No	No	No	354	331
ICI Novolux 3 ft cloches	11	18	45	No	No	Yes	No	No	No	444	416
Marmax	10·5	10	25	No	No	Yes	No	No	No	159	269
Pilc Supacloche Correx	7·5	15	37·5	Yes	No	No	No	No	Yes	167	188

Manufacturers and distributors

Brand name	Manufacturer/distributor
Chase Cloches	Expandite
Westray	Westray Cloches
Pilc Supacloche	Pilc Productions
Novolux and polythene tunnels	ICI
Marmax	Marmax Plastics
Transatlantic Plastic	Transatlantic Plastic
Poly-Gard	Wilmid Distribution
Planet	Planet Productions
Rumsey	Rumsey Clips
Calvert	Calvert Cultivation Co. Ltd
Essex	Essex Garden Products Ltd
TWE	Two Wests and Elliott

Correx may be obtained from Pilc Productions (see above) and other plastics from Transatlantic Plastics (see above).

Watering and irrigation equipment appendix

Manufacturers and distributors of watering equipment for outdoor use. Because the range of equipment goes from watering cans to automatic sprinklers price indications are meaningless and have therefore been omitted.

Brand name	Manufacturer/distributor
Access Seep-hose	Access Irrigation: plastic seep-hose and fittings
Agriframes	Agriframes: simple mist spray
Al-Ko	Al-Ko: hose, plastic hose fittings, sprinklers, well surveys and installation
Cameron	Cameron Irrigation: pulse sprinklers, mobile sprinklers, brass hose fittings, outdoor trickle lines, large-scale sprinkling units, all professional watering needs
CeKa	CeKa: plastic hose fittings
Gardena	Gardena Kress Kastner: plastic hose fittings
Barrie Grist	Barrie Grist: aluminium sprinkler pipe
Haws	Haws Elliott: galvanized and japanned watering cans, plastic watering cans, brass roses
Hozelock	Hozelock: sprinklers, plastic hose fittings
Melnor	Wilmid Distribution: sprinklers of all types, mobile sprinklers, hose reels, hose guns
Omnisector	Valentine Plastics: pulse sprinklers
T. Parker	T. Parker and Son: brass hose fittings, mobile sprinklers, wheeled water carrier
Pattisson	H. Pattisson: groundsmen's sprinklers, brass hose fittings, hose reels
Poly-Gard	Wilmid Distribution: ½ in. hose, plastic hose fittings, plastic watering cans, hose reels, sprinklers
Rain Bird	Plastic Tube and Conduit Co.: fully automatic watering system, sprinklers
Torspray	Tortube: aluminium mist sprinkler
Tricoflex	Valentine Plastic: variety of braided hose from ½ in. to 1½ in.
Voss	Voss Water Systems: hose, plastic hose fittings, sprinklers, hose reels
Wolf	Wolf Tools: hose, plastic hose fittings, sprinklers, hose reels

Grass cutting machinery appendix (SP = self propelled, RO = ride-on)

Brand name	Blade type	Propulsion type	Power type	Cutting widths (in.)	Rear roller	Four wheeled	Front or rear drive	Grass collection	Hover mower seat	Trailer	Price	Comments
Al-Ko	Rotary, sickle	Push	Electric, petrol	15, 19, 32	No	Yes	—	Yes	—	—	Low	
Allen Mayfield	Rotary, sickle, cylinder	SP	Petrol	32 rotary 48 sickle 30 cylinder	—	—	—	Yes	—	Yes	High	For commercial use but large gardens will be suitable
Allen National	Cylinder	RO	Petrol	68, 84	—	—	—	No	—	—	High	Specialized large cylinder mower for very large areas
Ariens	Rotary	RO	Petrol	26, 30, 38	—	—	—	Yes	—	—	Medium, high	
Atco	Rotary, cylinder	Push and SP	Electric, petrol	Cylinder: 12, 14, 17, 18, 20, 24, 30, 34 Rotary: 18, 21	Yes	Yes	Rear	Yes	—	Yes	Low, medium, high	Also mini gang mower. Range includes side wheel cylinder mowers
Barrus	Rotary	Push, SP	Electric, petrol	16, 19, 20, 22	No	Yes	Front, rear	Yes	—	—	Medium	
Black and Decker	Rotary, cylinder	Push	Electric	12	Yes	Yes	—	Yes	Yes	—	Low	
Crown	Rotary	Push	Petrol	18, 20, 21	—	—	—	—	Yes	—	Low, medium	

Brand	Type	Drive	Fuel	Cut widths							Notes
John Deere	Rotary	Push, RO	Petrol	18, 20, 30	No	Yes	—	Yes	—	—	Medium, high	
Flymo	Rotary, cylinder	Push, SP	Electric, petrol, none	Rotary: 12, 15, 18, 20, 30 Cylinder: 10, 14	No	Yes	—	Yes	Yes	Yes	Medium	The small cylinder mowers are not powered
Garda	Rotary	Push	Electric, petrol	12, 15, 18, 20	No	Yes	—	Yes	—	—	—	
Graveley	Rotary, flail	SP	Petrol	30, 40, 50 32 flail only	No	—	—	No	—	Yes	High	Professional equipment. Very versatile
Harry	Rotary	Push, SP	Electric, petrol	16, 19, 22	No	Yes	Rear	Yes	—	—	Low, medium, high	
Hayter	Rotary, cylinder	Push, SP	Petrol	12, 18, 19, 20, 21, 24, 30, 36	Yes	Yes	Rear	Yes	—	Yes	Medium, high	This range includes heavy duty rough cutters as well as lawn mowers
Honda	Rotary	Push, SP	Petrol	17, 21	No	Yes	Rear	Yes	—	—	High	Three forward speeds on some models
Husqvarna	Rotary, cylinder	Push, SP	Petrol, none	16, 18, 20	No	Yes	Rear	Yes	—	—	—	Side wheel cylinder mowers included
Landmaster	Rotary	Push, SP	Petrol	14, 18, 19	Yes	Yes	Rear	Yes	—	—	Medium, high	
Lawn-Boy	Rotary	Push, SP	Petrol	19, 21	No	Yes	Rear	Yes	—	—	Low, medium, high	The only electric start hand mowers

Grass cutting machinery appendix (*continued*)

Brand name	Blade type	Propulsion type	Power type	Cutting widths (in.)	Rear roller	Four wheeled	Front or rear drive	Grass collection	Hover mower seat	Trailer	Price	Comments
Lloyds	Cylinder	SP	Petrol	18, 21, 27	Yes	—	Rear	Yes	—	—	High	Probably the best cylinder mowers. Includes large side wheel mowers
M.T.D.	Rotary	RO	Petrol	26, 30	—	—	—	Yes	—	—	Medium	Mini gang available
Mountfield	Rotary	Push, SP, RO	Electric, petrol	14, 18, 21, 25	Yes	Yes	Front, rear	Yes	—	—	Medium, high	
Norlett	Rotary	Push, SP	Petrol	16, 19	Yes	Yes	Front, rear	Yes	—	—	Medium	Range includes two effective rough cutters, the Bushwakka and Gurkha
Qualcast	Rotary, cylinder	Push, SP	Petrol, electric, none	12, 14, 15, 18	Yes	Yes	Rear	Yes	Yes	—	Low, medium	Side wheel cylinder mowers included
Ransomes	Cylinder, flail, rotary	Cylinder, SP	Petrol	Cylinder: 18, 20, 24, 30, 36 Rotary: 32, 36, 48 Flail: 32	Yes	—	Rear	Yes	—	Yes	High	Mini gang mower available
Sheen	Sickle	Push, SP	Petrol	30	—	—	—	—	—	—	—	

Name	Type	Drive	Fuel	Cutting widths					Price	Notes
Simplicity	Rotary	Push, SP, RO	Petrol	19, 21, 20, 22, 26, 30	No	Yes	Rear	—	—	—
Snapper	Rotary	Push, SP, RO	Petrol	21, 25, 28, 33, 42	No	Yes	Rear	Yes	Medium, high	Six forward speeds on pedestrian rotaries. This is a big advantage
Solo	Rotary, sickle	Push, SP	Electric, petrol	18, 20 42 sickle	No	Yes	—	Yes	Medium, high	
Suffolk	Cylinder	SP	Petrol	12, 17, 19	Yes	No	Rear	Yes	Low, medium	Side wheel cylinder available
Templar	Rotary	Push	Petrol	15, 18, 20	No	Yes	—	Yes	Low	
Victa	Rotary	SP, push	Electric, petrol	18, 20, 21, 24	No	Yes	Rear	Yes	Low, medium, high	
Webb	Cylinder	Push, SP	Electric, petrol, none	12, 14, 18, 24	Yes	No	Rear	Yes	Low, medium, high	
Westwood	Rotary	Push, RO	Petrol	18, 19, 24	No	Yes	—	Yes	Low, medium	
Wolf	Rotary	Push, SP, RO	Electric, petrol	12, 14, 15, 18, 20, 22, 25	Yes	Yes	Rear	Yes	Low, medium, high	Induction electric motors
Wolseley	Rotary, cylinder	SP	Petrol	19, 23, 27, 30	No	Yes	Rear	No	High	Cutters for rough work and large areas

Manufacturers and distributors

Brand name	Manufacturer/distributor
Al-Ko	· Al-Ko Britain Ltd
Allen Mayfield	Allen Power Equipment
Allen National	Allen Power Equipment
Ariens	Norlett Ltd
Barrus	E. P. Barrus Ltd
Black and Decker	Black and Decker
Crown	Crown Horticultural Equipment
John Deere	John Deere Ltd
Flymo	Flymo Ltd
Garda	John Harston Ltd
Graveley	Autoturfcare
Harry	Kitbarns Ltd
Hayter	Hayters Ltd
Honda	Honda
Husqvarna	Hyett Adams
Landmaster	Boscombe Engineering
Lawn-Boy	Lawn-Boy
Lloyds	Lloyds
M.T.D.	E. P. Barrus Ltd
Mountfield	G. D. Mountfield Ltd
Norlett	Norlett Ltd
Qualcast	Birmid-Qualcast Ltd
Ransomes	Ransomes, Sims and Jefferies Ltd
Sheen	Sheen (Nottingham) Ltd
Simplicity	Stemport Marketing Co. Ltd
Snapper	Kitbarns Ltd
Solo	Solo Power Equipment (UK) Ltd
Suffolk	Birmid-Qualcast Ltd
Templar	Templar Tillers
Victa	Victa Mowers
Webb	Wolseley Webb
Westwood	Westwood Engineering Ltd
Wolf	Wolf Tools Ltd
Wolseley	Wolseley Webb

Supplementary lawn care equipment appendix

Brand name	Manufacturer/distributor
Al-Ko	Al-Ko: granular fertilizer spreader, push and tow models. Medium
Cooper Pegler	Cooper Pegler: pressure sprayers, towed sprayers, spray bars, lawn sprayers, spray shields. Medium/high
Corrie	J. B. Corrie: garden rollers
Dorman	Dorman Sprayer Co.: large wheeled sprayers, spray bars and booms. High
Driftmaster	Richmond Gibson Ltd: gravity fed roller distributors for liquids. Medium
Landmaster	Boscombe Engineering: scarifier for Landmaster Lion Cub and L88. Low
Little Wonder	Wolseley Webb: mains electric edge trimmer
Merry Tiller	Wolseley Webb: aerating, spiking, slitting tines for cultivator. Low
Mow-Rite	Mow-Rite Engineering: aerators for mowers, for towing and pushing. Medium/high
Nickerson	Nickerson Turfmaster: power scarifying machines. High
Norlett	Norlett: scarifying attachment for Beaver Powaspade. Low
T. Parker	T. Parker and Son: rollers, aerators, scarifiers, drag brushes, drag mats, boom sprayers, turfing irons, turf races
Pattisson	H. Pattisson and Co.: drag mats, drag brushes, turfing irons, turf races
Sheen	Sheen Ltd: small fork type aerators, wheeled aerators. Low
Sisis	Sisis Equipment: push aerators, 'Lawnman' turfcare outfit, power scarifiers. Medium/high
Wolf	Wolf Tools: scarifying rakes, fork type aerators, scarifier for rotary mowers, fertilizer distributors, power scarifiers. Low/medium/high

Other lawn care equipment may be obtained from various manufacturers: long handled shears are available from the companies listed in the appendix to hand cutting tools, and many tractor companies offer towed lawn spikers among their accessories and granular fertilizer distributors too.

Hand tools appendix

This appendix lists names of the companies mentioned in the hand tools chapter with their products. Because of the variety of equipment covered no price comparisons are given.

Electric cultivator from
Allen Power Equipment Ltd

Variety of hand tools including the West Country Spade from
Bulldog Tools

Mattock and other chopping hoes from
The Chillington Tool Co. Ltd

High-Hoe wheeled hoe from
Highlight Engineering

Wheeled hoe, scoop and seed drill from
Jalo Engineering

Lightweight spades from
Lysbro.
Agricessories Ltd

Fibreglass and stainless steel tools from
Nupla Products Ltd

Seed drill from
Richmond Gibson Ltd

Swoe and other hand tools from
Wilkinson Sword

Terrex spade and various unusual hand tools from
Wolf Tools Ltd

Hand pruning and cutting tools appendix

Quality is all important in this section and therefore price is less so. No price indications are given as these companies' prices are all comparatively expensive although most offer inexpensive versions of their tools.

Brand name	Manufacturer/distributor
Bushman	E. P. Barrus: pruning saws, bow saws
CeKa	CeKa: pruning saws, secateurs, loppers, knives, pole pruners
Felco	Burton McCall: secateurs, pole pruners
Gardena	Gardena Kress and Kastner: secateurs, small shears, electric shears
Honey Bros	Honey Bros: complete range of cutting and pruning equipment, safety harness, tree surgery tools
Rolcut	Rolcut: anvil secateurs, loppers, shears
Sandvik	Sandvik: secateurs, saws, shears, knives, pole pruners, loppers
Wilkinson Sword	Wilkinson Sword: secateurs, shears, loppers
Wolf	Wolf Tools: secateurs, shears, loppers, knives

Spraying equipment appendix

Spray booms, lances, jets, nozzles, extensions and crop guards are often interchangeable since they fit to the sprayer hose and such fittings are easily made. Therefore the range of attachments by one company will often fit the sprayer of another. The companies offering a good range of parts are listed for this reason.

Brand name	Manufacturer/distributor
ASL	ASL Airflow: range of small plastic pressure sprayers up to 14 pints capacity. Low
Cameron	Cameron Irrigation: quality brass and light alloy lances, guns, fan sprays, jets. High
Cooper Pegler	Cooper Pegler: quality pressure sprayers, knapsack sprayers, large tank sprayers, crop guards, nozzles, booms, lances, extensions, valves, pressure gauges. Medium and high
Dorman	Dorman Sprayer Co.: quality knapsack sprayers, double acting hand pump sprayers, power sprayers wheel mounted. High
Gardena	Gardena Kress and Kastner: plastic pressure sprayers. Medium
Hills	Hills Industries: plastic pressure sprayers. Low and medium
Poly-Gard	Wilmid Distribution: plastic pressure sprayers. Low
Solo	Solo Power Equipment: knapsack sprayers, power knapsack sprayers, pressure sprayers. Medium and high
Solo	Solo Sprayers: pressure sprayers, knapsack sprayers, double acting hand pumps, bucket pumps, guards, nozzles, lances. Medium and high
Tudor	Tudor Garden Products: plastic pressure sprayers. Low and medium
Wolf	Wolf Tools: electric sprayer. High

Hedge trimmers, chainsaws and brush cutters appendix

Name	Chainsaws Petrol	Chainsaws Electric	Hedgecutters Petrol	Hedgecutters Electric	Electric nylon line trimmers	Petrol brush cutters	Price	Manufacturer/ distributor
Al-Ko					Yes		Low	Al-Ko
Alpina	Yes						High	Glanfield Lawrence
Arrow			Yes				Medium	Paice and Son
Black and Decker		Yes		Yes	Yes		Low	Black and Decker
Carbra			Yes				—	Glanfield Lawrence
Danarm	Yes	Yes	Yes		Yes	Yes	Low, medium, high	Danarm
Easitrim			Yes				Medium	Allen Power
Echo	Yes					Yes	Low, medium, high	Trojan
Gardena				Yes			Medium	Gardena, Kress and Kastner
Graswip					Yes		Low	Thomas Edison
Hitachi		Yes					Low	E. P. Barrus
Homelite	Yes				Petrol trimmer		Low, medium, high	Trojan
Husqvarna	Yes						—	Hyett Adams
Jiffy					Yes		Medium	Allen Power
Kaaz						Yes	Medium, high	Paice and Son
Lombard	Yes						Medium, high	Glanfield Lawrence

Hedge trimmers, chainsaws and brush cutters appendix *(continued)*

Name	Chainsaws		Hedgecutters		Electric nylon line trimmers	Petrol brush cutters	Price	Manufacturer/ distributor
	Petrol	Electric	Petrol	Electric				
Minibrute		Battery					Low	Hyett Adams
McCulloch	Yes	Yes					Low, medium	Black and Decker
Oleo-Mac	Yes						Medium, high	E. P. Barrus
Poulan	Yes						Low, medium, high	Chain Saw Products
Preci-Tarpen				Yes			Low, medium, high	Preci-Tarpen
Sandvik				Yes			Low	Sandvik
Shingu-Shik			Yes				Medium	Chain Saw Products
Skil	Yes	Yes		Yes			Medium, high	Skil
Solo	Yes	Yes				Yes	Medium, high	Solo Power Equipment
Stihl	Yes						Medium, high	Stihl
Tas			Yes				Medium	Trojan
Tiger						Yes	Medium	E. P. Barrus
Tudor		Yes					Low	Tudor Products
Village Blacksmith		Yes					Low	Thomas Edison
Wolf				Yes	Yes		Medium	Wolf Tools
Webb			Yes	Yes			Medium	Wolseley Webb
Xenoah	Yes					Yes	Low, medium, high	Allen Power

The Hoffco Trimette attachment for turning your chainsaw into a nylon line weed trimmer, and the Carbra attachment for making your chainsaw into a hedge cutter, are available from Chain Saw Products and Danarm, among others.

The brush cutter attachment for the Shingu-Shik hedge cutter is also available from Chain Saw Products. All these pieces are reasonably priced.

Plant supports appendix

Brand name	Manufacturer/distributor
Agriframes	metal tube and netting supports for beans
East Anglian Wire Working and Engineering Co. Ltd	galvanized steel supports for border plants and begonias
Netlon	plastic ring supports for fixing to canes
Power Garden Products	galvanized steel supports for border plants
Rainbow	spring steel clips
Scottish War Blinded	galvanized steel supports for border plants
C. Sutton	bean and pea supports
Tortube	bean supports
Westray	'Link Stakes' in galvanized steel. Plastic plant ties

Fruit cages appendix

The price of fuit cages is roughly similar with C. Sutton probably being the cheapest and Knowle Nets the most expensive.

Brand name	Manufacturer/distributor
Agriframes	Agriframes: complete frame kits
Knowle Nets	Knowle Nets: aluminium tubes, netting, complete frame kits
Masterframe	C. Sutton: hortiballs, netting, complete frame kits
Netlon	Netlon: various plastic netting

Power cultivators appendix

In this appendix it is not sensible to give a comparative price index because it is not possible in many cases to determine exactly what constitutes a standard machine. Instead the general price categories are used – high, medium and low – which will give a broad indication of relative costs. When you decide on the exact specification of your choice you will be able to compare costs from the brochures which by then, I assume, you will have before you. The purpose of this appendix is to help you narrow the field of choice to manageable proportions. Note too that a 'yes' under any heading does not mean all machines qualify: for example a 'yes' appears under the *Reverse gear* column for Norlett but this means only that one or more of the Norlett machines is so equipped but not necessarily all Norlett machines. The codes FT and WD in the *Type* column mean forward tine and wheel driven respectively. The code WDFT means dual type machines. *Elect.* is an abbreviation for mains electric.

Power cultivators

Cultivator name	Engine size (hp)	Reverse gear	Forward gears	Range of attachments	Type	Price	Comments
Advon	4	No	Yes	Good	WD	Medium +, high	
Allen	8	Yes	Yes	Good	WD	High	No rotary digging. Plough only
Arun	3, 5, 6, 7	Yes	Yes	Good	WD	High	
BCS	8	Yes	Yes	Adequate	WD	High	Special attachments on application
Danarm	3, 5	No	No	Adequate	FT	Low	
John Deere	6	Yes	No	Not known	FT	High	
Ferrari	13, 18, 11	Yes	Yes	Good	WD	High	
Flymo	2	No	No	None	FT	Medium	
Honda	2½, 3½, 5, 7	Yes	Yes	Good	WDFT FT	Medium +, high	Steering clutches on some models
Howard	3½, 5½, 9, 11, 15	Yes	Yes	Adequate	FT	High	

Power cultivators *(continued)*

Cultivator name	Engine size (hp)	Reverse gear	Forward gears	Range of attachments	Type	Price	Comments
Iseki	4, 3, 3.6, 4.5	Yes	Yes	Good	FT WDFT	Medium +, high	Steering clutches on some models
Kubota	Not given	Yes	Yes	Good	WDFT FT	Medium +, high	Steering clutches on some models
Landmaster	Elect. 7, 4, 3	Yes	Yes	Good	FT WD Boom	Low +, medium +, high	
Merry Tiller	3, 4, 5, 7	Yes	Yes	Good	FT	Low +, medium +, high	
Monrotiller	5	Yes	Yes	Good	WD	High	Small machine of its type
Mountfield	3½, 4, 5	No	No	Adequate	FT	Medium	
Mow Rite	Battery	No	No	Limited	Boom	Low	
Norlett	Elect. 2½, 3, 4, 5, 7	Yes	Yes	Good	Boom WD FT	Low +, medium	

Qualcast	2, 4	Yes	Yes	Adequate	FT	Low	
S.E.P.	8, 10, 13, 14	Yes	Yes	Adequate	FT WD		Prices on application
Snapper	3, 4, 5	No	No	Adequate	FT	Low +, medium	
Solo	4, 5	No	Yes	Adequate	FT		Part of the Solo Combi range. See Chapter 4 on grass cutting
Stafor	Not given	Yes	Yes	Good	FT		
Templar	3, 4, 5	No	No	Adequate	FT	Low	Very good value
Terratiller	4, 5	No	No	Good	FT	High	
Tilsmith	3½, 4, 5, 8	Yes	Yes	Limited	FT	Low +, medium	
Westwood	2, 3, 4, 5	No	No	Adequate	FT	Low	

Manufacturers and distributors

Brand name	Manufacturer/distributor
Advon	Advon Engineers Ltd
Allen	Allen Power Equipment
Arun	Riverside Precision and Sheetmetal Ltd
BCS	Westwood Engineering Ltd
Danarm	Danarm Ltd
John Deere	John Deere Ltd
Ferrari	JHB Implements Ltd
Flymo	Flymo Ltd
Honda	Honda
Howard	Howard Rotavator Co. Ltd
Iseki	Chain Saw Products Ltd
Kubota	Kubota Tractors
Landmaster	Boscombe Engineering Ltd
Merry Tiller	Wolseley Webb
Monrotiller	*See* Terratiller
Mountfield	G. D. Mountfield Ltd
Mow-Rite	Mow-Rite Engineering Co. Ltd
Norlett	Norlett Ltd
Qualcast	Birmid
S.E.P.	Unit-Horse Tractors Ltd
Snapper	Kitbarns Ltd
Solo	Solo Power Equipment (UK) Ltd
Stafor	Hyett Adams Ltd
Templar	Templar Tillers
Terratiller	Mechanized Gardening
Tilsmith	Olcope Ltd
Westwood	*See* BCS

Trailers and barrows appendix

Companies manufacturing or distributing barrows and trailers.

Brand name	Manufacturer/distributor
Al-Ko	Al-Ko: metal trailer. Medium
Ballbarrow	Kirk-Dyson: plastic barrows. Medium
Corrie	J. B. Corrie and Son: two wheel barrows, conventional barrows. Low
High-Hoe Barrow	Highlight Engineering: two wheel barrow. Low
Link Trailers	Link-Hampson: trailers, hand trucks, large two wheel barrows, cultivator hitches. Medium and high
Packhorse	Bob Andrews Ltd: electric hand cart. High
Parker	T. Parker: wooden barrows, large two wheel metal hand truck. High
H. Pattisson	H. Pattisson: wooden barrows
Vulcan or VT	Vulcan Trucks: trailers, hand trucks, large two wheel barrows, cultivator hitches. Medium and high
Winget	Winget: dumper trucks. High
Wolf	Wolf Tools: two wheel barrow. High

Cultivator and tractor companies offer trailers as part of their accessory lists. As most tractor trailers are usable on all makes do not necessarily buy the same brand as your tractor. Better or cheaper ones may be available.

Leaf clearing equipment appendix

Brand name	Manufacturer/distributor
Billy Goat	Bob Andrews Ltd: vacuum leaf clearers, self-propelled and push models available. High
Case	Olcope Ltd: towed leaf sweeper. High
Helpmate	Helpmate Sweeping Machines: vacuum leaf clearers. High
Huff'n Puff	Bob Andrews Ltd: small vacuum leaf clearer. Medium
M.T.D.	E. P. Barrus: vacuum leaf clearer. High
Nickerson	Nickerson Turfmaster: power leaf sweepers, towed or self-propelled. High
Parkavac	T. Parker: vacuum leaf sweeper
Portablast	Bob Andrews Ltd: knapsack leaf blower. High
Winro	Bob Andrews Ltd: leaf blowers. High
Wolf	Wolf Tools: push or towed leaf sweepers. Low and medium

The trailer type vacuum models will be listed in the appropriate tractor accessory catalogues. Most of these trailer vacuums are made by the E-Z Rake company in America and if you have difficulty in obtaining a vacuum for your tractor or ride-on write directly to E-Z Rake.

Tractors appendix

In the following table the comment under the attachments range does not apply to towed accessories like a trailer or leaf sweeper. It applies only to accessories designed specifically for fitting to one machine or make. For example the Westwood has 'None' under the *attachments* range column but the Westwood tractor will pull many of the attachments offered by other manufacturers although you could not fit, for example, the hydraulic bulldozer blade designed specifically for a Graveley. Most companies offer a good range of fitments. Not all are readily available in this country and some can only be obtained by special order. If the distributor for your tractor is not stocking a particular accessory the distributor for another make may have it. If in trouble write direct to America for information.

The following abbreviations have been used.

LT Lawn tractor.   HS   Hydro-static.

GT Garden tractor.   Man.   Manual gear change

Tractors

Tractor name	Engine size (hp)	Tractor type	Drive type	Attachment range	Mower type	Hydraulic	Price	Comment
Al-Ko	8	LT	Man.	Limited	Rotary	No	Low	
Ariens	10, 14, 16	GT	HS, man.	Good	Rotary, cylinder	Yes	Medium, high	Special front mounted three gang cylinder mower
Bolens	8, 11, 14, 16, 20	LT, GT	HS, man.	Good	Rotary, sickle	Yes	Medium, high	
Case	8, 10, 14, 16	LT, GT	HS, man.	Good	Rotary, sickle	Yes	Medium, high	
John Deere	12, 16, 20	GT	HS, man.	Good	Rotary	Yes	High	
Graveley	10, 12, 16, 18	GT	Man.	Good	Rotary, forward rotary, sickle	Yes	Medium, high	All attachments shaft driven
International Harvester	10, 12, 14, 16	LT, GT	HS, man.	Adequate	Rotary	Yes	Medium, high	
M.T.D.	8, 11, 16	LT, GT	HS, man.	Adequate	Rotary, sickle	Yes	Low, medium, high	
Mountfield	11, 16	LT	Man.	Limited	Rotary	No	Low, medium	

Nickerson	8, 14	LT	Man.	None	Cylinder	No	High	The only all cylinder mower tractor
Roper	8, 11, 14, 16	LT, GT	HS, man.	Good	Rotary, sickle	Yes	Low, medium	
Simplicity	8, 10, 13, 16, 20	LT, GT	HS, man.	Good	Rotary	Yes	Medium, high	
Westwood	8, 11	LT	Man.	None	Rotary	No	Low, medium	All British. Good value
Wheel Horse	8, 10, 11, 12, 14, 16, 17	LT, GT	HS, man.	Good	Rotary	Yes	Low, medium, high	

Manufacturers and distributors

Brand name	Manufacturer/distributor
Al-Ko	Al-Ko
Ariens	Norlett
M.T.D.	E. P. Barrus
Bolens	Howard Rotavator
Case	Olcope
John Deere	John Deere
Graveley	Autoturfcare
International Harvester	Marshall Concessionaires
Mountfield	Mountfield
Nickerson Turfmaster	Nickerson Turfmaster
Roper	Allen Power

Miscellaneous appendix

Manufacturers and distributors offering equipment described in the miscellaneous chapter.

Brand name	Manufacturer/distributor
ASL	ASL Airflow Ltd: hand held flame wand
Barrus	E. P. Barrus: hand held, petrol engined hole borers
Mighty Mac	Merritstyle: compost shredder
Sheen	Sheen (Nottingham) Ltd: all flame guns, propane and paraffin fired
Solo	Solo Power Equipment Ltd: hand held, petrol engined hole borer

List of Addresses

ASL Airflow Ltd
Plume Street
Birmingham
B6 7RT

Access Irrigation Ltd
Crick
Northampton
NN6 7XS

Advon Engineers Ltd
11 St Johns Road
Hampton Wick
Kingston-Upon-Thames
Surrey

Agricessories Ltd
Broad Lane Works
Cottenham
Cambridge
CB4 4TP

Agriframes Ltd
Charlwoods Road
East Grinstead
Sussex

Agricaid Ltd
254 Braunstone Lane
Leicester
LE3 3AS

Al-Ko Britain Ltd
Albion Road
Carlton Industrial Estate
Barnsley
South Yorkshire

Allen Power Equipment
The Broadway
Didcot
Oxfordshire

Bob Andrews Ltd
The Garden Machine
 Centre
Sunningdale
Berkshire

Aspera Motors (England)
 Ltd
152/154 Commercial Road
Staines
Middlesex

Auriol (Guildford) Ltd
Passfield
Liphook
Hampshire

Autoturfcare*
2 Ladymead
Guildford
Surrey
GU1 1DL

E. P. Barrus Ltd
12–16 Brunel Road
Acton
London
W3 7UY

Birmid-Qualcast (Home
 and Garden Equipment)
 Ltd
Coleridge Street
Sunnyhill
Derby
DE3 7JT

Black and Decker
Cannon Lane
Maidenhead
Berkshire

Blackmore and Langdon
 Ltd
Pensford
Bristol

Boscombe Engineering
145 Sterte Road
Poole
Dorset

Briggs and Stratton
c/o Autocar Electrical
  Equipment Co. Ltd
640 Ripple Road
Barking
Essex

British Agricultural and
  Garden Machinery
  Association
Church Street
Rickmansworth
Hertfordshire

Bulldog Tools
Clarington Forge
Wigan
WN1 3DD

Burton McCall
Samuel Street
Leicester

Calvert Cultivation Co. Ltd
Rickmansworth
Hertfordshire

Cameron Irrigation Co. Ltd
Harwood Industrial Estate
Littlehampton
Sussex
BN17 5BR

CeKa Works Ltd
Pwllheli
Gwynedd
North Wales

Chain Saw Products Ltd
33 Broughton Street
Manchester
M8 8LZ

Chillington Tool Co. Ltd
PO BOX 45
Hickman Avenue
Wolverhampton
WV1 2BU

Cooper Pegler
PO BOX 27
Burgess Hill
Sussex

J. B. Corrie and Son
Petersfield
Hampshire

Cresent Plastics
838 Wickham Road
Croydon

Crown Horticultural
  Equipment
170 London Road
High Wycombe
Buckinghamshire

Danarm Ltd
Stafford Mill Estate
London Road
Stroud
Gloucester
GL5 2BP

John Deere Ltd
Langar
Nottingham
NG13 9HT

Dixon Gardening and
  Farming Aids
168 Springdale Road
Corfe Mullen
Wimborne
Dorset

Dorman Sprayer Co. Ltd
Brays Lane
Ely
Cambridge
CB7 4QL

East Anglian Wire Working
  and Engineering Co. Ltd
125 Fore Street
Ipswich
Suffolk

Thomas A. Edison Ltd
19 Binns Close
Torrington Trading Estate
Coventry
CV4 9TB

J. Ekis
The Old Forge
Denmead
Hampshire

Electricity Council
Millbank
London

Essex Garden Products Ltd
Well Lane
Danbury
Essex
CM3 4AD

Expandite
Western Road
Bracknell
Berkshire

E-Z Rake Inc
1001 South Ransdell Road
Lebanon
Indiana 46052
USA

Flymo Ltd
Aycliffe Industrial Estate
Darlington
Co. Durham

Gardena, Kress and
  Kastner
3 Ashville Way
Royston Road
Baldock
Hertfordshire

Glanfield Lawrence
  Concessionnaires
Victoria Road
Portslade
Brighton
East Sussex

Barrie Grist Irrigation
  Systems
Bearah Farm
West Ogwell
Newton Abbot
Devon

John Harston Ltd
Trowse
Norwich
NR14 8SY

Haws Elliott Ltd
Bescot Crescent
Walsall
West Midlands

Hayters Ltd
Spellbrook Lane
Bishops Stortford
Hertfordshire

Helpmate
Great Missenden
Buckinghamshire

Highlight Engineering Ltd
Dunnington
Yorkshire
YO1 5LP

Hills Industries Ltd
Pontygwindy Industrial
  Estate
Caerphilly
Mid Glamorgan
CF8 1XF

Honda
Power Road
London
W4

Honey Brothers (Sales) Ltd
New Pond Road
Peasmarsh
Guildford
Surrey

Howard Rotavator Co. Ltd
Saxham
Bury St Edmunds
Suffolk

Hozelock Ltd
Haddenham
Aylesbury
Buckinghamshire
HP17 8JD

Chester Hudson
Stream Farm
Horam
Heathfield
Sussex
TN21 0BP

Hyett Adams Ltd
Oldends Lane
Stonehouse
Gloucestershire
GL10 2SY

ICI
Garden and Household
  Products Division
Woolmead House East
Woolmead Walk
Farnham
Surrey
GU9 7UB

J. H. B. Implements Ltd
  (Ferrari)
Ickburgh
Nr Thetford
Norfolk
IP26 5JG

Jalo Engineering
Mill Lane
Wimborne
Dorset

Jenks and Cattell (Garden
  Tools) Ltd
Wednesfield
Wolverhampton
WV11 3PU

Kirk-Dyson Ltd
Leafield Trading Estate
Corsham
Wiltshire
SN13 9UD

Kitbarns Ltd
97 East Hill
London
SW18 2QD

Knowle Nets
20 East Road
Bridport
Dorset

Kohler
J. H. Hancox Ltd
Wood Lane
Earlswood
Solihull
West Midlands

Kubota Tractors
Hut Green
Whitley Bridge
Yorkshire
DN14 0RX

Lawn-Boy
Railway Road
Downham Market
Norfolk
PE38 9DX

Ledger Selby
Ardfern House
By Lochgilphead
Argyll
Scotland
PA31 8QN

A. J. Likeman
Springfield Rise
Hednesford
Staffordshire

Link Trailers
Link Hampson Ltd
5 Bone Lane
Newbury
Berkshire

Lloyds and Co.
Birds Hill
Letchworth
Hertfordshire
SG6 1JE

Marmax Plastics Ltd
Willow Drive
Longfield Road
Twyford
Berkshire

Marshall Concessionaires
  Ltd
Oxford Road
Brackley
Northampton

Mechanized Gardening
Great Gransden
Sandy
Bedfordshire
SG19 3AY

Merritstyle
Lyon Industrial Estate
Hartspring Lane
Watford
Hertfordshire

G. D. Mountfield Ltd
Reform Road
Maidenhead
Berkshire
SL6 8DO

Mow-Rite Engineering Co.
Basingstoke Road
Swallowfield
Reading
Berkshire

Netlon Ltd
Mill Hill
Blackburn
Lancashire

Nickerson Turfmaster Ltd
Fullbridge Mill
Fullbridge
Maldon
Essex

Norlett Ltd
Dormer Road
Thame
Oxfordshire
OX9 3UE

Nupla Products
Norwich House
13 Southampton Place
London
WB1A 2AY

Olcope Ltd
East Anglian Trading Co.
5 Guardian Road
Norwich
NR5 8PB

Paice and Son
Felbridge
East Grinstead
Sussex

T. Parker and Sons Ltd
Worcester Park
Surrey

H. Pattisson and Co. Ltd
Stanmore Hill Works
Stanmore
Middlesex
HA7 3HD

Pilc Productions
2 Leigh Way
Weaverham
Northwich
Cheshire

Planet Products Ltd
59 St Mary Church Street
London
SE16

The Plastic Tube and
  Conduit Co. Ltd
Irrigation Division
Sterling Works
Bath Road
Aldermaston
Berkshire

Preci-Tarpen
Chapel Street
Syston
Leicester

R.S.J. Plastics Ltd
PO BOX 3
Bedwas Road
Caerphilly

Ransomes Sims and
  Jefferies Ltd
Nacton Works
Ipswich
IP3 9QG

Richmond Gibson Ltd
Salisbury Road
Downton
Salisbury
Wiltshire

Riverside Precision and
  Sheetmetal Ltd
Ford Lane
Arundel
Sussex

Rolcut Ltd
Blatchford Road
Horsham
Sussex

Rumsey
20 Beacon Down Avenue
Plymouth
Devon

Sandvik
Manor Way
Halesowen
West Midlands

Scottish War Blinded
Room C
Linburn
Wilkieston
By Kirknewton
West Lothian
EH27 8DU

Sheen (Nottingham) Ltd
Greasley Street
Bulwell
Nottingham
NG6 8NH

Sisis Equipment
  (Macclesfield) Ltd
Shoreclough Works
Hulley Road
Macclesfield
Cheshire

Skil Ltd
1B Thames Avenue
Windsor
Berkshire

Solo Power Equipment
  (UK) Ltd
Industrial Estate
Pedmore Road
Brierley Hill
West Midlands

Solo Sprayers Ltd
Brunel Road
Leigh-on-Sea
Essex

Stemport Marketing Co.
  Ltd
Pembroke Road
Aylesbury
Buckinghamshire

C. Sutton Ltd
North Mills
Bridport
Dorset

Tecumseh *see* Aspera
  Motors

Templar Tillers
Halifax Road
High Wycombe
Buckinghamshire

Tortube Products
Tamar View Industrial
  Estate
Saltash
Cornwall

Trojan Ltd (Agricultural
  Division)
Hillside
The Square
Forest Row
East Sussex

Tudor Garden Products
Ystrad Mynach
PO BOX 1
Hengoed
Mid Glamorgan
CF8 7XD

Two Wests and Elliott
103 Storforth Lane
  Trading Estate
Chesterfield
Derbyshire
S41 0QB

Uni-Horse Tractors Ltd
George Bayliss Road
Droitwich
Worcestershire

V.T. Trucks
Unit 11
10 Nuffield Estate
Poole
Dorset

Valentine Plastics
Colham Mill Road
West Drayton
Middlesex
UB7 7AS

Victa Mowers
Victa (UK) Ltd
Rutherford Road
Daneshill West
Basingstoke
Hampshire
RG24 0QY

Villiers
Wolverhampton Industrial
  Engines
Marston Road
Wolverhampton
WV2 4NN

Voss Water Systems
Blenheim Road
High Wycombe
Buckinghamshire

Westray Cloches
15 Church Road
Upper Boddington
Daventry
Northamptonshire

Westwood Engineering
  Ltd
Bell Close
Plympton
Plymouth
Devon

Wilkinson Sword
Sword House
Totteridge Road
High Wycombe
Buckinghamshire

Wilmid Distribution
Mount Street
Birmingham

Winget Ltd
Rochester
Kent
ME2 4AA

Wolf Tools Ltd
Ross-on-Wye
Herefordshire

Wolseley Webb
Electric Avenue
Witton
Birmingham
B6 7JA

Index

Numbers in *italic* refer to line drawings